JIM MANTHORPE (seen here bivvying on the summit of Sgurr Fhuaran in Scotland's Western Highlands) is a wildlife cameraman and writer. He has written and updated dozens of Trailblazer guidebooks over the years, from Ladakh to Canada. But it is in the Highlands, where he is based, that he spends most of his time. He has a particular love for wild places and wildlife and has filmed eagles, otters and orcas for various BBC shows including *Springwatch*. He is also the author of *Scottish Highlands Hillwalking*, *Tour du Mont Blanc*, *South Downs Way* and *Iceland Hiking*, all from Trailblazer.

Author

Great Glen Way

First edition: 2017; this second edition 2021

Publisher Trailblazer Publications
The Old Manse, Tower Rd, Hindhead, Surrey, GU26 6SU, UK
info@trailblazer-guides.com, ⌨ trailblazer-guides.com

British Library Cataloguing in Publication Data
A catalogue record for this book is available from the British Library

ISBN 978-1-912716-10-4

© Trailblazer 2017, 2021: Text and maps

Series editor: Anna Jacomb-Hood
Editor: Henry Stedman **Layout**: Nick Hill **Additional research**: Nicky Slade
Proof-reading: Daniel McCrohan & Jane Thomas **Cartography**: Nick Hill
Illustrations: © Nick Hill (pp71-3); Rev CA Johns (pp62-4) **Index**: Jane Thomas
Photographs (flora) and pp162-3: © Bryn Thomas
All other photographs: © Jim Manthorpe

All rights reserved. Other than brief extracts for the purposes of review no part of
this publication may be reproduced in any form without the written consent of the
publisher and copyright owner.

The maps in this guide were prepared from out-of-Crown-
copyright Ordnance Survey maps amended and updated by Trailblazer.

Acknowledgements

From Jim: I'd like to thank the many travellers I met who gave me tips and good vibes
along the trail and also the readers who sent in suggestions and updates for this edition, particularly Hannah Orr, Randall Plant and Philip Scriver. Heartfelt gratitude goes to Claire,
Oren and Zara who, as always, sent me on my way with love and biscuits. And thank you
to my good friend Liz Proudlock for the local knowledge, the banter and a shed to sleep in.
   Finally, thank you to the wonderful Trailblazer team: Henry Stedman for editing,
Nicky Slade for additional research, Daniel McCrohan for proof-reading and Jane Thomas
for the index, Nick Hill for layout and the cartography and Bryn Thomas for the opportunity to write about something I love doing.

A request

The author and publisher have tried to ensure that this guide is as accurate and up to date as
possible. Nevertheless, things change. If you notice any changes or omissions that should be
included in the next edition, please contact us at Trailblazer (⌨ info@trailblazer-guides.com).
A free copy of the next edition will be sent to persons making a significant contribution.

Warning: long-distance walking can be dangerous

Please read the notes on when to go (pp13-15) and outdoor safety (pp53-7). Every effort
has been made by the author and publisher to ensure that the information contained herein
is as accurate and up to date as possible. However, they are unable to accept responsibility
for any inconvenience, loss or injury sustained by anyone as a result of the advice and information given in this guide.

PHOTOS – Front cover & this page: View north along Loch Ness from the stone shelter (see p117) on the Fort Augustus to Invermoriston high route. **Overleaf**: Looking west
from the 'Viewcatcher' (see p124) above Invermoriston towards the mountains of Kintail.

Updated information will be available on: ⌨ **trailblazer-guides.com**

Printed in China; print production by D'Print (☎ +65-6581 3832), Singapore

Great Glen
WAY

FORT WILLIAM TO INVERNESS

38 large-scale maps & guides to 15 towns and villages

PLANNING – PLACES TO STAY – PLACES TO EAT

JIM MANTHORPE

TRAILBLAZER PUBLICATIONS

Contents

INTRODUCTION

The Great Glen Way

PART 1: PLANNING YOUR WALK

Practical information for the walker

Budgeting 28

Itineraries

What to take

Getting to and from the Great Glen Way

PART 2: MINIMUM IMPACT WALKING & OUTDOOR SAFETY

Minimum impact walking

Outdoor safety

PART 3: THE ENVIRONMENT & NATURE

Conserving Scotland's nature

Contents

ABOUT THIS BOOK

This guidebook contains all the information you need. The hard work has been done for you so you can plan your trip without having to consult numerous websites and other books and maps.

When you're packed and ready to go, there's comprehensive public transport information to get you to and from the trail and detailed maps (1:20,000) and town plans to help you find your way along it. It includes:

● All standards of accommodation with reviews of campsites, hostels, B&Bs, guesthouses and hotels
● Walking companies if you want a self-guided or group/guided holiday, baggage-carrying services if you just want your luggage carried, and an accommodation-booking agency if you want someone else to book your accommodation
● Itineraries for all levels of walkers
● Answers to all your questions: when to go, degree of difficulty, what to pack, and how much the whole walking holiday will cost
● Walking times in both directions and GPS waypoints
● Cafés, pubs, tearooms, takeaways, restaurants and shops for buying supplies
● Rail, bus and taxi information for all places along the path
● Street plans of the main towns and villages both on and off the path
● Historical, cultural and geographical background information

---

❏ MINIMUM IMPACT FOR MAXIMUM INSIGHT

Nature's peace will flow into you as the sunshine flows into trees. The winds will blow their freshness into you and storms their energy, while cares will drop off like autumn leaves. **John Muir** (one of the world's earliest and most influential environmentalists, born in 1838)

Walking in wild places is about opening ourselves up to all that is 'green'. Treading lightly and with respect we give ourselves a precious chance to tap into the curative power of the natural world. Physical contact with the land makes us more in tune with it and as a result we feel all the more passionate about protecting it.

It is no surprise then that, since the time of John Muir, walkers and adventurers have been concerned about the natural environment; this book seeks to continue that tradition. There is a detailed, illustrated chapter on the wildlife and conservation of the Highlands as well as a chapter devoted to minimum impact walking with ideas on how we can broaden that ethos.

By developing a deeper ecological awareness through a better understanding of nature and by supporting rural economies, local businesses, sensitive forms of transport and low-impact methods of farming and land-use we can all do our bit for a brighter future. In the buzzwords of today there can be few activities as 'environmentally friendly' as walking.

INTRODUCTION

The Great Glen Way opened in 2002 and is the fourth official long-distance path in Scotland. It runs for 79 miles (127km) from Fort William to Inverness, connecting Scotland's west coast with its east, following the length of the Great Glen. The glen is one of Scotland's most significant landscape features; it is both a fault line and a glacial trough, effectively splitting the Highlands in two with the North-West Highlands on one side and the Grampian mountains on the other. For anyone wanting to cross from one side of the Highlands to the other this is the obvious place to do it as there is no mountain barrier to hinder you. The main A82 road utilises the glen, as does Thomas Telford's Caledonian Canal which links the three major lochs that partly fill the glen: lochs Lochy, Oich and Ness.

The Great Glen Way runs for 79 miles (127km) following the length of the Great Glen

The Great Glen Way begins at the marker post (**above**) at the fort in Fort William and ends at the castle in Inverness (**below**).

The Great Glen Way makes use of the canal's towpath in places, particularly at the southern end, but for the most part it avoids the road and canal, following instead the forestry tracks as well as a disused railway line and an old drovers' road. Some stretches can be a little monotonous as they negotiate the dense conifer plantations but the route is varied and takes in loch shore, hill, moor, beautiful Caledonian pine forest and birch woodland. There is plenty for the wildlife enthusiast with red squirrels, ospreys and golden eagles. And

INTRODUCTION

history buffs will find ancient castles, Jacobite battle sites and a WWII training area. All this and I haven't even mentioned the Loch Ness Monster.

It takes about a week to complete the Way but if you only have a day or two the good transport links make it easy to do one or more of the suggested day and weekend walks.

For those who feel 79 miles isn't enough, the Great Glen Way can be tagged on to the 96-mile West Highland Way that ends where the Great Glen Way starts in Fort William. Combining the two gives an uninterrupted long-distance path of 175 miles (282km), all the way from Glasgow to Inverness.

Above: You're unlikely to catch even a glimpse of the Loch Ness monster (see p123) – other than this sculpture in Fort Augustus.

Below: The locks at Corpach, at the southern end of the Caledonian Canal (see p84). The Great Glen Way makes use of the canal's towpath in places.

History of the Great Glen Way

From the Iron Age, when people lived in *crannogs* (see p113) on the water, to the 18th-century Jacobite uprisings, when clansmen and government troops fought over territory in the glen and to the building of Wade's roads (see p93) in response to the uprisings, the Great Glen has been used as a thoroughfare for travellers.

Today it's a natural route for long-distance walkers. The Great Glen Way was first proposed way back in the 1970s by the

Above: WWII landing craft practice site, near Achnacarry (see p94), where some of the training was done for the D-Day landings.

INTRODUCTION

INTRODUCTION

Above: Telford's Bridge, (Invermoriston Old Bridge, see p120) was completed in 1813.

Scottish Rights of Way Society and came to fruition thanks to the co-operation of a number of organisations: Highland Council, Scottish Natural Heritage, Inverness and Nairn Enterprise, Lochaber Limited, Forestry Commission Scotland, Visit Scotland and British Waterways. The Way was the fourth long-distance path to be created in Scotland, following on from the West Highland Way, Southern Upland Way and Speyside Way.

It cost half a million pounds to create, nearly half of which came from European Union funding. It's always hard to say how much money the route generates through increased tourism to the villages and towns along the Way but it is probably around £2 million per year.

In 2002 Prince Andrew officially opened the route in Inverness. The choice of Inverness for the official opening caused something of a hoo-ha at the time, as it was felt that Fort William was the start of the walk and Inverness the end. But Prince Andrew happened to have an engagement in Inverness on the same day as the proposed opening ceremony so he was snapped up to cut the ribbon there.

The late Tony Dyer, then Countryside Officer for the Highland Council and a key person in getting the Way up and running, pointed out at the time that it's perfectly acceptable to walk the route in either direction, although walking south to north was the preferred choice because 'the weather is behind you'.

INTRODUCTION

How difficult is it?

Long-distance walking aficionados will tell you that the Great Glen Way is one of the easier of Britain's long-distance paths, and they are not wrong. For the most part, certainly on the southern half, the walking is on low, level and easy-to-navigate forestry tracks and canal towpaths with plenty of way-marking signposts to keep you right.

The Great Glen Way is one of the easier of Britain's long-distance paths ... but ... seventy-nine miles is still a fair old hike.

But don't be lulled into a false sense of security. Seventy-nine miles is still a fair old hike and walking 10 miles or more a day requires stamina. If you are new to long-distance walking don't make the mistake of carrying too heavy a rucksack as this can turn a pleasant walk into a painful endurance exercise. The

Below: Stone shelter and viewpoint above Alltsigh, looking south over Loch Ness.

Above: Old commando boat station,
Bunarkaig (see p95).

northern half of the trail with its steep ascents and descents and high, moorland walking is the toughest section but, if you are walking in the recommended direction of south to north, you should have built up a bit of fitness by the time you get to that part of the walk.

One of the hardest aspects of the Great Glen Way is what you will be walking upon. Forestry tracks and canal towpaths, of which there are many on the Way, are hard-wearing surfaces and can be punishing on your feet. Nevertheless, those long-distance walking aficionados are right: this is one of the easier trails that Britain has to offer and is well within the capabilities of any reasonably fit person.

How long do you need?

If you are staying in the villages along the way, the even spacing of those villages at roughly 10- to 15-mile distances helps to dictate the rate at which you knock off the miles and thus how long the whole walk takes. Most walkers take six or seven days to complete the 79 miles.

Most walkers take six or seven days to complete the 79 miles

Unless you are wild camping it is quite hard to find accommodation between the villages so your itinerary really is limited. If you are dead set on completing the Way in as fast a time as you can manage it is possible to double up on some of the sections. Of course, while it can be very satisfying to finish a walk in record time, in doing so you sacrifice the pleasure of seeing things along the way, stopping off at cafés, enjoying the wildlife and the views. If that's more your thing it may be possible to stretch your walk out to eight days. The suggested itineraries on p32 give options both for fast walkers and for those who prefer a more leisurely pace.

If you really are just intent on getting it over and done with, you can sign up to the Great Glen Ultra Race (see box p14) which follows the 71 miles from Banavie to Inverness in less than 24 hours. At the time of research the record is

See p32 for some suggested itineraries covering different walking speeds

held by Mike Raffan who, in 2014, completed the route in a mind-boggling 10 hours 48 minutes and 43 seconds.

When to go

SEASONS

The **main walking season** in Scotland is from the Easter holiday (March/April) through to

The best months to walk the Great Glen Way are June and September

October. Balancing all the variables – such as weather, number of other walkers, midges and available accommodation – the best months to walk the Great Glen Way are June and September.

In the Highlands there's a west–east split in climate. It is generally, though not always, drier in the east while the west gets the full force of Atlantic low-pressure systems and their associated weather fronts. In other words, you are more likely

Below: Old Inverlochy Castle (see p82) dates back to 1280.

to get wet the closer you are to Fort William. The Inverness area, meanwhile, is one of the driest regions of Scotland. That's dry in Highland terms!

Spring

April is unpredictable in terms of the weather. It can be warm and sunny, though blustery days with showers are more typical and snow may often still be lying on the hills. On the plus side, the land is just waking up to spring, there

INTRODUCTION

❏ **FESTIVALS AND ANNUAL EVENTS**

Year-round

● **Great Glen Rangers events** (🖳 www.outdoorhighlands.co.uk/long-distance-trails/great-glen-way-2/events/) The Highland Council ranger service that manages the Great Glen Way holds a number of events throughout the year, aimed at connecting people with the natural world. Activities include star-gazing, foraging for wild food and bushcraft. Check their website for details.

February/March

● **Fort William Mountain Festival** (🖳 www.mountainfestival.co.uk) A hugely popular event held in **February** or **March** at The Nevis Centre (see p76). This week-long extravaganza began life as a mountain film festival but has grown to showcase not just films but all sorts of lectures and exhibitions.

July to September

● **Great Glen Ultra Race** (🖳 runyabam.com/race-information/great-glen-ultra/) This 71-mile race, held annually on the first Saturday in **July**, follows the Great Glen Way from Banavie to Inverness. Super-fit runners are given 22 hours to complete the race.

● **Glenurquhart Highland Gathering** (🖳 www.glenurquhart-highland-games .co.uk) There are Highland Games held in towns and villages across the Highlands every summer but this one, held annually on the last Saturday in **August** in Drumnadrochit (see pp131-5), is one of the most well established and popular. It was conceived in 1945 when the local people were looking to bring a little joy back to the community following the war years. Around 3000 people from near and far attend the event to witness the traditional caber toss and hammer throw. There is also a pipe band and Highland dancing.

● **Loch Ness Marathon** (🖳 www.lochnessmarathon.com) A walk in the park compared to the Great Glen Ultra Race, this marathon has to be one of the most beautiful there is. It follows a route along the south-eastern side of Loch Ness with a finish in Inverness city centre. It takes place in late **September** or early **October** every year.

● **Ben Race** (🖳 www.bennevisrace.co.uk) If you are in the Ben Nevis area on the first Saturday in **September** try to watch the Ben Race when up to 600 fell-runners reach the summit and return to the glen in ludicrously short times. This spectacle began in 1895 when William Swan ran to the top and back down in 2 hours 41 minutes. At the time of writing the men's record stands at 1 hour 25 minutes 34 seconds, and the women's 1 hour 43 minutes and 25 seconds (both set in 1984, by Kenny Stuart and Pauline Haworth respectively).

November

● **Inverness Film Festival** Held in early November at Eden Court Theatre (see p145) in Inverness, the festival has screenings of mainstream and art-house films as well as low-budget movies from local film-makers. The website seems not to have been updated since 2018 even though the festival is still running, so you'll have to look elsewhere for schedules.

won't be many other walkers about and you shouldn't encounter any midges. As far as the weather is concerned, **May** can be a great time for walking in Scotland; the temperature is warm, the weather is as dry and clear as can be expected, wild flowers are out in their full glory and the midges have yet to reach an intolerable level. However, the Way is exceptionally busy at this time of year and it can be a night-mare finding accommodation.

Above: The locks at Fort Augustus (see p113).

Many B&Bs take bookings in January or earlier for people walking in May. This is not the time to go if you like walking in solitude. You'd be far better off going in **June** which has all the advantages of May without the crowds.

Summer

The arrival of hordes of tourists in **July** and **August** along with warm, muggy weather brings out the worst in the midges. On many days you'll be wondering what all the fuss is about; that's until you encounter a still, overcast evening when you'll swear never to set foot in the Highlands again. Campers are the ones who should really take note of this as everyone else can escape the torture behind closed windows and doors. On some weekends it can feel as if the whole world has arrived in the Highlands; traffic is nose to tail on the roads and many hostels and B&Bs are fully booked days in advance. Surprisingly, there can also be a fair amount of rain in these months.

Autumn

A slower pace of life returns when the school holidays come to an end. Early **September** is a wonderful and often neglected time for walking, with fewer vis-itors and the midges' appetites largely sated. Towards the end of the month and

Below: Ben Nevis, in the centre of this photo (see pp160-4) from across Loch Lochy.

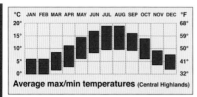

Average max/min temperatures (Central Highlands)

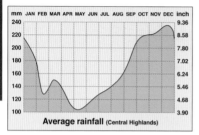

Average rainfall (Central Highlands)

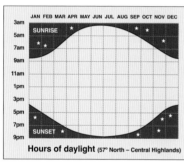

Hours of daylight (57° North – Central Highlands)

into **early October** the vivid autumn colours are at their best in the woods and on the hills but you are starting to run the risk of encountering more rain and stronger winds. The air temperature, however, is still quite mild.

Winter
Late October and **early November** can occasionally be glorious with crisp clear days, but this is also the start of winter; the days are shortening, the temperature has dropped noticeably and many seasonal B&Bs, hostels, campsites and shops have closed.

You need to be pretty hardy to walk between late **November** and **mid March**. True, some days can be fantastically bright and sunny and your appreciation will be heightened by snow on the hills and few people around. You are far more likely, however, to encounter the weather the Highlands are famous for; driving rain and snow for days on end on the back of freezing northerly winds.

TEMPERATURE & RAINFALL
January temperatures are on average 1-6°C and July temperatures are on average 10-18°C. The annual **rainfall** for the West Highlands is about 2000mm (80 inches); as you progress north-east you are likely to encounter drier weather, but don't count on it! The annual average in the Fort William area can be as much as 3000mm while in Inverness it is closer to 750mm.

DAYLIGHT HOURS
If walking in autumn, winter and early spring, you must take account of how far you can walk in the available light. It may not be possible to cover as many miles as you would in summer. The table gives the sunrise and sunset times for each month at latitude 57° North. This runs across the southern tip of Loch Lomond, about 50 miles south of Fort William, giving a realistic picture of daylight for the Great Glen Way. Depending on the weather you will get a further 30-45 minutes of usable light before sunrise and after sunset.

Above: Looking north up Loch Ness towards Foyers from the high path above Fort Augustus.
Below: The Viewcatcher sculpture (see p125) above Loch Ness.
Overleaf, clockwise from top left: **1**. Urquhart Castle (see p131) and Loch Ness by Drumnadrochit. **2**. Loch Oich from high on the Invergarry route. **3**. Engine at Old Invergarry railway station. **4**. River Oich and Bridge of Oich (p109) at Aberchalder. **5**. The view south along Loch Ness from just north of Drumnadrochit.

Practical information for the walker

ROUTE FINDING

The official symbol of the Great Glen Way, and all Scottish national trails, is a thistle in the middle of a hexagon. You will see waymarker posts and signposts the length of the Way to help you stay on track. Navigation is easy and with the aid of the maps in this book it should be quite straightforward to follow the route.

The southern half of the Way follows the Caledonian Canal towpath and broad forestry tracks. The only danger is going into auto-pilot on these long trails and missing a turning, especially if you are blethering away to a friend while you walk. Just keep an eye on the maps in the book so that you know when to pay attention for significant junctions. The northern half of the route crosses some high, featureless moorland which can often be shrouded in low cloud and fog. The path, however, is obvious and so long as you stick to it and don't go wandering off across the moor there should be no need to get your compass out.

Using GPS with this book

Whilst traditionalists will scoff, more open-minded walkers will accept that GPS technology can be an inexpensive, well-established if non-essential, navigational aid. In no time at all a GPS receiver, given a clear view of the sky, will establish your position and altitude in a variety of formats to within a few metres. These days, most **smartphones** have a GPS receiver built in and mapping software available to run on them (see p40).

Most of the maps throughout the book include **numbered way-points** along the route. These correlate to the list on pp152-4 which gives the OS grid reference and a description. You can download the complete list for free as a GPS-readable file (that doesn't include the text descriptions) from the Trailblazer website: 🖥 **trailblazer-guides.com**. It's also possible to buy state-of-the-art digital mapping to import into your GPS unit (see p40), but it's not the most reliable

---

(Opposite) **Top**: Boats moored on the Caledonian Canal.
Bottom: Wild camping (see p19) beside Loch Lochy.

❏ **For information on how COVID-19 could affect your walk see p46**

way of navigating and the small screen on your pocket-sized unit will invariably fail to put places into context or give you the 'big picture'. Traditional OS paper maps (see p38-40), whilst bulkier, are always preferable.

Another way of using a GPS unit is to download a **track log** of the route from the internet. Where waypoints are single points like cairns, a track log is a continuous line like a path that appears on your GPS screen; all you have to do is keep on that line – as with a car sat-nav. Many of these 'user-generated' track logs available online are imperfect, however, because it takes an extremely trail-savvy and committed person to record a perfect track log without any gaps or confusing diversions.

The fact is thousands have managed the walk without GPS. However, all those thousands will also have had their frustrating moments of navigational uncertainty, and reliable technology now exists to minimise mistakes and wasted time. Correctly using this book's GPS data could get you back on track and dozing in front of the pub fireplace or tucked up in bed all the sooner.

ACCOMMODATION

The Great Glen Way passes through a number of villages which are conveniently spaced to make logical end points to each day's walk. The only places where accommodation is sparse are at Gairlochy, and between Drumnadrochit and Inverness. For the former, it's possible to make a 3-mile detour to the village of Spean Bridge, but for the latter you really have no choice but to fit the 19 miles between Drumnadrochit and Inverness into one day, unless you are camping.

Elsewhere along the Way there is plenty of B&B accommodation but this is a popular tourist destination so book ahead to avoid being stranded. Outside the peak summer and Easter seasons it may be quieter but some of the accommodation closes for winter. The town and village facilities table (see pp30-1) shows

❏ **Book accommodation in advance!**
Always book your accommodation in advance. Not only does this ensure you have a bed for the night but it gives you an opportunity to find out more about the place, check the price and see what's included.

Most B&Bs and hotels can now be booked through a website, either their own or an agency's; however, booking by phone or email is best because you can check details more easily. Also, in general, it is best to book direct – online agencies may seem to have a good rate but you are likely to get the best deal if booked with the relevant B&B or hotel. Expect to have to pay a deposit when booking in advance.

If you have to cancel please telephone your hosts; it will save a lot of worry and possibly allow them to provide a bed for someone else.

You may also want to consider using the services of an accommodation-booking agency (see p26); they charge a fee but save you a considerable amount of work.

the availability of accommodation and in the route guide section of this book there is detailed information on the options available in each town and village.

Camping

It's quite possible to camp the whole way and, if you wish to lighten your load while walking, there are baggage-carrying companies who will drive your kit to your next destination (see p26). **Wild camping** is permitted in the wilds of Scotland thanks to the Scottish Outdoor Access Code (see p50) although it is not permitted to camp on designated historic monuments, of which the Caledonian Canal is one. There are, however, organised campsites at the end of each stage of the walk and three official 'wild' campsites (see box below) as well; some spots suitable for wild camping are noted on the maps.

Hostels

These offer budget accommodation and are generally popular with a young crowd, although not exclusively so. Many people of all ages prefer the camaraderie and opportunity to meet fellow walkers that such accommodation provides.

A dorm bed (often bunk beds) costs around £16-22pp (though can go up to £30), but many hostels now have private rooms which are a little more expensive, at around £20-40pp, which is still – usually – cheaper than a B&B. However, the

---

❏ Trailblazer rest sites – wild campsites

There are three of these well-named campsites or **rest sites** (see below) on the Way and all are in a beautiful location by the water's edge. They are designed for small tents, for single-night stays only, and are essentially 'wild' campsites, albeit with an

official stamp on them. Conceived with canoeists in mind; walkers are welcome to make use of them too. They have designated flat areas for pitching, fire sites and compost toilets. The rest sites are as follows: **Glas-dhoire**, Loch Lochy, see p95; **Leitirfearn**, Loch Oich, see p104; and **Kytra Lock**, see p107.

To use the **compost toilets** you will need a key; the 'facilities access charge' for this is £10pp and you can keep the key for the duration of the walk. Keys are available either from **Corpach Sea**

Glas-dhoire Trailblazer wild campsite

Lock Office (Mar to early Nov daily 8.30am-5.30pm, early Nov to Mar Mon-Fri 9am-4.30pm), or **Seaport Marina in Inverness** (May/June to end Sep daily 9am-6pm, end Sep to May/June Mon-Thur 9.15am-5pm, Fri to 4.30pm). It's best to arrange this in advance by calling ☎ 01463-725500; they will also give you the mobile number for the Corpach lock-keeper in case the keeper is out of the office when you arrive. If you can't arrive during the office hours a key can be posted to you but there is likely to be a postal charge. The key must be returned at the end of your walk – it can either be handed in, put through the post box at the relevant office, or posted back.

For additional information visit 🖥 www.scottishcanals.co.uk/canals/caledonian-canal/; click on Paddling and then click on Great Glen Canoe Trail map.

beds may not be as comfortable as those in a B&B, the rooms are more basic and breakfast is not included in the rate, though sometimes can be provided.

The Scottish Youth Hostels Association (SYHA; general enquiries ☎ 01786 891400, reservations Mon-Fri 9am-5pm ☎ 0345 293 7373, 🖳 hostellingscot land.org.uk) has a hostel in Inverness and one in Glen Nevis near Fort William; three other hostels are affiliated to the SYHA and there are also some independent hostels (see p31) on/near the Way.

Bed and breakfast

Most walkers opt for a bed and breakfast (B&B) as they offer comfortable, private accommodation with a hearty breakfast in the morning; just what is needed after a hard day's walk. The larger B&Bs usually have a choice of rooms: **singles** (one single bed), **doubles** (one double bed), **twins** (two single beds) and **triple/quad rooms** (often called family rooms) which comprise a double bed along with one or two singles, or bunk beds. Single rooms are not very common; if you are alone you may find you have to take a double or twin and pay a single occupancy charge to compensate for the loss of a bed space to the owner. B&B owners are often proud to boast that all rooms are **en suite**. This enthusiasm has led some to squeeze a cramped shower and loo cubicle into the corner of a bedroom. Establishments without en suite rooms are sometimes preferable as you may get sole use of a bathroom. See also p29 and p75.

Airbnb

The rise and rise of Airbnb (🖳 airbnb.co.uk) has seen private homes and apartments opened up to overnight travellers on an informal basis. Do check thoroughly what you are getting and the precise location. Places tend to come and go far more frequently than 'normal' B&Bs. There are several Airbnb establishments along the Great Glen Way, most of them in Fort William and Inverness, though more and more are appearing around Loch Ness too. It might be worth checking the website as more may appear in rural areas. At its best, this is a great way to meet local people in a relatively unstructured environment, but do be aware that these places are not registered B&Bs, so standards may vary, yet prices may not necessarily be any lower than for those of a B&B.

Guesthouses, hotels, pubs and inns

Guesthouses and **hotels** usually offer a little more than a B&B and while the former is often a home with rooms set aside for guests, the latter is a dedicated accommodation provider. There is often a residents' lounge, room service and an evening meal on offer (at additional cost). Consequently prices are often higher, ranging from £35pp to £80pp. The poshest hotels will charge even more than this during the peak summer season. A posh hotel may not be the natural fit for a muddy walker, but should you feel the need for some pampering you will find quality hotels in Fort Augustus, Drumnadrochit and Inverness.

Pubs and **inns** vary in quality where accommodation is concerned. The better ones are akin to a good hotel while others offer basic rooms and a lot of noise from the bar below. Prices match the quality with the cheaper ones around £25-35pp and the better ones around £35-45pp.

FOOD AND DRINK

Breakfast and lunch

Although you may expect a bowl of Scottish porridge for your B&B **breakfast**, you're more likely to be offered a bowl of cereal or muesli followed by a full plate of bacon, eggs, black pudding and baked beans as well as toast and marmalade; ideal for setting you up for a day on the trail. If you prefer something lighter, a continental breakfast is normally available.

You will need to carry a packed **lunch** with you some days; your accommodation host may well be able to prepare one, if requested in advance. If you stick to the logical daily stages between villages you will have no problem picking up some lunch from the village shop at the start of the day's walk. On some stages there may be somewhere to pick up lunch during the day but not always. Where you really need to plan ahead is for the long stretch between Banavie and Laggan (see p86) where there is no food at all. The last food shop is the Co-op in Corpach while the last eatery is The Moorings Hotel at Banavie. If you get stuck you will have to make the 3-mile detour from Gairlochy to Spean Bridge to pick up food

---

❑ **Scottish food**

For too long Scotland, and most of Britain for that matter, neglected its once fine local food culture. Things are starting to change although there is still little regional differentiation on many menus along the Way. As highly subsidised mass-produced food enters Britain from across the globe on the back of 'free trade', local small-scale producers find it hard to compete. Pub grub bows to the economic dictates of freezer and microwave, rather than the sanity of home-grown specialities. At the end of a hard day on the trail your staple diet is more likely to be scampi and chips or lasagne, than cock-a-leekie or crappit heids.

This is a shame; one of the great joys of travel is to embrace the spirit of a place and there is no better way of doing this than by sampling food that is grown and produced locally. By doing so you feed the local economy and strengthen regional identity; a direct benefit to the locality that is giving you, the traveller, so much. Now and then you will come across brave places attempting to breathe life back into rural culinary traditions and these should be actively supported. Keep an eye out for **Taste of Scotland** (🖳 taste-of-scotland.com) signs indicating places serving good quality, fresh Scottish produce.

Some traditional dishes include:
- **Arbroath smokies** – smoked haddock
- **Bannocks** – oatcakes baked in an oven and served with cheese
- **Bridies** – minced beef pies
- **Cock-a-leekie** – chicken and leek soup with prunes
- **Clapshot/tatties and neeps** – originating from Orkney, this is a combination of mashed potatoes, turnips, chives and butter or dripping; it usually accompanies haggis
- **Crappit heids** – lobster-stuffed haddock heads
- **Cullen skink** – smoked haddock and potato soup
- **Haggis** – minced lamb's or deer's liver and a collection of other meaty offal bits
- **Porridge** – boiled oats, often eaten for breakfast
- **Scotch broth** – a thick soup of lamb, vegetables, barley, lentils and split peas
- **Stovies** – fried potatoes and onion mixed with left-over meat and baked in an oven

there. There is a similar dearth of food on the 19 miles between Drumnadrochit and Inverness (see p135); only the very basic Abriachan Eco-Café offering simple treats (if it is open). For this stage it's best to stock up on lunch in Drumnadrochit, particularly as this is a long, strenuous day's walk.

Use the information in the village and town facilities table (see pp30-1) and in Part 4 to plan ahead.

Evening meals

Stumbling across a good **pub** when you're on a long walk is like manna from heaven. Not only a good place to revive flagging spirits in the middle of the day or early afternoon, the local pub (or 'hotel') is often your only choice for an evening meal. Many have à la carte restaurants, but most walkers choose something from the cheaper bar menu washed down by a pint of real ale and perhaps a nip of malt whisky to bring the day to a contented close. Menus often include at least one vegetarian option.

In the larger villages, such as Fort Augustus and Drumnadrochit, you'll have a wider choice with **takeaways** serving anything as long as it's fried, and good **restaurants** dishing up culinary selections from round the world.

Buying camping supplies

Campers who wish to cook their own meals each night will find **food** supplies from the local village shops at the start and end of each stage of the Way. The only exception is at Gairlochy where you have three options: make the three-mile detour to Spean Bridge, combine the two days into one and walk from Fort William to Laggan, or carry enough food with you for two days. The last chance to stock up on the first day is at the Co-op in Corpach.

Buying **fuel** for stoves is surprisingly difficult, but it should be possible to last on a couple of gas canisters for the whole walk. There are plenty of outdoor shops in Fort William where you can buy gas and liquid fuels.

Drinks and drinking

Whisky Scotland is world famous for its alcohol production and most pubs and hotel bars have a good selection of whisky and beer. Scotch whisky, 'the water of life', is distilled from malted barley and other cereals and is either a blend, or a single malt made in one distillery. A connoisseur can tell the difference between single malts distilled in different parts of the country such as the West Coast, East Coast, Lowlands, Highlands, Isle of Islay... the list goes on, and many happy evenings can be spent brushing up on this neglected skill without coming to any conclusion about which is best. **Ben Nevis Distillery**, in Fort William (see p76), is the only distillery in the Great Glen.

Beer Traditional British ale, beer, bitter, call it what you like, is the product of small-scale regional breweries who have created a huge diversity of strengths and flavours through skill and craftsmanship. Real ale continues to ferment in the cask so can be drawn off by hand pump or a simple tap in the cask itself. It should not be confused with characterless, industrially produced beer whose fermentation is stopped by pasteurisation and therefore needs the addition of gas to give it some life and fizz. Traditionally the Highlands have not been a happy hunting ground for the real ale enthusiast, but this has changed; there has been a resurgence in craft brewing and the walker in Scotland shouldn't find it hard to track down a few quality pints, with around 80 breweries (some of them tiny craft breweries) now operating north of the border.

Beer from the following Scottish **breweries** is worth looking out for: An Teallach (🖳 anteallachale.wordpress.com), Cairngorm (🖳 cairngormbrewery .com), Orkney (🖳 orkneybrewery.co.uk), Broughton Ales (🖳 broughtonales .co.uk), Innis & Gunn (🖳 innisandgunn.com), Black Isle (🖳 blackislebrewery .com), Inveralmond (🖳 inveralmond-brewery.co.uk), Caledonian (🖳 caledo nianbeer.com) and Isle of Skye (🖳 skyeale.com) among others. Another particularly interesting pint to try is Fraoch Heather Ale (🖳 williamsbrosbrew .com/beer/fraoch), which is flavoured with heather flowers to give you a real taste of the country you're walking over.

Water Spring water, 'a noble, royal, pleasant drink' as the Highland poet Duncan Ban Macintyre would have it, is readily available for the taking along much of the Great Glen Way, but if you wish to drink directly from gushing burns, use a little common sense. Although the Great Glen Way crosses a rural landscape it is a heavily used landscape. There are a lot of people living in the Great Glen and, in places, quite a few farm animals so the water may not be as clean as it could be. The freshest water is higher up, particularly on the section between Fort Augustus and Drumnadrochit. See p54 for further information on when and how to purify water.

It's best to stock up with a day's worth of water in the villages at the start of each day. You can fill up your water bottle in public toilets, or alternatively ask in shops, cafés or pubs if they would mind filling it up; most people are happy to do so.

MONEY

There are **ATMs/cash machines** in Fort William, Corpach, Fort Augustus, Drumnadrochit and Inverness. Note that some ATMs (not those at banks) charge you for making a cash withdrawal (usually the Link machines that are sometimes found in shops and post offices; note, too, that some readers using cards issued by banks abroad have had them rejected by Link machines).

Most shops take **credit or debit cards** and have a **cashback** service so you can obtain cash, though usually only if you buy something at the same time.

Small independent shops generally prefer you to pay in **cash** as do most B&Bs, bunkhouses and campsites; fewer places accept a **cheque** now.

The table on pp30-1 indicates the whereabouts of post offices and banks.

Getting cash from a post office

Most banks in Britain have agreements with the post office allowing customers to make cash withdrawals using their debit card at post offices throughout the country. This is a useful facility on the Great Glen Way where there are more post offices than banks. To find branches and check their services contact the Post Office (☎ 0345-722 3355, 🖳 postoffice.co.uk/branch-finder).

PLANNING YOUR WALK

❏ **Information for foreign visitors**

● **Currency** The British pound (£) comes in notes of £50, £20, £10 and £5, and coins of £2 and £1. The pound is divided into 100 pence (usually referred to as 'p', pronounced 'pee') which come in 'silver' coins of 50p, 20p, 10p and 5p, and 'copper' coins of 2p and 1p. Although Scotland uses pounds sterling like the rest of the UK they do have their own sterling bank notes which can confuse visitors from abroad who are used to the more ubiquitous Bank of England notes south of the border. To confuse matters even more Scottish bank notes are not issued by a central bank as they are in England but by three retail banks (RBS, Bank of Scotland and Clydesdale), so there is not one but three styles of bank notes in circulation. On top of that, Bank of England notes are also common. All four styles of notes are pounds sterling and are widely accepted throughout Scotland.

A guide to currency **exchange rates** can be found on 🖥 xe.com/ucc; however, the actual rate used by post offices, banks and travel agents varies.

● **Business hours** Most **village shops** are open Monday to Friday 9am-5pm and Saturday 9am-12.30pm. Many open for longer than this and some open on Sundays as well. Occasionally you'll come across a local shop that closes at lunchtime on one day during the week, usually a Wednesday or Thursday; this is a throwback to the days when all towns and villages had an 'early closing day'.

Supermarkets are open Monday to Saturday 8am-8pm (sometimes up to 15 hours a day, closing at 10pm) and on Sunday from about 9am to 5 or 6pm, though main branches of supermarkets can only open for six hours on a Sunday; most choose 10am-4pm or 11am-5pm.

Main **post offices** generally open Monday to Friday 9am-5pm and Saturday 9am-12.30pm; **banks** typically open at 9.30/10am Monday to Friday and close at 3.30/4pm, though in some places both post offices and banks may open only two or three days a week and/or in the morning, or limited hours, only. **ATMs (cash machines)** located outside a bank, shop, post office or petrol station are open all the time, but any that are inside will be accessible only when that place is open; see also p23.

Pub hours are less predictable; although many open daily 11am-11pm, opening hours in rural areas and during quieter periods (early weekdays, or in the winter months) are often more limited: typically opening hours are Monday to Saturday 11am-3pm & 5 or 6-11pm, and Sunday 11am/noon-3pm & 7-10.30/11pm.

The last entry time to most **museums and galleries** is usually half an hour/an hour before the official closing time.

● **Public (bank/national) holidays** Most businesses in Scotland are shut on 1st & 2nd January, Good Friday (March/April), the first & last Monday in May, the first Monday in August, 25th and 26th December; some businesses also close on St Andrew's Day, 30th November. If a bank holiday is on a weekend the Monday after the weekend usually becomes the holiday day.

● **School holidays** School holiday periods in the Highlands are generally: a two-week break mid October, two weeks around Christmas/New Year, a few days in late February, two weeks around Easter, and six weeks from early July to mid August.

● **Documents/entry charges** If you are a member of a National Trust (NT) organisation in your country bring your membership card as you should be entitled to free, or discounted, entry to National Trust for Scotland properties and sites in Scotland.

● **Travel/medical insurance** At the time of writing the **European Health Insurance Card** (EHIC) entitles EU nationals (on production of their card) to necessary medical treatment under the UK's National Health Service (NHS) while on a temporary visit here. It is unlikely this will be the case after Brexit but it may depend on your home country. However, this is not a substitute for proper medical cover on your travel insurance for unforeseen bills and for getting you home should that be necessary.

Also consider cover for loss or theft of personal belongings, especially if you're camping or staying in hostels, as there may be times when your luggage is unattended.

● **Weights and measures** Although the country is generally metricated, milk in Britain can still be sold in pints (1 pint = 568ml), as can beer in pubs. Most other **liquids** including petrol (gasoline) and diesel are sold in litres.

Road distances can also continue to be given in miles (1 mile = 1.6km) rather than kilometres, and yards (1yd = 0.9m) rather than metres.

The population remains divided between those who still use inches (1 inch = 2.5cm) and feet (1ft = 0.3m) and those who are happy with centimetres and millimetres; you'll often be told that 'it's only a hundred yards or so' to somewhere, rather than a hundred metres or so.

Most **food** is sold in metric weights (g and kg) but the imperial weights of pounds (lb: 1lb = 453g) and ounces (oz: 1oz = 28g) are often displayed too.

The **weather** – a frequent topic of conversation – is also an issue: while most forecasts predict temperatures in °C (centigrade), many people continue to think in terms of °F (Fahrenheit); see temperature chart on p16 for conversions.

● **Time** During the winter the whole of Britain is on Greenwich Mean Time (GMT). The clocks move one hour forward on the last Sunday in March, remaining on British Summer Time (BST) until the last Sunday in October.

● **Smoking** Smoking in enclosed public places is banned. The ban relates not only to pubs and restaurants, but also to B&Bs, hostels and hotels. These latter have the right to designate one or more bedrooms where the occupants can smoke, but the ban is in force in all enclosed areas open to the public – even in a private home such as a B&B. Should you be foolhardy enough to light up in a no-smoking area, which includes pretty well any indoor public place, you could be fined £50, but it's the owners of the premises who suffer most if they fail to stop you, with a potential fine of £2500.

● **Telephones** The international access code for Britain is ☎ 44, followed by the area code minus the first 0, and then the number you require. Within the UK, to call a number with the same code as the landline phone you are calling from, the code can be omitted: dial the number only. It is cheaper to ring at weekends (from midnight on Friday till midnight on Sunday), and after 7pm and before 7am on weekdays. To protect against vandalism some public phones accept debit/credit cards only; the minimum cost for a call is 60p.

Mobile (cell) phone reception is not particularly reliable along the Great Glen Way. While you may get a signal in Fort William and Inverness it's best not to rely on your phone on the Way. Generally speaking the signal is often better on higher, open ground than it is down in the depths of the glen, but not always. If you're using a mobile phone that is registered overseas, consider buying a local SIM card to keep costs down; also remember to bring a universal adaptor so you can charge your phone.

● **Emergency services** For police, ambulance, fire and mountain rescue dial ☎ 999, or the EU standard number ☎ 112.

PLANNING YOUR WALK

OTHER SERVICES

Most of the settlements through which the Way passes have little more than a **general store**, a **post office** and a **public telephone**. Post offices can be very useful if you have discovered you are carrying too much in your rucksack and want to send unnecessary items home to lighten your load.

Where they exist, special mention has also been made in Part 4 of other services which are of use to walkers such as **laundrettes**, **internet access**, **pharmacies/chemists**, **medical/health centres**, **outdoor equipment shops** and **tourist information centres**.

WALKING COMPANIES

For walkers wanting to make their holiday as easy and trouble free as possible there are several specialist companies offering a range of services from luggage transport to fully guided group tours.

Baggage carriers

This is one service that's well worth the money! The following companies offer a baggage-carrying service either direct to your campsite/accommodation each night or to a drop-off point in each village from about £45-65 per rucksack for the whole Way; all you need to carry is a small daypack with essentials in it. If you are finding the walk harder than expected you can always join one of these services at a later stage. Note that they will take camping gear.

● **Great Glen Baggage Transfer** (☎ 01320-351322, 🖥 greatglenbaggagetrans fer.co.uk; Fort Augustus) Will collect and drop off bags for £60 per bag for a minimum of two bags, and maximum weight of 18kg per bag. If arranged in advance they can meet you at the start and end of the walk to transfer you to/from your accommodation. The service is available in either direction for either the whole or part of the walk. Solo walkers should contact them for a discounted rate.

● **Loch Ness Travel** (☎ 01456-450550, 🖥 lochnesstravel.com; Drumnadrochit) Operate the service along the entire route in both directions between Easter and mid October. Maximum weight 18kg per bag. Options available to drop-off/ collect baggage at Fort William and Inverness locations. Their Loch Ness Shuttlebus transfers walkers from Drumnadrochit via Loch Laide/Ladycairn or Blackfold for those wishing to divide the longest (20-mile) section from Drumnadrochit to Inverness into two more manageable 'chunks' by staying two nights in Drumnadrochit.

Self-guided holidays

The following companies provide all-in customised packages which usually include detailed advice and notes on itineraries and routes, maps, accommodation booking, daily baggage transfer, and transport arrangements at the start and end of your walk. The companies listed offer the walk from south to north with a range of itineraries (generally taking from **five to seven days** for the whole walk). However, most also **tailor-make holidays** including from north to south.

● **Absolute Escapes** (☎ 0131-240 1210, 🖳 absoluteescapes.com; Edinburgh)
● **AMS-Outdoors** (☎ 0141-812 7370, 🖳 scottish-walks.com; Glasgow)
● **C-N-Do Scotland** (☎ 01786-445703, 🖳 cndoscotland.com; Stirling)
● **Celtic Trails** (☎ 01291-689774, 🖳 celtictrailswalkingholidays.co.uk; Chepstow) Offers whole trail over six or seven days.
● **Contours Walking Holidays** (☎ 01629-821900, 🖳 contours.co.uk; Derbyshire)
● **Discovery Travel** (☎ 01983-301133, 🖳 discoverytravel.co.uk; York)
● **Easyways** (☎ 01324-714132, 🖳 easyways.com; Falkirk)
● **Explore Britain** (☎ 01740-650900, 🖳 explorebritain.com; Durham)
● **Gemini Walks** (☎ 01324-410260, 🖳 geminiwalks.com; Stirlingshire)
● **Great British Walks**, formerly known as The Walking Holiday Company (☎ 01600-713008, 🖳 great-british-walks.com; Monmouth, Wales)
● **Let's Go Walking** (☎ 01837-880075, 🖳 letsgowalking.com; Devon)
● **Macs Adventure** (☎ 0141-530 7163, 🖳 macsadventure.com; Glasgow) Offers 3 itineraries: 'Escape' from Fort Augustus to Inverness in 5 days, the whole trail in 7-9 days, and an 'In Comfort' tour in 9 days/8 nights.
● **Make Tracks Walking Holidays** (☎ 0131-229 6844, 🖳 maketracks.net; Edinburgh)
● **Mickledore Travel** (☎ 017687-72335, 🖳 mickledore.co.uk; Keswick)
● **North-West Frontiers** (☎ 01997-421474, 🖳 nwfrontiers.com; Strathpeffer) Offers the whole trail in 8 days.
● **NorthWest Walks** (☎ 01257-424889, 🖳 northwestwalks.co.uk; Wigan)
● **Sherpa Expeditions** (☎ 0800-008 7741, 🖳 sherpaexpeditions.com; London)
● **Transcotland** (☎ 01887-820848, 🖳 transcotland.com; Perthshire)
● **Wilderness Scotland** (☎ 01479-898529, 🖳 wildernessscotland.com; Aviemore)

Group/guided walking tours

Fully guided tours are ideal for individuals wanting to travel with others and for groups of friends wanting to be guided. Packages usually include meals, accommodation, transport arrangements, mini-bus backup, baggage transfer, as well as a qualified guide. Few companies offer guided walks on the Great Glen Way, perhaps because the walk is quite easy to follow your own. However, if you like to walk with a guide contact the following companies:

● **Caledonian Discovery** (☎ 01397-772167, 🖳 caledonian-discovery.co.uk; Corpach, Fort William) offers a walking holiday with an experienced guide and with accommodation on board a barge so there is no need to pack and unpack each day. It is also not necessary to walk every day; alternative activities are available including cycling, canoeing, and relaxing!
● **Thistle Trekking** (☎ 01228-710252, 🖳 thistletrekking.co.uk; Cumbria) Offers an 8-day holiday with 6 days of walking.
● **HF Holidays** (☎ 020-3974 8865, 🖳 hfholidays.co.uk) Offers a 7-night holiday staying first at their own country house in Glen Coe and then at a hotel in Inverness.

WALKING WITH A DOG

There is nothing stopping you taking your dog along the Great Glen Way. The only issue may arise from over-excited dogs wishing to take a dip in the canal. In places the sides are sheer, particularly at the locks, so any water-borne pooch may struggle to get out. Well-behaved dogs, however, will enjoy the walk just as much as their owners (see pp155-6).

OTHER OPTIONS FOR THE GREAT GLEN WAY

The Great Glen isn't just for walkers. There are two other official routes from Fort William to Inverness: one for cyclists and one for canoeists.

Mountain-biking

The Great Glen Way is primarily a walkers' route but it is possible to cycle it if you have the right bike. South of Fort Augustus the route is, for much of the way, on broad, level towpaths, forestry tracks and some short sections of road but north of Fort Augustus things get decidedly more hilly and, for long stretches, the trail is rougher, narrower and steeper. You would need a mountain bike or hybrid bike for this section. For road-bike users, follow Sustrans Route 78. This follows the Great Glen Way north to Fort Augustus and then picks up the quiet single-track roads on the east side of Loch Ness all the way to Inverness. It is 66 miles and takes between two and five days from end to end.

You can hire bikes in Fort William (see p76) and Inverness (see p146).

Canoeing

The third and final way to 'do' the Great Glen is probably the most relaxing: by canoe. The Great Glen Canoe Trail is an official route that opened in 2012 and follows the Caledonian Canal and lochs Lochy, Oich and Ness; a distance of 60 miles. Competent canoeists will find little difficulty with the route while novices can join a guided group. There is more information at ▱ greatglen canoetrail.info.

Budgeting

If you're **camping**, most sites charge around £8-10 per person (pp) so you can get by on as little as £14-16pp per day using the cheapest sites and the free 'wild' sites as often as possible. This assumes you would be cooking all your own food from staple ingredients rather than eating convenience food.

Most people find that the best-laid plans to survive on the bare minimum fall flat after a couple of hard days' walking or in bad weather. Assuming the odd end-of-day drink and the occasional pub meal or takeaway, a budget of £22-28pp is more realistic.

A **hostel** bed costs £16-30pp. Every SYHA hostel and most independent hostels have a self-catering kitchen and the larger ones offer breakfast (£4.50-7.50), packed lunches (£6.50) and evening meals (about £7/10/12 for 1/2/3 courses). Allowing £35-45pp per day will enable you to have the occasional meal out and enjoy sampling a few of the local brews. If you don't want to cook in a hostel's kitchen or are planning on eating out most nights add another £12 per day.

If you're staying in **B&B-style accommodation**, you won't be cooking for yourself. Bearing that in mind, B&B prices vary enormously but expect to pay around £35pp. The more simple B&Bs will charge closer to £25pp while those that consider themselves something special can be as much as £50pp. (Rates are based on two people sharing a room.) Overall £50-75pp per day is a rough guide based on spending £25-35pp on a packed lunch, evening pub meal and a couple of drinks. If staying in a guesthouse or hotel expect to spend £65-85pp per day.

If you are travelling alone you must also expect to pay a **single occupancy supplement**; this may mean paying the full room rate in the peak season. See also p20.

Don't forget to set some money aside, perhaps £100-150, for the inevitable **extras**: postcards, bus/train fares, taxis, whisky and beer, using a baggage-transfer service, or any changes of plan.

Itineraries

Walkers are individuals. Some like to cover large distances as quickly as possible, others are happy to stroll along stopping whenever the fancy takes them. You may want to walk the Great Glen Way all in one go, tackle it over a series of weekends or use the trail for linear day walks; the choice is yours. To accommodate these differences this guidebook has not been divided into rigid daily stages which often leads to a fixed mindset of how you should walk. Instead, it's been designed to make it easy for you to plan your own perfect itinerary. Nevertheless the villages along the Way are evenly spaced offering a logical way to divide the walk into daily sections.

The **overview map** and **stage maps** (see the end of the book) and **table of village and town facilities** (see pp30-1) summarise the essential information.

Alternatively, to make it even easier, have a look at the **suggested itineraries** (see pp31-2) and simply choose your preferred type of accommodation and speed of walking. There are also suggestions on pp33 for those who want to experience the best of the trail over a day or a weekend; the **public transport map and table** on pp44-5 may also be useful at this stage.

Having made a rough plan, turn to **Part 4**, where you will find summaries of the route; full descriptions of accommodation, places to eat and other services in each village and town; as well as detailed trail maps.

				VILLAGE AND
Place name (Places in brackets are a short walk off the Great Glen Way)	**Distance from previous place** approx **miles km** (Distances in brackets indicate how far the place is from the nearest point on the Great Glen Way)	**ATM (cash machine) /bank**	**Post Office**	**Tourist Information Centre (TIC)**
Fort William	MILES KM	✔	✔	TIC
Caol	2½ 4	✔	✔	
(Corpach)	(½ 1)	✔	✔	
Banavie	1 1.5			
Gairlochy	6½ 10.5			
(Spean Bridge)	3½ 5.5 (from Gairlochy)	✔	✔	
Glas-dhoire	9½ 15.5 (from Gairlochy)			
Laggan Locks (jctn)	2½ 4			
Laggan	1 1.5			
(Loch Oich route)				
Leitirfearn	4 6.5 (from Laggan on Loch Oich route)			
Invergarry	*5 8*		✔	
(Invergarry Link Route)				
Aberchalder	2 3 (from Leitirfearn)			
	3 5 (from Invergarry)			
Kytra Lock	3 5			
Fort Augustus	3 5	✔	✔	
Invermoriston	9½ 15.5			
(Alltsigh)	4½ 7 (from Invermoriston)			
Grotaig	9½ 15.5 (from Invermoriston)			
Drumnadrochit	5 8	✔	✔	
Abriachan	7 11.5			
Inverness	13 21	✔	✔	TIC

WHICH DIRECTION?

Most walkers head south to north which is reflected in the layout of this book. There are other practical reasons for heading north rather than south; the prevailing wind and rain (south-westerly) is behind you, as is the sun, and the gentler walking is at the start giving you time to warm up before tackling the steeper climbs north of Fort Augustus.

That said, there is no reason why you shouldn't walk in the other direction, especially if just tackling a part of the Way. The maps in Part 4 give timings for

TOWN FACILITIES

Eating Place ✔ = one; ✔✔ = two; ✔✔✔ = 3+	Food Store	Campsite (✔) = Trailblazer rest site or wild camping spot	Hostel (SYHA) H = independent hostel	B&B-style accommodation ✔ = one ✔✔ = two; ✔✔✔ = 3+	Place name (places in brackets are a short walk off the Great Glen Way: see opposite for distances)
✔✔✔	✔		H	✔✔✔	**Fort William**
✔✔✔	✔				**Caol**
	✔				(Corpach)
✔✔				✔	**Banavie**
		(✔)			**Gairlochy**
✔✔✔	✔	✔		✔✔✔	(Spean Bridge)
		(✔)			**Glas-dhoire**
✔		(✔)			**Laggan Locks (jctn)**
	✔		H	✔✔	**Laggan**
					(Loch Oich route)
		(✔)			**Leitirfearn (Loch Oich route)**
✔	✔		H	✔✔✔	*Invergarry*
					(Invergarry Link route)
		(✔)			**Aberchalder**
		(✔)			**Kytra Lock**
✔✔✔	✔	✔	H	✔✔✔	**Fort Augustus**
✔✔	✔	✔(Invercoille)		✔✔✔	**Invermoriston**
			H	✔	(Alltsigh)
✔					**Grotaig**
✔✔✔	✔	✔	H	✔✔✔	**Drumnadrochit**
✔		(✔) & ✔		✔	**Abriachan**
✔✔✔	✔	✔	H/SYHA	✔✔✔	**Inverness**

PLANNING YOUR WALK

both directions and, as route-finding instructions are on the maps rather than in blocks of text, it is straightforward using this guide back to front.

SUGGESTED ITINERARIES

These itineraries (see p32) are suggestions only; adapt them to your needs. They have been divided into different accommodation types and each table has itineraries to encompass different walking paces. **Don't forget to add your travelling time before and after the walk.**

CAMPING

Night	Relaxed pace Place	Approx distance miles	km	Medium pace Place	Approx distance miles	km	Fast pace Place	Approx distance miles	km
0	Fort William			Fort William			Fort William		
1	Gairlochy	11½	18.5	Gairlochy	11½	18.5	Glas-dhoire§	23	37
2	Glas-dhoire§	11½	18.5	Glas-dhoire§	11½	18.5	Fort Augustus	15½	25
3	Leitirfearn§	7½	12	Leitirfearn§	7½	12	Drumnadrochit	24	39
4	Kytra Lock§	5	8	Inver Coille	14½	23.5	Inverness	20	31.5
5	Inver Coille	9½	15	Drumnadrochit	17½	28			
6	Drumnadrochit	17½	28	Inverness	20	31½			
7	Abriachan	7	11.5						
8	Inverness	13	21	§ Trailblazer rest site (wild campsite)					

STAYING IN HOSTELS

Night	Relaxed pace Place	Approx Distance miles	km	Medium pace Place	Approx Distance miles	km	Fast pace Place	Approx Distance miles	km
0	Fort William			Fort William			Fort William		
1	Gairlochy*	11½	18.5	Gairlochy*	11½	18.5	Laggan	23½	38
2	Laggan	13	20.5	Laggan	13	20.5	Invermoriston**	22½	36
3	Invergarry	5	8	Fort Augustus	13	21	Drumnadrochit	14½	23.5
4	Fort Augustus	9	14.5	Alltsigh	14	22.5	Inverness	20	31.5
5	Invermoriston**	9½	15	Drumnadrochit	10	16			
6	Alltsigh	4½	7	Inverness	20	31.5			
7	Drumnadrochit	10	16	* No hostel but alternative accommodation available					
8	Inverness	20	31.5	at Spean Bridge (3 miles from Gairlochy, take a taxi)					

** No hostel but alternative accommodation available

STAYING IN B&B-STYLE ACCOMMODATION

Night	Relaxed pace Place	Approx Distance miles	km	Medium pace Place	Approx Distance miles	km	Fast pace Place	Approx Distance miles	km
0	Fort William			Fort William			Fort William		
1	Banavie	3½	5.5	Gairlochy†	10	16	Laggan	23½	37.5
2	Gairlochy†	6½	10.5	Laggan	13	20.5	Invermoriston	21½	34.5
3	Laggan	13	20.5	Fort Augustus	12	19.5	Drumnadrochit	14½	23.5
4	Fort Augustus	12	19.5	Invermoriston	9½	15	Inverness	20	31.5
5	Invermoriston	9½	15	Drumnadrochit	14½	23.5			
6	Drumnadrochit	14½	23.5	Inverness	20	31.5			
7	Abriachan††	6½	10.5	†No B&Bs in Gairlochy (take a taxi to Spean Bridge)					
8	Inverness	13½	21	†† Only one place to stay (Rivoulich Lodge)					

DAY AND WEEKEND WALKS

If you don't have time to walk the whole Way in one shot, there's nothing stopping you from picking off the highlights in just a day or weekend. The following suggestions take in some of the best of the Great Glen Way and have good public transport links (see pp43-6) at the start and finish. The weekend walk is also do-able in a day if you are fit and up for a long day.

Day walks

● **Laggan to Fort Augustus (see pp99-113)** An easy low-level (9½-mile/15km) walk following the old railway line by the shore of Loch Oich and the canal towpath. There are lovely views across the loch, and the stretch of the canal to Fort Augustus is one of the prettiest on its entire length.

● **Fort Augustus to Invermoriston high route (see pp116-18)** Probably the second most spectacular day; a 9-mile/14.5km walk. After a steep ascent out of Fort Augustus you are rewarded with a wonderful high-level romp across the moors with far-ranging views across Loch Ness and the Great Glen.

● **Invermoriston to Drumnadrochit (see pp122-31)** This is most people's highlight section, a 14½-mile/23.5km walk that, similar to the previous suggestion, starts with a steep ascent and then follows an undulating route across hill and moor, high above Loch Ness. There is also some beautiful Caledonian pine forest and spectacular views over rugged hills and the full length of Loch Ness.

● **Loch Oich circuit (see pp99-107)** This combines the two route choices from Laggan to Aberchalder, making a neat 13-mile/21km circuit around Loch Oich. The west side of the loch follows the old railway line through beautiful birch and oak woodland while the Invergarry side follows forestry tracks through conifer plantations but the route here is higher and offers better views across the loch and glen.

Weekend walks

● **Fort Augustus to Drumnadrochit (see pp116-131)** This route combines the two day walks suggested above to give a whole weekend of high-level walking, above the expanse of Loch Ness, with a convenient overnight stay in Invermoriston. The overall walk is 23½ miles/38km.

HILLWALKING SIDE TRIPS

The majesty of the Highlands can only be fully grasped by climbing out of the glens and onto the summits. The Great Glen Way passes below Ben Nevis (see pp160-4), the highest mountain in Scotland, and two fine munros above Loch Lochy (see pp96-8), presenting the well-equipped walker with a wonderful opportunity for a few days' hillwalking.

If you have been bitten by the hill-bagging bug take a look at Trailblazer's *Scottish Highlands Hillwalking Guide*.

Although not particularly high when compared with other mountains round the world, the Scottish mountains can be dangerous for the unprepared at any time of year. Read 'Mountain Safety' on p53, and also 'Access' on pp51-2 to make sure your planned walk doesn't interfere with other users of the hills.

What to take

How much you take with you is a very personal decision which takes experience to get right. For those new to long-distance walking the suggestions below will help you strike a sensible balance between comfort, safety and minimal weight.

KEEP YOUR LUGGAGE LIGHT

In these days of huge material wealth it can be a liberating experience to travel **as light as possible** to learn how few possessions we really need to be safe and comfortable. It is all too easy to take things along 'just in case' and these little items can soon mount up. If you are in any doubt about anything on your packing list, be ruthless and leave it at home.

To liberate themselves entirely from their luggage, many people now make use of **baggage-carrying companies** (see p26).

HOW TO CARRY IT

The size of your **rucksack** depends on how you plan to walk. If you are camping along the Way you will need a pack large enough to hold a tent, sleeping bag, cooking equipment and food; 65-75 litres' capacity should be ample. If you are going to stay in B&Bs or hostels you should be able to get all you need into a 30- to 40-litre pack. However, if planning to self-cater in hostels you may need to aim for the larger end of that pack scale to accommodate your food, although you won't need to carry too much as you can restock along the way.

The rucksack should have a stiffened back system and either be fully adjustable, or exactly the right size for your back. If you carry the main part of the load high and close to your body with a large proportion of the weight carried on your hips (not on your shoulders) by means of the padded hip belt you should be able to walk in comfort for days on end. Play around with different ways of packing your gear and adjusting all those straps until you get it just right. It's also handy to have a **bum/waist bag** or a very light **day pack** in which you can carry your camera, guidebook and other essentials when you go off sightseeing or for a day walk.

Pack similar things in different-coloured **stuff sacks** so they are easier to pull out of the dark recesses of your pack. Put these inside **waterproof rucksack liners**, or tough plastic sacks, that can be slipped inside your pack to protect everything from the inevitable rain. It's also worth taking a **waterproof**

rucksack cover; most rucksacks these days have them 'built in' to the sack but you can also buy them separately for less than a tenner.

Of course, if you decide to use one of the baggage-carrying services (see p26) you can pack most of your things in a **suitcase** and simply carry a small day-pack with the essentials you need for the day's walking.

FOOTWEAR

Boots

Your boots are the **single most important item** that can affect the enjoyment of your walk. In summer you could get by with a light pair of trail shoes if you're carrying only a small pack, although they don't give much support for your ankles and you'll get wet, cold feet if there is any rain. Some of the terrain is rough so a good pair of walking boots would be a safer option. They must fit well and be properly broken in. A week's walk is not the time to try out a new pair of boots. Refer to pp54-5 for some blister-avoidance strategies.

If you plan to climb Ben Nevis (see pp160-4) or the Loch Lochy munros (see pp96-8), good boots are essential.

Socks

The traditional wearing of a thin liner sock under a thicker wool sock is no longer necessary if you choose a high-quality sock specially designed for walking. A high proportion of natural fibres makes them much more comfortable. Three pairs are ample. Some people, however, still prefer to use thin liner socks (silk being best) as these are much easier to wash than thick socks, so you can change them more regularly than thick socks.

Extra footwear

Some walkers like to have a second pair of shoes to wear when they are not on the trail. Trainers, sport sandals or flip flops are all suitable as long as they are light.

CLOTHES

Scotland's wet and cold weather is notorious; even in summer you should come prepared for wintry conditions. It can also be spectacularly glorious so clothes to cope with these wide variations are needed. Experienced walkers pick their clothes according to the versatile layering system: a base layer to transport sweat from your skin; a mid-layer or two to keep you warm; and an outer layer or 'shell' to protect you from any wind, rain or snow.

Base layer

Cotton absorbs sweat, trapping it next to the skin which will chill you rapidly when you stop exercising. A thin lightweight **thermal top** made from synthetic material is better as it draws moisture away, keeping you dry. It will be cool if worn on its own in hot weather and warm when worn under other clothes in cooler conditions. A spare top would be sensible. You may also like to bring a **shirt** for wearing in the evening.

Mid-layers

From May to September a woollen jumper or mid-weight polyester **fleece** will suffice. For the rest of the year you will need an extra layer to keep you warm. Both wool and fleece, unlike cotton, stay reasonably warm when wet.

Outer layer

A **waterproof jacket** is essential year-round and will be much more comfortable (but also more expensive) if it's also 'breathable' to prevent the build-up of condensation on the inside. This layer can also be worn to keep the wind off.

Leg wear

Whatever you wear on your legs it should be light, quick-drying and not restricting. Many British walkers find polyester tracksuit bottoms comfortable. Poly-cotton or microfibre trousers are excellent. Denim jeans should never be worn; if they get wet they become heavy and cold, and bind to your legs.

A pair of **shorts** is nice to have on sunny days. Thermal **longjohns** or thick tights are cosy if you're camping and necessary for winter walking. **Waterproof trousers** are necessary most of the year but in summer could be left behind if your main pair of trousers is reasonably windproof and quick drying. **Gaiters** are not needed unless you come across a lot of snow in winter.

Underwear

Three changes of what you normally wear is fine. Women may find a **sports bra** more comfortable because pack straps can cause bra straps to dig into your shoulders.

Other clothes

A **warm hat** and **gloves** should be carried at all times of the year. Take two pairs of gloves in winter. In summer you should carry a **sun hat**. A small **towel** will be needed if you are not staying in B&Bs. If camping in summer a **head net** to protect you from the midges can be invaluable. These can be bought at various places along the Way.

TOILETRIES

Only take the minimum: a small bar of **soap** in a plastic container (unless staying in B&Bs) which can also be used instead of shaving cream and for washing clothes; a tiny tube of **toothpaste** and a **toothbrush**; and one roll of **loo paper** in a plastic bag. If you are planning to defecate outdoors you will also need a lightweight **trowel** for burying the evidence (see p49 for further tips). In addition a **razor**; **tampons/sanitary towels**; **deodorant**; a high-factor **sun screen**; and a good **insect repellent** for the midges (see p55) should cover all your needs.

FIRST-AID KIT

You need only a small kit to cover common problems and emergencies; pack it in a waterproof container.

A basic kit will contain **paracetamol** or **aspirin** for treating mild to moderate pain and fever; **plasters/Band Aids** for minor cuts; '**moleskin**', '**Compeed**', or '**Second Skin**' for blisters; a **bandage** for holding dressings, splints, or limbs in place and for supporting a sprained ankle, an **elastic knee support** (tubigrip) for a weak knee, a small selection of different-sized **sterile dressings** for wounds; **porous adhesive tape**; **antiseptic wipes**; **antiseptic cream**; **safety pins**; **tweezers**; **scissors**.

GENERAL ITEMS

Essential
Although navigation along the Way is not difficult it's always a good idea to have a **compass** or **GPS** in your rucksack, particularly for the high sections of the Way north of Fort Augustus. An emergency **whistle** for summoning assistance (see p57) is also very useful, as are the following: a **water bottle** or **pouch** holding at least one litre; a **torch** (flashlight) with spare bulb and batteries in case you end up walking after dark; **emergency food** which your body can quickly convert into energy (see p53); a **penknife**; a **watch** with an alarm; and several degradable **plastic bags** for packing out any rubbish you accumulate.

If you're not carrying a sleeping bag or tent you may wish to consider taking an emergency plastic **bivvy bag**, although it's not strictly necessary.

Useful
Many would list a **camera** as essential but it can be liberating to travel without one once in a while – however, if you do take one remember to take spare batteries or your camera's battery charger and also look at pp154-5 for notes on landscape photography; a **notebook** can be a more accurate way of recording your impressions; a **book** to pass the time on train and bus journeys or for the evenings; a pair of **sunglasses** in summer or when there's snow on the ground; **binoculars** for observing wildlife; a **walking stick** or poles to take the shock off your knees on the steepest sections which are between Fort Augustus and Drumnadrochit; and a **vacuum flask** for carrying hot drinks.

Most walkers carry **mobile/cell phones** (don't forget to bring the charger) but it is important to remember that the network may not provide full coverage of the area through which you are walking owing to the terrain (see box p25).

CAMPING GEAR

If you're camping you will need a decent **tent** (or bivvy bag if you enjoy travelling light) able to withstand wet and windy weather with netting on the entrance to keep the midges at bay; a three-season **sleeping bag** will cope with most eventualities although many walkers will be able to make do with one rated for one or two seasons – it's a personal choice; a **sleeping mat**; a **stove** and **fuel** (fuel can be picked up from the outdoor shops in Fort William; bottles of meths and the various gas cylinders are readily available, Coleman fuel is sometimes harder to find); a **pan** with a lid that can double as a frying pan/plate

PLANNING YOUR WALK

is fine for two people; a **pan handle**; a **mug**; a **spoon**; and a wire/plastic **scrubber** for washing up (there's no need for washing-up liquid and, anyway, it should never be used in streams, lochs or rivers).

Incense sticks to burn in your tent have been recommended as a midge repellent. Put them out before you go to sleep, though.

MONEY

There are few banks on the Great Glen Way so most of your money will need to be carried as **cash**, especially if you do not have an account with a bank that has an agreement with the Post Office (see p23).

A **debit card** is the easiest way to withdraw money either from banks or cash machines and that or a **credit card** can often be used to pay in larger shops, restaurants and hotels. Having a **cheque book** could be useful for paying at B&Bs that do not accept cards, even though supermarkets and shops may not accept them now.

MAPS

The hand-drawn maps in this book cover the trail at a scale of 1:20,000, which is a better scale than any other map currently available, and we've also included

---

❏ SOURCES OF FURTHER INFORMATION
Trail information
● **Great Glen Way websites** The **Highland Council** (🖳 highland.gov.uk) website has a wealth of online information including a downloadable pdf booklet to the Way. Click on 'Tourism and visitor attractions', then 'Long distance routes', then 'The Great Glen Way'. The council is also responsible for the **The Great Glen Way Ranger Service** which has a useful website with trail news and events information (see box p14).

Tourist information
● **Tourist information centres (TICs)** Many towns and villages in Scotland have a TIC, though these have been re-branded as **Visit Scotland iCentres**. They provide all manner of locally specific information for visitors and an accommodation-booking service (for which there is a £4 booking fee; a 10% discount is also payable but is deducted from the rate at your chosen accommodation).
  There are iCentres bookending the Way in Fort William (p76) and Inverness (p145).

Tourist boards For general information on the whole of Scotland contact **VisitScotland** (🖳 visitscotland.com), formerly the Scottish Tourist Board. The website has separate pages to the regions, including the **Highlands**, as well as an accommodation-booking service. However, their accommodation entries are not specific to the Great Glen Way so it is harder to navigate their lists for accommodation close to the trail. This book is a much better resource for finding a bed near the Way.

Organisations for walkers
● **Backpackers Club** (🖳 backpackersclub.co.uk) Aimed at people who are involved or interested in lightweight camping through walking, cycling, skiing, canoeing, etc. They produce a quarterly magazine, provide members with a comprehensive advisory

plenty of detail and information so you should not need any other map if you're walking just the Way.

However, if you prefer to have maps the **Ordnance Survey** (🖳 ordnance survey.co.uk) Explorer maps (orange cover) at a scale of 1:25,000 (£8.99) are excellent but you need three maps (Nos 392, 400 and 416) to cover the whole trail (two if you don't mind missing out the first few miles from Fort William on sheet 392). Alternatively, there are the Landranger maps (pink cover), Nos 41 (again, not essential as it only covers the first few miles of the Way), 34 and 26 at a scale of 1:50,000 (£8.99).

The best-buy map (£14.50) of the Way is published by **Harvey** (🖳 harvey maps.co.uk) with the trail arranged in strips at a scale of 1:40,000. Its coverage either side of the trail is limited.

If you want to climb Ben Nevis see p163 for details of recommended maps. For the Loch Lochy munros (see pp96-8) you must also take a map so that you can navigate accurately with a compass; maps for the Loch Lochy munros are Explorer 1:25k No 400 or Landranger 1:50k No 34.

Members of **Ramblers** (see box below) can borrow maps from their organisation's library; as can members of the **Backpackers Club** (see box below) who can also purchase them at a discount through their map service.

and information service on all aspects of backpacking, organise weekend trips and also publish a farm-pitch directory. Membership is £20/30 individual/family per year.
● **British Mountaineering Council** (🖳 thebmc.co.uk) Promotes the interests of British hillwalkers, climbers and mountaineers. Among the many benefits of membership are an excellent information service, a quarterly magazine and travel insurance designed for mountain sports. Annual membership is £39.95/19.97*, family membership £69.80/34.90* (*direct debit special offer), concessions (unemployed, students, U18s) £25.35.
● **The Long Distance Walkers' Association** (🖳 ldwa.org.uk) Annual membership (Jan-Dec), at £18/25.50 individual/family, includes three copies of *Strider* magazine a year giving details of challenge events and local group walks as well as articles on the subject. Information on 730 long-distance paths is presented in their *UK Trailwalker's Handbook*.
● **Mountaineering Council of Scotland** (MCS; 🖳 mountaineering.scot) The MCS is the main representative body for mountaineers and hillwalkers in Scotland. Among the many benefits of membership is a very useful information service. Membership is £30.50, £19 for unemployed, seniors and students, or £33.50 families; 50% discount for first year if pay by direct debit.
● **Ramblers** (formerly Ramblers' Association; 🖳 ramblers.org.uk) Looks after the interests of walkers throughout Britain. They publish a large amount of useful information including their quarterly *Walk* magazine (£3.60 to non-members), and have an extensive map library that is free to members. Membership costs £35.85/47.85/23 individual/joint/concessionary. Their website also has information about walking in Scotland (🖳 ramblers.org.uk/scotland).

Digital maps

There are numerous software packages that provide Ordnance Survey (OS) maps for a PC, smartphone, tablet or GPS. Maps are supplied by direct download over the internet. The maps are then loaded into an application, also available by download, from where you can view them, print them and create routes on them. **Memory Map** (🖥 memory-map.co.uk) currently sell OS 1:25,000 mapping covering the whole of the UK for £75.

For a subscription of £3.99 for one month or £23.99 for a year (on their current offer) **Ordnance Survey** (see p39) will let you download and then use their UK maps (1:25,000 scale) on a mobile or tablet without a data connection for a specific period.

Harvey (see p39) sell their Great Glen Way map (1:40,000 scale) as a download for £20.49 for use on any device.

RECOMMENDED READING

General guidebooks

There are several good guidebooks for exploring away from the trail. Footprint, Lonely Planet and Rough Guides all produce a *Scotland* guide for the whole country and all three also publish guides to the *Scottish Highlands and Islands* for travelling in the remoter parts of the Highlands.

Flora and fauna field guides

Scottish Birds by Valerie Thom and *Scottish Wild Flowers* by Michael Scott (both Collins) are ideal pocket-sized field guides to take with you. The *RSPB Handbook of Scottish Birds*, by Peter Holden and Stuart Housden, is published by Bloomsbury.

Getting to and from the Great Glen Way

The gateways to the Great Glen Way are Fort William and Inverness; both can be reached easily by rail and road, but only Inverness has an airport. If you are opting to walk just a section of the Way, there are many onward buses along the length of the Great Glen.

NATIONAL TRANSPORT

By rail

The best way to reach both Fort William and Inverness from the south of England is the comfortable overnight (Sunday to Friday only) **sleeper service from London's Euston** station (the train divides at Edinburgh Waverley station) with accommodation either in single or twin cabins, or seats. Tickets can be bought up to 12 months in advance and reservations are essential; for details contact Caledonian Sleeper (💻 sleeper.scot, ☎ 0330-060 0500 or from overseas +44 141-555 0888). Travel in peak periods and on a Friday may be more expensive than at other times.

The West Coast rail line, operated by **Virgin Trains** (☎ 0871-977 4222, 💻 virgintrains.co.uk), provides frequent rail services to Glasgow from London Euston and is connected to other lines from the rest of Britain. From Glasgow, ScotRail (see box p44) provides services to Fort William on the stunning West Highland Line.

London North Eastern Railway (☎ 03457 225333, 💻 lner.co.uk) operates a direct daytime service from London Kings Cross to Inverness (Highland Chieftain; daily 1/day) as well as frequent services to Edinburgh; see box p44 for details of services from Edinburgh to Inverness.

Timetable and fare information can be obtained from **National Rail Enquiries** (☎ 03457-484950; 24hrs; 💻 nationalrail.co.uk) or the relevant train companies. The cheapest tickets for Virgin's services can be booked only 24 weeks in advance; it is best to buy one as early as possible as only a limited number of tickets are sold at discounted prices. It helps to be as flexible as possible and don't forget that most cheap tickets carry some restrictions, so check what they are before you buy your ticket. Tickets can be bought direct from Virgin, or from websites such as 💻 thetrainline.com and 💻 qjump.co.uk. However, there may be additional charges such as a booking fee, or for using a debit/credit card.

If you plan to take a bus when you arrive consider getting a plusbus ticket (💻 plusbus.info) and if you want to book a **taxi** Traintaxi's website (💻 train taxi.co.uk) gives details of the companies operating at railway stations.

By coach

Travel by coach is usually cheaper than by train but does take longer. Advance bookings carry discounts so be sure to book at least a week ahead.

National Express (☎ 0871-781 8181, 🖥 nationalexpress.com) is the principal coach (long-distance bus) operator in Britain. There are no services to Fort William but the 592 operates daily (overnight) from London to Inverness with a change at Perth. Note that tickets booked over the phone are now subject to a £2 charge. Another company to consider is **Megabus** (🖥 megabus.com), which operates between London and Inverness and also from London to Glasgow via Manchester.

For details of bus/coach services from Glasgow to Fort William and Inverness see box p44).

By car

Both Fort William and Inverness are simple to get to by car from anywhere in Britain using the motorway network. However, you always need to think about **parking** while you walk; there are long-stay car parks at Fort William railway station (free parking) and at Rose Street Multi-storey car park in Inverness (£7

PLANNING YOUR WALK

❏ **GETTING TO BRITAIN**

● **By air** Fort William doesn't have an airport; its closest airport is **Inverness** (🖥 invernessairport.co.uk), which has direct flights from several places in Europe. There are more international flights to **Edinburgh** (🖥 edinburghairport.com), **Glasgow** (🖥 glasgowairport.com), and **Prestwick** (🖥 glasgowprestwick.com), near Glasgow. From all of these it is about 3-5 hours by bus or train to Fort William or Inverness.

For further details about airlines that fly to Inverness, Glasgow and Edinburgh, and the destinations served, visit the respective airport's website.

● **From Europe by train Eurostar** (🖥 eurostar.com) operates a high-speed passenger service via the Channel Tunnel between Paris/Brussels and St Pancras International station in London. From there it is a short walk to Euston and Kings Cross stations for trains to Fort William and Inverness.

For more information about rail services from Europe contact your national rail service provider, or Railteam (🖥 railteam.eu).

● **From Europe by coach Eurolines** (🖥 eurolines.de) works with several long-distance coach operators across mainland Europe to provide an integrated network connecting some 500 destinations to the UK, where it links with the National Express network (see above). Megabus (🖥 megabus.com) also provides services from destinations in mainland Europe to London.

● **From Europe by car Eurotunnel** (🖥 eurotunnel.com) operates 'le shuttle' train service for vehicles via the Channel Tunnel between Calais and Folkestone taking one hour, if all goes as it should, between the motorway in France and the motorway in Britain.

There are numerous **ferry** routes between the major North Sea ports, as well as across the Irish Sea and the English Channel. A useful website for information about the many options and the ferry operators is 🖥 directferries.com.

> ❏ **Traveline Scotland**
> The best way to plan local travel to and from the Great Glen Way is by using the
> 'Plan your journey' tab on 🖳 **travelinescotland.com**. Alternatively download their
> app: 🖳 travelinescotland.com/apps.

first day, £5/day thereafter), but overall it is probably easier to use public transport. There's then no need to worry about the cost of parking, the safety of your
temporarily abandoned vehicle while walking, or needing to allow time to pick
up your car after the walk. Quite apart from that, you'll simply feel your holiday
has begun the moment you step out of your front door, rather than having to
wait until you've slammed the car door behind you.

By air
The closest airport to Fort William is Inverness, though Glasgow and Edinburgh
are not much further away. For details of flights to any of these airports see box
opposite. With many bargain tickets available and short flight times this can
seem an alluring way to cover large distances. Bear in mind, however, the time
and expense of travelling to and from the airports and the extra time you need
to allow for check-in. Air travel is also by far the least environmentally sound
option (see 🖳 chooseclimate.org for the true costs of flying).

LOCAL TRANSPORT

The **public transport map** (p45) gives an overview of routes which are of particular use to walkers. The **public transport table** on p44 gives the approxi-
mate frequency of services in both directions, the relevant stops, and contacts
for detailed timetable information. See also box above.

By train
There is no railway the length of the Great Glen. The only line that may be of
use is on the first stage of the walk where trains on the Glasgow to Fort William
and Mallaig line stop at Spean Bridge, Banavie and Corpach. For exploring further afield before and after your walk the line to Mallaig will take you to the
ferry terminal for ferries to the Isle of Skye. In summer a special 'Hogwarts'
steam train (The Jacobite; 🖳 westcoastrailways.co.uk) runs along the Fort
William to Mallaig line. Scenes from the *Harry Potter* films were filmed on the
line, most notably at the Glenfinnan viaduct.
    From Inverness there are trains to Kyle of Lochalsh (for an alternative route
to Skye) and north to Wick and Thurso, for ferries to Orkney. Contact Scotrail
(see box p44) for train timetables and tickets or National Rail (see p41).

By bus
The Great Glen is a major communication route between the West and East
Highlands so there are plenty of bus services between Fort William and

PLANNING YOUR WALK

❏ **PUBLIC TRANSPORT SERVICES**

Notes: The details below were correct at the time of writing but services and operators change so it is essential to check before travelling.

Many of the services listed operate year-round; however, they may operate less frequently in the winter months (generally late October to late May).

Services operate with the same frequency in the opposite direction.

Drivers are generally happy to pick up passengers at intermediate points between bus stops as long as it is safe so to do and the intending passenger has made a clear signal.

At the time of writing **Citylink bus services don't accept dogs** but Stagecoach's do, though at the discretion of the driver.

Bus services

Scottish Citylink (☎ 0871-266 3333, 🖵 citylink.co.uk)

913	Edinburgh to Fort William, daily 1/day
914	Glasgow to Fort William, daily 4/day (1/day winter)
915	Glasgow to Uig via Fort William, Spean Bridge, Laggan Locks, Laggan swing bridge, Invergarry, Kyle of Lochalsh & Sconser, daily 1/day plus 1/day to Portree (1/day winter)
916	route as above to Uig, daily 1/day
917	Portree (Skye) to Inverness via Kyle of Lochalsh, Dornie, Shiel Bridge, Invermoriston, Lochside Hostel, Urquhart Castle, Drumnadrochit & Lochend, daily 4/day
919	Fort William to Inverness via Spean Bridge, Laggan Locks, Laggan swing bridge, Invergarry (A82), Fort Augustus, Invermoriston, Lochside Hostel, Urquhart Castle, Drumnadrochit & Lochend, 6/daily
961	Ullapool to Inverness, 2/day
M90	Edinburgh to Inverness via Perth, Pitlochry (3/day) & Aviemore (6/day), daily 9/day
G10	Glasgow to Inverness, daily 3/day plus Mon-Fri 2/day

Stagecoach in the Highlands (Fort William ☎ 01397 702373, Inverness ☎ 01463-233371, 🖵 stagecoachbus.com)

17/17A	Inverness to Tomich via Drumnadrochit & Cannich, Mon-Sat 3/day

Shiel Buses (☎ 01967-431272, 🖵 shielbuses.co.uk)

500	Mallaig to Fort William, Mon-Sat 4/day, Sat 1/day, Sun 1/day in summer

West Coast Motors (☎ 01586 552319, 🖵 westcoastmotors.co.uk)

918	Oban to Fort William, Mon-Sat 2/day (note: Citylink tickets are valid)

Train services

Scotrail (☎ 0344-811 0141, 🖵 scotrail.co.uk)

● Glasgow Queen Street to Mallaig via Crianlarich, Roy Bridge, Spean Bridge, Fort William, Banavie, Corpach, Glenfinnan, Arisaig & Morair, Mon-Sat 4/day, Sun 2/day (daily plus 1/day Fort William to Mallaig)

● Glasgow Queen Street to Inverness via Perth, Mon-Sat 5/day, Sun 3/day

● Edinburgh to Inverness via Perth, Mon-Sat 6/day, Sun 3/day

● Inverness to Kyle of Lochalsh (for Skye), Mon-Sat 4/day, Sun 2/day

● Inverness to Wick via Thurso, Mon-Sat 4/day, Sun 2/day

● Inverness to Aberdeen, Mon-Sat 11/day, Sun 5/day

PLANNING YOUR WALK

Inverness. However, where the Way veers away from the main A82 road public transport becomes less reliable or non-existent. The two main blackspots are around Gairlochy and Clunes, and between Abriachan and Grotaig on the Drumnadrochit to Inverness northern section. However, all the main villages on the Way are frequented by buses. This makes it easy, with a bit of careful bus timetable studying, to base oneself in one place for a few nights and use the buses to get to and from each stage of the walk without having to carry a heavy pack each day. Fort Augustus is a good base in being roughly halfway between Fort William and Inverness.

The two main bus operators along the Great Glen are Scottish Citylink and Stagecoach; see box p44 for contact details. A useful feature is that Scottish

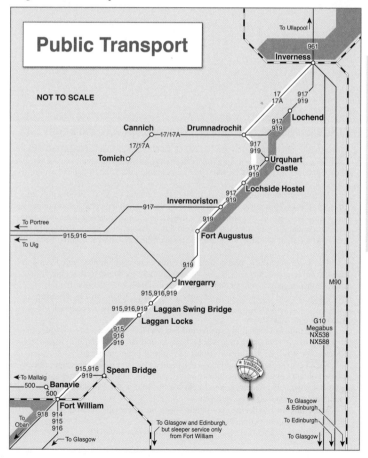

PLANNING YOUR WALK

Citylink single and return tickets are valid on Stagecoach services in the Highlands.

The most useful service is Citylink's 919 service which stops off at all the main villages along the Great Glen Way. Citylink's other services from Glasgow, Edinburgh and Inverness to Skye all run through part of the Great Glen so there are plenty of buses to allow you to reach different stages of the walk at most times of the day. If you're travelling with a dog, however, check their current dog-carrying policy as at the time of research only dogs small enough to fit in a carrier under your seat were allowed on board.

❏ HOW COVID-19 COULD AFFECT GREAT GLEN WAY WALKERS

This edition was about to go to press just as COVID-19 struck but has been rechecked since then. At the time of writing, many businesses were open again, but we don't know what the situation will be when you are planning your walk, or indeed walking. Things to bear in mind are:

Most **accommodation** was back open in the summer of 2020, albeit with some changes. The exception was the SYHA hostels. Virtually all the campsites were open but shared shower/toilet facilities were often closed. Some B&Bs/guesthouses had reduced the number of rooms that they were letting out at any one time and only let rooms which share facilities to families because of the problems of cleaning between guests.

The majority of **pubs, restaurants and cafés** were open but they were having to adapt to comply with any restrictions. In general these mean reduced opening hours and a limited menu; booking a table in advance and table service only (though some were only offering takeaway or meals served outdoors). It may still be necessary to wear a face mask when you go into (or move around) a pub, café or restaurant but not when you are sitting down.

At the time of writing most **train and bus services** had reduced timetables but hopefully by summer 2021 they will be back to normal. However, it is likely face coverings will still be required on (or in) all forms of public transport.

Social distancing shouldn't be a problem when you are **walking** except perhaps where you are passing through a town or village. You will need to open and close gates but if you are concerned, you might like to wear a glove to do this, or take a small bottle of hand-sanitiser with you.

Museums and galleries may require booking (especially for tours) and also restrict the number of people inside at any one time.

For further information visit 🖥 gov.scot/coronavirus-covid-19/.

Minimum impact walking

Walk as if you are kissing the Earth with your feet **Thich Nhat Hanh**

Scotland's large and sparsely populated countryside is no wilderness. The bare open hills have lost most of their forest cover through centuries of felling and meddling with the complex ecosystem, but it is still the wildest land you will find anywhere in Britain and as such it has attracted large numbers of visitors for over a century. They come for the fresh air, natural beauty and opportunity to explore. The popularity of these wild places has boomed over the last decade or two, no doubt because they are an antidote to the hectic, urban lifestyles that so many of us endure. Re-connecting with the natural world is not just a tonic, it is a necessity if we are, as individuals and as a society, going to live fulfilling lives and survive the dystopian existence we are creating for ourselves.

But as more and more of us look for headspace in wild country, so pressure on the environment increases and the potential for conflict with other land-users is heightened. Everyone has a right to this natural heritage but with it comes a responsibility to care for it too.

By following some simple guidelines while walking the Great Glen Way you can have a positive impact, not just on your own well-being but also on local communities and the environment, thereby becoming part of the solution.

ECONOMIC IMPACT

Support local businesses

Rural businesses and communities in Britain have been hit hard in recent years by a seemingly endless series of crises. The countryside through which the Great Glen Way passes is no exception and there is a lot that the walker can do to help. Playing your part today involves much more than simply closing the gate and not dropping litter; there is something else you can do – **buy local** – and with it come huge social, environmental and psychological benefits.

Look and ask for local produce to buy and eat. Not only does this cut down on the amount of pollution and congestion that the transportation of food creates, so-called 'food miles', but also ensures you are supporting local farmers and producers. It's a fact of life that money spent at local level – perhaps in a market, or at the greengrocer, or in an independent pub – has a far greater impact for good on that community than the equivalent spent in a branch of a national chain store or restaurant. If you can find local food which is also organic so much the better.

While no-one would advocate that walkers should boycott the larger supermarkets, which after all do provide local employment, it's worth remembering that businesses in rural communities rely heavily on visitors for their very existence. If we want to keep these shops and post offices, we need to use them.

ENVIRONMENTAL IMPACT

By choosing a walking holiday you have already made a positive step towards minimising your impact on the wider environment. By following these suggestions you can also tread lightly along the Great Glen Way.

Use public transport whenever possible
Traffic congestion in the Highlands during peak holiday times is becoming more and more of a nightmare. Conversely public transport to and along the Great Glen Way is excellent and the more people who use it the better the services will become. This not only benefits visitors but also local people and the environment.

Never leave litter
Leaving litter shows a total disrespect for the natural world and others coming after you. As well as being unsightly, litter kills wildlife, pollutes the environment and can be dangerous to farm animals.

Please carry a degradable bag so you can dispose of your rubbish in a bin in the next village. It would be very helpful if you could pick up litter left by other people too.

● **Is it OK if it's biodegradable?** Not really. Apple cores, banana skins, orange peel and the like are unsightly, encourage flies and wasps and ruin a picnic spot for others. Using the excuse that they are natural and biodegradable just doesn't cut any ice. When was the last time you saw a banana tree in Scotland?
● **The lasting impact of litter** A piece of orange peel left on the ground takes six months to decompose; silver foil 18 months; a plastic bag 100 years; clothes 15 years; and an aluminium drinks can 85 years.

Erosion
● **Stay on the main trail** The effect of your footsteps may seem minuscule but when they are multiplied by several thousand walkers each year they become rather more significant. Avoid taking shortcuts, widening the trail or creating more than one path; your boots will be followed by many others.
● **Consider walking out of season** Maximum disturbance by walkers coincides with the time of year when nature wants to do most of its growth and repair. In high-use areas, like that along much of the Way, the trail never recovers. Walking at less busy times eases this pressure while also generating year-

round income for the local economy. Not only that, but it may make the walk a more relaxing experience for you as there are fewer people on the path and there's less competition for accommodation.

Respect all wildlife
Care for all wildlife you come across on the Way; it has just as much of a right to be there as you. Tempting as it may be to pick wild flowers leave them so the next people who pass can enjoy them too. Don't break branches off or damage trees in any way.

If you come across wildlife keep your distance and don't watch for too long. Your presence can cause considerable stress particularly if the adults are with young or in winter when the weather is harsh and food scarce. Young animals are rarely abandoned. If you come across deer calves or young birds keep away so that their mother can return.

The code of the outdoor loo
'Going' in the outdoors is a lost art worth reclaiming, for your sake and everyone else's. As more and more people discover the joys of the outdoors this is becoming an important issue. In some parts of the world, where visitor pressure is higher than in Britain, walkers and climbers are required to pack out their excrement; this could one day be necessary here. Human excrement is not only offensive to our senses but, more importantly, can infect water sources.

● **Where to go** Wherever possible **use a toilet**. Public toilets are marked on the trail maps in this guide and you will also find facilities in pubs, cafés and campsites. There are composting toilets at the Trailblazer rest sites (wild campsites) but you will need a key to use them (see box p19).

The Great Glen Way is not a wilderness area and the thousands of walkers using it each year mean you need to be as sensitive as possible.

If you do have to go outdoors choose a site at least **30 metres away from running water** and 200 metres away from high-use areas such as huts. Carry a small trowel and **dig a hole** about 15cm (6") deep in which to bury your excrement. It decomposes quicker when in contact with the top layer of soil or leaf mould. Use a stick to stir loose soil into your deposit as this speeds up decomposition even more. Do not squash it under rocks as this slows down the composting process. If you have to use rocks to hide it make sure they are not in contact with your faeces. Also ensure you do not dig any holes on ground that is, or could be, of historic or archaeological interest.

● **Toilet paper and tampons** Toilet paper takes a long time to decompose whether buried or not. It is easily dug up by animals and can then blow into water sources or onto the trail. The best method for dealing with it is to **pack it out**. Put the used paper inside a paper bag which you place inside a (degradable) plastic bag (or two). Then simply empty the contents of the paper bag at the next toilet you come across and throw the bag away. You should also pack out **tampons** and **sanitary towels** in a similar way; they take years to decompose and may be dug up and scattered about by animals.

❑ THE SCOTTISH OUTDOOR ACCESS CODE

Scotland has its own 'Countryside code' for those looking to enjoy the outdoors. The full code runs to 67 pages, a copy of which can be found on their website 💻 outdoor access-scotland.scot. However, they also publish a brief summary of the code, the main points of which are listed below.

Take personal responsibility for your own actions
You can do this by:
● Caring for your own safety by recognising that the outdoors is a working environment and by taking account of natural hazards;
● Taking special care if you are responsible for children as a parent, teacher or guide to ensure that they enjoy the outdoors responsibly and safely.

Respect people's privacy and peace of mind
● Use a path or track, if there is one, when you are close to a house or garden;
● If there is no path or track, keep a sensible distance from houses and avoid ground that overlooks them from close by;
● Take care not to act in ways which might annoy or alarm people living in a house; and at night, take extra care by keeping away from buildings where people might not be expecting to see anyone and by following paths and tracks.

Help land managers and others to work safely and effectively
You can do this by:
● Following any precautions taken or reasonable recommendations made by the land manager, such as to avoid an area or route when hazardous operations, such as tree felling and crop spraying, are underway;
● Checking to see what alternatives there are, such as neighbouring land, before entering a field of animals;
● Never feeding farm animals;
● Avoiding causing damage to crops by using paths or tracks, by going round the margins of the field, by going on any unsown ground or by considering alternative routes on neighbouring ground; and by leaving all gates as you find them;
● Not hindering a land management operation, by keeping a safe distance and following any reasonable advice from the land manager.

Care for your environment
You can do this by:
● Not intentionally or recklessly disturbing or destroying plants, birds and other animals, or geological features;
● Following any voluntary agreements between land managers and recreation bodies;
● Not damaging or disturbing cultural heritage sites;
● Not causing any pollution and by taking all your litter away with you.

Keep your dog under proper control
● Never let it worry or attack livestock;
● Never take it into a field where there are calves or lambs;
● Keep it on a short lead or under close control in fields with farm animals;
● If cattle react aggressively and move towards you, keep calm, let the dog go and take the shortest, safest route out of the field;
● Keep it on a short lead or under close control during the bird breeding season (usually April to July) in areas such as moorland, forests, grassland and loch shores;
● Pick up and remove any faeces if your dog defecates in a public open place.

Wild camping

Along the Great Glen Way there are several informal sites where you are allowed to camp wild. There is deep, lasting pleasure to be gained from living outdoors close to nature but all too often people ruin that enjoyment for those who come after them. Camping without any facilities provides a valuable lesson in simple, sustainable living where the results of all your actions, from going to the loo to washing your plates in a stream, can be seen. Follow these suggestions for minimising your impact and encourage others to do likewise.

● **Be discreet** Camp alone or in small groups, spend only one night in each place and pitch your tent late and move off early.
● **Never light a fire** The deep burn caused by camp fires, no matter how small, seriously damages the turf and can take years to recover. Cook on a camp stove instead. Be aware that accidental fire is a great fear for farmers and foresters; take matches and cigarette butts out with you to dispose of safely.
● **Don't use soap or detergent** There is no need to use soap; even biodegradable soaps and detergents pollute streams and lochs. You won't be away from a shower for more than a couple of days. Wash up without detergent; use a plastic or metal scourer, or failing that, a handful of fine pebbles from a stream or some bracken or grass.
● **Leave no trace** Enjoy the skill of moving on without leaving any sign of having been there: no moved boulders, ripped up vegetation or dug drainage ditches. Check your campsite before heading off; pick up any litter that you or anyone else has left, so leaving it in at least as good a state as you found it, if not better.

ACCESS

The Great Glen Way, as a designated 'Long Distance Footpath', is a right of way with open access to the public. Access laws in Scotland were for many years very different from those in England and Wales largely due to an uneasy tradition of 'freedom to roam' going back many centuries. This freedom to roam was, until recently, little more than a moral right rather than a legal one. This changed with the Land Reform (Scotland) Act 2003 that established statutory rights of access to land and inland water for outdoor recreation and came into effect in February 2005. The law now states that there is a right of access to land that is considered, among other designations, moorland and mountain.

Walkers need to be aware of the wider access situation, especially if planning to leave the Way to explore some of the remoter country around it. In the past there has been some conflict between the interests of large sporting estates and walkers. The new access legislation relies on an attitude of co-operation between landowners and those wishing to use the land for peaceful recreation. Hillwalkers therefore have a responsibility to be considerate to those using the land for other purposes such as farming, forestry and deer stalking. Equally, landowners must respect the right of walkers to exercise their right to roam responsibly. If everyone follows the Scottish Outdoor Access Code (see box opposite) conflicts can be minimised. Walkers should pay particular attention to their access rights with regard to the lambing and deer-stalking seasons (see

MINIMUM IMPACT & OUTDOOR SAFETY

below). For more information see **Scottish Rights of Way Society** (🖥 scotways .com), a charity that works to develop and protect public rights of way.

Other points to consider on the Great Glen Way
● Unlike many long-distance paths that can resemble an obstacle course, you will find very few stiles or gates on the Great Glen Way. Where gates do occur they should be easy to open but if you do have to climb over one, always do so at the hinged end.
● Walkers should take special care on country roads. Cars travel dangerously fast on narrow winding lanes. To be safe, walk facing the oncoming traffic and carry a torch or wear highly visible clothing when it's getting dark. Conversely, if you are driving, go carefully on country roads and park your car with consideration for others' needs; never block a gateway.
● Make no unnecessary noise. Enjoy the peace and solitude of the outdoors by staying in small groups and acting unobtrusively. Avoid noisy and disruptive behaviour which might annoy residents and other visitors and frighten farm animals and wildlife.

Deer-stalking
Large areas of the Highlands have been actively managed for deer shooting, or stalking as it is known, since the 19th century when it became fashionable for the aristocracy and the newly rich industrialists to partake in all forms of field sports. Little has changed today except that the wealthy now come from all over the world and contribute £30 million to the Highland economy every year providing much-needed income for many estates.

Shooting deer for sport (sport-shooting) is a Highland tradition and is partly responsible for the deer population spiralling out of control, doubling in number since the early 1960s. Some estates actively maintain a high density of red deer to ensure their clients, who pay handsomely for a day's stalking, have something to shoot. Deer-stalking can also be an important conservation measure; there is a growing number of conservation-minded estates who operate their deer culls to reduce numbers, contrasting with traditional sport-shooting estates that keep the numbers high. Reducing numbers leads to a healthier herd of deer and aids vegetation recovery and habitat improvement. It is a role that the wolf would have played when this native Scottish species was still extant in the Highlands. The loss of this vital component of Highland ecology has been devastating with knock-on effects for other species. Deer numbers have shot up; their browsing activity prevents recovery of the native woodland that has been so severely depleted. Without a cull, or fenced exclosures, the recovery of the native woodland would be impossible.

Access restrictions during the deer-culling seasons should therefore be respected and you should try to cause the minimum of disturbance. Stags are culled between 1st July and 20th October, hinds are culled between 21st October and 15th February. Details of access restrictions are usually posted on signs in the vicinity of stalking activities and on the internet at 🖥 outdoor access-scotland.scot/practical-guide-all/heading-scottish-hills.

Outdoor safety

The Great Glen Way is not a particularly difficult or dangerous walk and with common sense, some planning and basic preparation most hazards and hassles can easily be avoided. The information given here is just as valid for walkers out on a day walk as for those walking the entire Way. See also p46 (COVID-19).

AVOIDANCE OF HAZARDS

Always make sure you have suitable **clothes** (see pp35-6) to keep you warm and dry, whatever the conditions, and a spare change of inner clothes. A **compass**, **whistle**, **torch** and **first-aid kit** should also be carried. Take plenty of **food** and **water** (see p37) with you for the day. You will eat far more walking than you do normally so make sure you have enough, as well as some high-energy snacks, such as chocolate, dried fruit or biscuits, in the bottom of your pack for an emergency. Stay alert and know exactly where you are throughout the day. The easiest way to do this is to **regularly check your position** on the map. If visibility suddenly decreases with mist and cloud, or there is an accident, you will be able to make a sensible decision about what action to take based on your location.

Walking alone

If you are walking alone you must appreciate and be prepared for the increased risk. It is always a good idea to leave word with somebody about where you are going; you can always ring ahead to your accommodation and let them know you are walking alone and what time you expect to arrive. Don't forget to contact whoever you have left word with to let them know you've arrived safely. Carrying a mobile phone can be useful though you cannot rely on getting good reception.

Mountain safety

If you plan to climb any of the mountains along the Great Glen Way there are further precautions you need to take. You must always take a **map** and **compass** with you on the Scottish mountains and be able to navigate accurately with them as paths are rare and visibility often poor. In addition to the emergency equipment, food and clothes you would normally carry, you may also want to take a **survival bag**.

In **summer** the temperature on the summits of Scottish mountains can be as much as 12°C lower than in the glen so take an extra warm layer and always pack a **hat** and **gloves**. Gales carrying sleet, hail and snow can blow in with little warning at any time of the year; be prepared.

In **winter** you should not venture onto the hills unless you are a competent mountaineer. The typical Arctic conditions require crampons, ice axe and specialist clothing as well as knowledge of snow conditions, avalanche and cornices.

Mountain guides

If you feel your skills need polishing there are some experienced mountain guides and instructors in the region who run courses (and also provide accommodation) such as **West Coast Mountain Guides** (☎ 01397-532022, 🖳 west coast-mountainguides.co.uk).

WEATHER FORECASTS

The weather in Scotland can change with incredible speed. At any time of the year you must be prepared for the worst. Most hotels, some B&Bs and TICs will have pinned up somewhere a summary of the weather forecast. Alternatively you can get a forecast through **Mountain Weather Information Service** 🖳 mwis.org.uk) or reports that also take in the whole country: 🖳 bbc.co.uk/weather, or 🖳 metoffice.gov.uk.

WATER

You need to drink lots of water while walking; 2 to 4 litres a day depending on the weather. If you're feeling drained, lethargic or just out of sorts it may well be that you haven't drunk enough. Thirst is not a reliable indicator of how much you should drink. The frequency and colour of your urine is better and the maxim, 'a happy mountaineer always pees clear' is worth following.

Tap water is safe to drink unless a sign specifies otherwise. In upland areas above habitation and away from intensively farmed land walkers have traditionally drunk straight from the stream and many continue to do so with no problems. It must be said, however, that there is a very small but steadily increasing risk of catching giardia from doing this. Just a few years ago this disease was only a threat to travellers in the developing world. As more people travel some are returning to the UK with the disease. If one of these individuals defecates too close to a stream or loch that water source can become infected and the disease transmitted to others who drink from it. If you want to minimise the risk either purify the water using a filter or iodine tablets, or collect water only from a tap.

Far more dangerous to health is drinking from natural water sources in the lowlands. The water may have run off roads, housing or agricultural fields picking up heavy metals, pesticides and other chemical contaminants that we humans use liberally. Such water should not be drunk; find a tap instead.

BLISTERS

You will prevent blisters by wearing worn-in, comfortable boots and looking after your feet; air them at lunchtime, keep them clean and change your socks regularly. If you feel any 'hot spots' on your feet while you are walking, stop immediately and apply a few strips of zinc oxide tape and leave it on until it is pain free or the tape starts to come off.

If you have left it too late and a blister has developed you should surround it with 'moleskin' or any other 'blister kit', such as Compeed, to protect it from abrasion. Popping it can lead to infection. If the skin is broken keep the area clean with antiseptic and cover it with a non-adhesive dressing material held in place with tape.

BITES

For the summer-time walker these few bugs which bite are more irritating than dangerous.

Midges

The Gaelic name for this annoying blood-sucker is *meanbh-chuileag* – tiny fly. When you see its diminutive size it's inconceivable to think that it can cause such misery, but it never works alone. The culprits are the pregnant females who critically need a regular supply of fresh blood to develop their eggs. On finding a victim she sends out a chemical invitation to other hungry females and you are soon enveloped in a black gyrating cloud. A single bite would pass unnoticed, but concurrent bites are itchy and occasionally mildly painful.

The key to dealing with this wee beastie is understanding its habits. The main biting season is from June to August, so planning a holiday outside this time obviously makes sense. For many though, this is not an option. It's worth knowing that the midge is also extremely sensitive to light and only comes out when the sun's radiation is below a certain intensity; dawn, dusk, long summer twilight hours and dull overcast days are its favourite hunting times. The message for campers is to get into your tent early, get up late and not to camp in conifer forests which can often be dark enough to trigger a feeding frenzy.

The other factor on your side is wind. It only needs a gentle breeze of 5½mph to keep the midge grounded. Try to camp on raised ground which will catch any hint of a breeze or, if you're walking on a still, overcast day, keep moving. The apparent wind created is often enough to keep them away. Insect repellents vary in effectiveness with different brands working for different people. The simplest methods are often the best: long-sleeved shirts, trousers and midge-proof headnets are all worth wearing, preferably in a light colour which the midges find less attractive. Weirdly, Avon Skin So Soft, a moisturising body lotion, has proved to be the most effective repellent against midges and is even now sold in many camping shops along the way. The insect repellent Smidge is also very effective.

When all is lost and there is nothing you can do to keep them away, try to seek solace from the final words of George Hendry's fascinating little book, *Midges in Scotland*, '… the Scottish Highlands remain one of the most under-populated landscapes with a timelessness difficult to find anywhere at the start of the twenty-first century … If, as seems likely, the biting midge is a significant factor in limiting our grossest capacities for unsustainable exploitation then this diminutive guardian of the Highlands deserves our lasting respect.'

Ticks

Ticks are small, wingless creatures with eight legs which painlessly bury their heads under your skin to feed on your blood. After a couple of days' feasting they will have grown to about 10mm and drop off. There is a very small risk that they can infect you with **Lyme Disease**. Because of this you should check your body thoroughly after a walk through long grass, heather or bracken; the tick's favoured habitat.

If you find a tick, remove it promptly. Use fine point tweezers and grasp the tick where its head pierces your skin; do not squeeze its body. Tug gently and repeatedly until the tick lets go and falls off. Be patient, this will take time. Keep the area clean with disinfectant and over the next month watch for any flu-like symptoms, a spreading rash or lasting irritation at the site of the bite which could indicate Lyme Disease. If any of these symptoms appear see a doctor and let them know you suspect Lyme Disease. It is treatable with antibiotics but the sooner you catch it the easier this will be.

Prevention is always better than cure so wear boots, socks and trousers when walking through or sitting on long grass, heather and bracken.

For further information look up ▣ lymediseaseaction.org.uk.

Horseflies and mosquitoes
In July and August **horseflies**, or *clegs*, can be a nuisance on warm bright days. Their bite is painful and may stay inflamed for a few days.

There are several species of **mosquito** in Scotland which tend to bite at night leaving an itchy, painful mark. Insect repellents such as Jungle Formula or Autan may help deter horseflies and mosquitoes but they do not offer a permanent solution. You can take other preventative measures such as wearing a midge net over your head (available from outdoor shops and local village shops throughout the Highlands) and wearing light-coloured clothing: most insects are attracted to dark colours. If you are bitten, rest assured that Scottish mosquitoes and horseflies carry no nasty viruses or diseases. The worst that will happen is that the bite will become itchy and swollen for a day or two. To soothe the affected area, cover it with an antihistamine gel.

Adders
The adder is the only venomous snake present in the British Isles. It is very rare to be bitten by one and deaths are even rarer, although children and pets are more vulnerable. In the unlikely event of a bite you should stay calm and try to move as little as possible to prevent the venom circulating quickly. Send a companion to call for help.

Prevention is better than cure. If you see an adder, give it a wide berth and move on. It will only attack if you provoke it. Adders are active on warm, sunny days, so look out for them in open, grassy areas. See also p70.

SUNBURN

Even on overcast days the sun still has the power to burn. Sunburn can be avoided by regularly applying sunscreen, remembering your lips and ears, and by wearing a hat to protect your face and the back of your neck. Those with fair skin should consider wearing a light, long-sleeved top and long trousers rather than T-shirt and shorts.

HYPOTHERMIA

Also known as exposure, this occurs when the body can't generate enough heat to maintain its normal temperature, usually as a result of being wet, cold, unprotected from the wind, tired and hungry. It is easily avoided by wearing suitable clothing, carrying and eating enough food and drink, being aware of the weather conditions and checking the morale of your companions.

Early signs to watch for are feeling cold and tired with involuntary shivering. Find some shelter as soon as possible and warm the victim up with a hot drink and some chocolate or other high-energy food. If possible give them another warm layer of clothing and allow them to rest until feeling better.

If allowed to worsen, strange behaviour, slurring of speech and poor co-ordination will become apparent and the victim can quickly progress into unconsciousness, followed by coma and death. Quickly get the victim out of wind and rain, improvising a shelter if necessary. Rapid restoration of bodily warmth is essential and best achieved by bare-skin contact: someone should get into the same sleeping bag as the patient, both having stripped to their underwear, with any spare clothing under or over them to build up heat. Send urgently for help.

HYPERTHERMIA

Hyperthermia occurs when the body generates too much heat, eg heat exhaustion and heatstroke. Not ailments that you would normally associate with the Highlands of Scotland, these are serious problems nonetheless.

Symptoms of **heat exhaustion** include thirst, fatigue, giddiness, a rapid pulse, raised body temperature, low urine output and, if not treated, delirium and finally a coma. The best cure is to drink plenty of water.

Heatstroke is more serious. A high body temperature and an absence of sweating are early indications, followed by symptoms similar to hypothermia (see above) such as a lack of coordination, convulsions and coma. Death will follow if treatment is not given instantly. Sponge the victim down, wrap them in wet towels, fan them and get help immediately.

DEALING WITH AN ACCIDENT

- Use basic first aid to treat any injuries to the best of your ability.
- Work out exactly where you are.
- Try to attract the attention of anybody else who may be in the area. The **emergency signal** is six blasts on a whistle, or six flashes with a torch.
- If possible leave someone with the casualty while others go for help. If there is nobody else, you have a dilemma. If you decide to get help leave all spare clothing and food with the casualty.
- Telephone ☎ **999** and ask for the police. They will alert the volunteer mountain rescue team.
- Report the exact position of the casualty and their condition.

THE ENVIRONMENT & NATURE

Nature is our medicine. **Henry D Thoreau**

The Great Glen Way passes through a range of habitats, from the loch-side woodlands, both native and non-native, to the high ground above Loch Ness. There are tumbling burns, slow-flowing rivers, country lanes festooned with wildflowers on their verges, heather moorland and open hill. While much of Scotland's native wildlife has been exterminated, thanks to historical persecution, this is still the stronghold for some of the rarest habitats and species in the British Isles.

It would take a book several times the size of this to list the thousands of species which you could come across on your walk. A brief description of the more common animals and plants you may encounter as well as some of the more special species for which Scotland is well known is given on pp61-73. If you want to know more refer to the field guides listed on p40.

Conservation issues are also explored on the premise that to really learn about a place you need to know more than the names of all the plants and animals in it. It is just as important to understand the interactions going on between them and man's relationship with this ecological balance.

Conserving Scotland's nature

[Since 1945] the normal landscape dynamics of human adaptation and natural alteration had been replaced by simple destruction. The commonest cause was destruction by modern agriculture; the second, destruction by modern forestry.
Oliver Rackham *The Illustrated History of the Countryside*

The statistics of how the Scottish land has been treated over the last 70 years do not make comfortable reading. More than half of the hedgerows which existed at the end of WWII have been pulled up; a quarter of the broadleaved woods have disappeared; a third of heather moorland has been destroyed; half the lowland peat mires have been lost. These are all important habitats for a diverse range of wildlife species. When they are replaced by monocultural conifer plantations or sheep grassland the rich web of plant and animal life also disappears leaving behind a poor substitute for nature's bounty.

❏ **The Great Glen fault**

The Great Glen may be a mighty glen but it could be even mightier than you realised. The glen represents a major fault line in the earth's crust that runs way beyond Scottish shores, running west past Northern Ireland out into the Atlantic and north as far as Svalbard in the High Arctic.

At one time the two land masses either side of the glen would have been separated from one another by an ancient sea. Around 430 million years ago the North-West Highlands, on the north side of the glen, formed part of the continent of Laurentia, which is now known as Canada. On the southern side of the glen the Grampian mountains would have belonged to a much smaller land mass called Avalonia. The two land masses collided at an angle forming a series of fault lines with the Great Glen fault being the biggest, 3km wide and stretching 40km into the earth. While the fault was active the land on the north side shifted 200km relative to the land on the south side.

Since the creation of the fault a succession of ice ages have scoured out the weakened rock along its length. The last Ice Age, around 12,000 years ago, would have seen a sheet of ice about a kilometre thick covering much of the Highlands, with only the highest peaks poking above the surface. The grinding of the ice over thousands of years has left behind the wonderful landscape of mountain and glen that we see today.

If you are interested in the fascinating geology of the Great Glen you can learn more at **Lochaber Geopark Visitor Centre** in Fort William (see p76).

The stark results of this destruction are highlighted by the decline in Scotland's farmland birds over the last 35 years. The numbers of skylark, bullfinch and linnet for example have diminished by almost two-thirds, while partridge numbers are down by three-quarters. Species of all kinds have suffered similar fates as habitats continue to be destroyed.

Nature conservation arose tentatively in the middle of the 19th century out of concern for wild birds which were being slaughtered to provide feathers for the fashion industry. As commercial exploitation of land has increased over the intervening century so too has the conservation movement. It now has a wide sphere of influence throughout the world and its ethos is upheld by international legislation, government agencies and voluntary organisations.

SCOTTISH NATURAL HERITAGE (SNH)

This is the main government body concerned with the preservation of wildlife and landscape in Scotland. SNH (🖳 nature.scot) manages the 43 **National Nature Reserves** (NNRs; 🖳 nnr.scot) to conserve some of the best examples of Scotland's varied habitats. Along with the land owned and managed by voluntary conservation groups there are some 75 **local nature reserves** across Scotland creating refuges for many endangered species.

However, about 94% of Scottish land is in the hands of foresters and farmers who generally put economic returns above concern for habitat and wildlife. SNH has the difficult job of protecting this land from the grossest forms of damage using a complex array of land designations and statutory mechanisms, all shortened (throughout the UK) to mind-boggling acronyms.

One of the most important designations and one that covers 12.9% of Scotland is **Site of Special Scientific Interest** (SSSI; there were 1423 at the time of writing). These range in size from those of just a few acres protecting natural treasures such as wild-flower meadows, important nesting sites or a notable geological feature, to vast swathes of upland, moorland and wetland. Owners and occupiers of 'triple SIs' as they are often known, have to abide by strict guidelines and must notify SNH of any proposed actions which would affect the land. There are 40 areas in Scotland designated as a **National Scenic Area** (NSA). This has provided some recognition for outstanding landscapes such as Ben Nevis and Glen Coe, just south of the Great Glen Way. Along with these designations Scotland has two **national parks** to call its own in the shape of Loch Lomond and the Trossachs, and the Cairngorms.

These are all encouraging steps but on their own will never provide complete protection. New developments such as roads and housing still get pushed through in so-called protected areas under the guise of being in the public interest and some landowners ignore the designations, and suffer the rather insignificant penalties when it is in their interest to do so. There is still a long way to go before all our land is treated as something more than just an economic resource to be exploited.

CAMPAIGNING AND CONSERVATION ORGANISATIONS

Voluntary organisations started the conservation movement back in the mid 1800s and they are still at the forefront of developments. Independent of government but reliant on public support, they can concentrate their resources either on acquiring land which can then be managed purely for conservation purposes, or on influencing political decision-makers by lobbying and campaigning.

Managers and owners of land include: the **Royal Society for the Protection of Birds** (RSPB; 🖳 rspb.org.uk/whatwedo/scotland), which manages 213 nature reserves, 77 of which are in Scotland, and is the largest voluntary conservation body in Europe with over a million members; and the **National Trust for Scotland** (🖳 nts.org.uk) which, with about 300,000 members, is Scotland's largest conservation charity. It protects, through ownership, both countryside and historic buildings.

Lesser known but equally important groups include: the **John Muir Trust** (🖳 johnmuirtrust.org) which is dedicated to safeguarding and conserving wild places (the trust owns and manages about 50,000 acres/20,000 hectares in the Scottish Borders, Skye, Knoydart, Sutherland, Perthshire and Lochaber, including Ben Nevis); **Trees for Life** (🖳 treesforlife.org.uk), a group committed to the regeneration of the Caledonian Forest (see box opposite) in the Highlands; **Woodland Trust** (🖳 woodlandtrust.org.uk) who own lots of woodlands across the UK including Urquhart Bay at Drumnadrochit (see p131); **Scottish Wildlife Trust** (🖳 scottishwildlifetrust.org.uk) which covers all aspects of conservation across Scotland through a network of local groups; and the Scottish branch of **Butterfly Conservation** (🖳 butterfly-conservation.org/in-your-area/scottish-office).

Lobbying groups, such as the **Association for the Protection of Rural Scotland** (⌨ aprs.scot) also play a vital role in environmental protection by raising public awareness and occasionally co-operate with government agencies such as SNH when policy needs to be formulated. A huge increase in membership over the last 20 years and a general understanding that environmental issues can't be left to government 'experts' is creating a new and powerful lobbying group; an informed electorate. For details about Scottish Wildcat Action see p69.

Historic Environment Scotland (formerly Historic Scotland; ⌨ historic environment.scot) is a public body with responsibility for the historic environment of Scotland. This includes historic buildings and sites, of which there are three under its care on the Great Glen Way: Old Inverlochy Castle (see p82), Bridge of Oich (see p105) and Urquhart Castle (see p131).

Flora and fauna

TREES

In the past 500 years we have destroyed over 99 per cent of our equivalent of the rain-forests. **David Minns** *The Nature of Scotland*

The woods of Caledon

When the Romans arrived in Scotland almost 2000 years ago they named it Caledonia or 'wooded heights'. By the time Samuel Johnson and James Boswell toured the country in 1773 it was possible to remark, 'A tree might be a show in Scotland as a horse in Venice'. The tree cover which so amazed the Romans consisted of oak in the lowlands, with Scots, or Caledonian, pine in the Highlands. This is still Scotland's natural pattern of woodland and it has existed for 7000 years, since the end of the last Ice Age. However, today less than 1% of the original woods remain.

❏ **The Caledonian pine forest**
The Caledonian pine forest is characterised by Scots pine, birch and aspen among other species, with an understorey dominated by juniper and ling. It is an important habitat for many species including pine martens, red squirrels and capercaillie. To gaze over an extensive remnant of Caledonian pine forest is to witness one of the ancient glories of the Highlands. The forest is the essence of Highland Scotland and when you consider this fact it is even more devastating to acknowledge that only 1% of the original forest remains today. On the 79 miles of the Great Glen Way you will see almost none of it. The positive news is that in places the forest is recovering, in no small part thanks to forward-thinking estates and organisations such as **Trees for Life** (see opposite) who have planted over a million native trees in an attempt to restore what has been lost. Forestry & Land Scotland (formerly the Forestry Commission) also continues to restore Scots pine to many areas.

There are a few old granny pines on the Way north of Invermoriston and north of Alltsigh but the best examples require a detour from the path. The most accessible is **Arkaig Community Forest** near Achnacarry (see box p95).

THE ENVIRONMENT & NATURE

Before the Romans tree cover had already been much reduced by Neolithic peoples. As the population expanded over the following centuries so the forests continued to shrink as land was converted to agriculture. In more recent times large areas of timber were felled for industry and warfare. However, from the 18th

Birch (with flowers)

century onwards it was the more subtle processes of sheep grazing and the management of land for field sports that ensured that once the trees were gone they would never return. Overgrazing the land with sheep and deer (which eat young trees) and the burning of heather to maintain the grouse moors have meant that new trees never get established.

Indigenous trees on the Way

There are some glorious examples of **oak woodland** along the Way, in particular around Loch Oich. There are two native species of oak: the common, or pedunculate, (*Quercus robur*) and the sessile (*Q. petraea*); you are most likely to see the latter on the Great Glen Way. The oak woods are far more diverse than their single species name would suggest.

Elm (*Ulmus glabra*), **hazel** (*Corylus avellana*) and **ash** (*Fraxinus excelsior*; see illustration) intermingle with the oaks on good soil while pioneer species such as **rowan** (*Sorbus aucuparia*), **silver birch** (*Betula pendula*) and **downy birch** (*B. pubescens*) and the much-rarer **aspen** (*Populus tremula*) congregate on poorer soils along with **holly** (*Ilex aquifolium*). Pioneer species play the vital role in a forest ecosystem of improving the soil. In a natural system unaffected by man they would gradually be succeeded by longer-lived species such as oak and Scots pine. Being hardy, brave lone rowans and birches are often to be seen growing in inaccessible ravines or high up on crags where they are safe from sheep and deer. In wet marshy areas and along rivers and streams you'll find **alder** (*Alnus glutinosa*).

Hazel (with flowers)

Sadly there is little left of the once-majestic **Caledonian pine** (*Pinus sylvestris*) forests which would have covered so much of Scotland in the distant past. Some of the oldest Scots pines in

Ash (with seeds)

THE ENVIRONMENT & NATURE

Scotland are over 500 years old, they can grow up to 120ft (36m) high and can have a girth of 12ft (3.6m). They are easily identified by their reddish brown upper trunk and pairs of blue-green needles about 2 inches (5cm) long.

The so-called pinewoods also support **juniper** (*Juniperus communis*), **birch** (*Betula pendula* and *B. pubescens*) and **willow** (*Salix spp.*). For more on the Caledonian pine forest see box p61.

Alder (with flowers)

Conifer plantations

On the face of it the 20th century was a boom time for trees in Scotland. Tree cover leapt from a disastrous 4% at the start of the 20th century to 14% by the end (although still rather poor when compared with other European countries such as France with 27% and Germany with 30%). What these figures disguise is that over 90% of this planting was in conifer plantations; certainly no substitute for oak and Scots pine, and in terms of land use and ecology, about as far removed from the native forests as it is possible to get while still growing trees.

The mass planting of the uplands with conifers was fuelled by the need for a strategic reserve of timber after two world wars. The low-quality land in the hills supported marginal sheep farming and was of little value to agriculture. Why not utilise it for

Juniper (with berries)

growing timber? The Forestry Commission (now Forestry & Land Scotland: a government agency funded by the tax payer) needed a tree which grew fast with little management and at low cost. The **Sitka spruce** (*Picea sitchensis*), a native of North America, fitted the bill. Industrial methods of cultivation totally inapplicable to remote parts of the British uplands could be used and soon gangs of contract workers were ploughing up the land behind caterpillar tractors.

The 2000 square miles (3000 sq km) made into forest by the Forestry Commission was substantially added to during the 1970s and '80s when tax arrangements allowed many wealthy private investors to use forestry as a way to shelter their earnings. These short-sighted policies produced the eye-sores accurately described as 'blanket forestry'; same-age trees planted close together in neat regimented rows enclosed by miles of straight-running deer-proof fencing.

The visual impact is almost inconsequential when compared to their **ecological impact**. Once mature the plantations cannot support much wildlife as the close canopy allows little light to penetrate to the forest floor. Nothing else can

❏ **Oak leaves showing galls**
Oak trees support more kinds of insects than any other tree in Britain and some affect the oak in unusual ways. The eggs of gall-flies cause growths known as galls on the leaves. Each of these contains a single insect. Other kinds of gall-flies lay eggs in stalks or flowers, leading to flower galls, growths the size of currants.

grow and as a consequence few animals venture into this sterile environment.

As with all monocultures pests easily build up and have to be controlled with chemicals. The deep ploughing and use of heavy machinery damages soil structure and also leads to a higher incidence of flash-floods as drainage patterns are altered. It has also been found that acid rain gets trapped in the trees and is released into the streams during a downpour killing young fish and invertebrates. What's more, the end product from this environmentally damaging land-use is a low-grade timber used mainly for paper, a hideous waste of a valuable raw material. Perversely and misleadingly this is often advertised as 'paper from sustainable forestry'.

Thankfully, now that we have entered the 21st century, even big business is beginning to recognise the importance of conservation and environmentally friendly practices. While there are still many stands of tightly packed sitka spruce across Scotland, Forestry & Land Scotland does now have an active conservation programme (see box p68) through which they plant native species and leave clear areas, particularly around streams and rivers, to encourage wildlife.

FLOWERS

Wood margins

Wood margins along the trail provide the best displays of wild flowers. In early summer look out for the pink flowers of **red campion** (*Silene dioica*), **wood cranesbill** (*Geranium sylvaticum*) and the more fragile **herb robert** (*Geranium robertianum*) along with the bright yellow displays of **creeping** and **meadow buttercup** (*Ranunculus repens* and *R. acris*).

In summer **broad-leaved willowherb** (*Epilobium montanum*) and **foxgloves** (*Digitalis purpurea*) make an appearance in hedges and woods while **rosebay willowherb** (*Chamerion angustifolium*) often colonises the sides of footpaths and waste ground.

The tall white-flowering heads of members of the carrot family, such as **sweet cicely** (*Myrrhis odorata*), **cow parsley** (*Anthriscus sylvestris*) and **hogweed** (*Heracleum sphondylium*), are another familiar sight along verges. In the autumn the hedgerows produce their edible harvest of delicious blackberries which can be eaten straight from the thorny **bramble** (*Rubus fruticosus*) and rose-hips of the **dog rose** (*Rosa canina*), best made into a syrup which provides 20 times the vitamin C of oranges.

Common Butterwort
Pinguicula vulgaris

Early Purple Orchid
Orchis mascula

Spear Thistle
Cirsium vulgare

Bell Heather
Erica cinerea

Heather (Ling)
Calluna vulgaris

Wood Sorrel
Oxalis acetosella

Rosebay Willowherb
Epilobium angustifolium

Common Vetch
Vicia sativa

Common Fumitory
Fumaria officinalis

Meadow Cranesbill
Geranium pratense

Water Avens
Geum rivale

Red Campion
Silene dioica

Common Dog Violet
Viola riviniana

Honeysuckle
Lonicera periclymenum

Dog Rose
Rosa canina

Self-heal
Prunella vulgaris

Germander Speedwell
Veronica chamaedrys

Herb-Robert
Geranium robertianum

Lousewort
Pedicularis sylvatica

Rowan (tree)
Sorbus aucuparia

Yellow Rattle
Rhinanthus minor

Common Knapweed
Centaurea nigra

Ramsons (Wild Garlic)
Allium ursinum

British Bluebell
Hyacinthoides non-scripta

Marsh Marigold
Caltha palustris

Meadow Buttercup
Ranunculis acris

Gorse
Ulex europaeus

Tormentil
Potentilla erecta

Birdsfoot-trefoil
Lotus corniculatus

Ox-eye Daisy
Leucanthemum vulgare

St John's Wort
Hypericum perforatum

Primrose
Primula vulgaris

Cowslip
Primula veris

Common Ragwort
Senecio jacobaea

Hemp-nettle
Galeopsis speciosa

Cotton Grass
Eriophorum angustifolium

Grassland

There is much overlap between the hedge/woodland-edge habitat and that of pastures and meadows. You will come across **common birdsfoot-trefoil** (*Lotus corniculatus*), **germander speedwell** (*Veronica chamaedrys*), **tufted** and **bush vetch** (*Vicia cracca* and *V. sepium*) and **meadow vetchling** (*Lathyrus pratensis*) in both.

Often the only species you will see in heavily grazed pastures are the most resilient. The emblem of Scotland, the thistle, is one of these. The three most common species are **creeping thistle**, **spear thistle** and **marsh thistle** (*Cirsium arvense*, *C. vulgare* and *C. palustre*). Among them you may find **common ragwort** (*Senecio jacobaea*), **yarrow** (*Achillea millefolium*), **sheep's** and **common sorrel** (*Rumex acetosella* and *R. acetosa*), and **white** and **red clover** (*Trifolium repens* and *T. pratense*).

Other widespread grassland species include **Scottish bluebell** (*Campanula rotundifolia*), known as harebell in England, delicate yellow **tormentil** (*Potentilla erecta*) which will often spread up onto the lower slopes of mountains along with **devil's-bit scabious** (*Succisa pratensis*). Also keep an eye out for orchids such as the **fragrant orchid** (*Gymnadenia conopsea*), **common spotted orchid** (*Dactylorhiza maculata*) and **early purple orchid** (*Orchis mascula*).

Woodland

Springtime is when the woods are at their best. In birch and oak woods during May and June the floor will be dotted with **primroses** (*Primula vulgaris*), **wood anemones** (*Anemone nemorosa*), **dog's mercury** (*Mercurialis perennis*), **lesser celandine** (*Ranunculus ficaria*), **wood sorrel** (*Oxalis acetosella*), **wild hyacinth** (*Hyacinthoides non-scripta*, called bluebell in England), **common** and **small cow-wheat** (*Melapyrum pratense* and *M. sylvaticum*) and **common dog-violets** (*Viola riviniana*).

Moorland

Common **heather** (*Calluna vulgaris*), see box p66, or ling, is the flower most often associated with the Scottish moors bursting into purple blooms at the end of summer. Its natural habitat is the native pine woods but the regular burning of the moors as part of their management for grouse shooting keeps it regenerating on open ground. **Bell heather** (*Erica cinerea*) has larger flowers and is usually found on dry peaty soils; **cross-leaved heath** (*Erica tetralix*) prefers wetter boggier ground. Other members of the heather family include **blaeberry** (*Vaccinium myrtilis*, called bilberry in England), **bog bilberry** (*V. uliginosum*) and **cowberry** (*V. vitis-idaea*) which all have edible berries. In boggy areas look for **bog myrtle** (*Myrica gale*), **common** and **harestail cottongrass** (*Eriophorum angustifolium* and *E. vaginatum*) and the incredible carnivorous **great sundew** (*Drosera anglica*) which traps and digests small insects.

(Opposite – Flora and fauna) Top: Native to Scotland, shaggy Highland cattle (see p69) are descended from the wild ox. **Centre**: You'll be lucky to spot the elusive pine marten (*Martes martes*) but they are to be found along the Great Glen Way. **Bottom left**: Common spotted orchid (*Dactylorhiza maculata*). **Bottom right**: Great sundew (*Drosera anglica*), a carnivorous plant found in boggy areas.

❏ Heather
To a fool who cries 'Nothing but heather!' where in September another
Sitting there and resting and gazing around
Sees not only the heather but blaeberries
With bright green leaves and leaves already turned scarlet,
Hiding ripe blue berries; and amongst the sage-green leaves
Of the bog-myrtle the golden flowers of tormentil shining;
And on the small bare places, where the little Blackface sheep
Found grazing, milkworts blue as summer skies;
And down in neglected peat-hags, not worked
Within living memory, sphagnum moss in pastel shades
Of yellow, green and pink; sundew and butterwort
Waiting with wide-open sticky leaves for their tiny winged prey;
And nodding harebells vying in their colour
With the blue butterflies that poise themselves delicately upon them,
And stunted rowan with harsh dry leaves of glorious colour.
'Nothing but heather!' – How marvellously descriptive! And incomplete!

Hugh MacDiarmid *Lucky Poet*

Heather is an incredibly versatile plant which is put to many uses. It provides fodder for livestock, fuel for fires, an orange dye and material for bedding, thatching roofs, basketwork and brooms. It is still used in place of hops to flavour beer and the flower heads can be brewed to make a good tea. It is said that Robert Burns used to drink such a 'moorland tea' made from heather tops and the dried leaves of blackberry, speedwell, bilberry, thyme and wild strawberry.

Bees are also responsible for heather honey, widely acclaimed the world over. In high summer the heather moorlands are in bloom and the bees will collect pollen exclusively from this source. The result is a much sought-after dark amber honey full of flavour.

On drier heaths you can't miss the prickly **whin** (*Ulex europaeus*) bushes, called gorse in England, with their yellow flowers, and the similar but spineless bushes of **broom** (*Cytisus scoparius*).

Mountain
If you explore some of the mountains along the way you may come across alpine plants, in particular **starry**, **purple**, **yellow** and **mossy saxifrage** (*Saxifraga stellaris*, *S. oppositifolia*, *S. aizoides* and *S. hypnoides*) whose dramatic name means 'rock-breaker'. Other flowers to look out for are **alpine lady's-mantle** (*Alchemilla alpina*), **trailing azalea** (*Loiseleuria procumbens*) and **northern bedstraw** (*Galium boreale*).

MAMMALS

The animal most frequently associated with the Scottish Highlands is the **red deer** (*Cervus elaphus*), justifiably referred to as 'the monarch of the glen'. This is Britain's largest land mammal and one that most walkers will have a good chance of seeing. They can be found either in their preferred habitat of natural woodland or out on the open hills, a harsh environment to which the red deer has had to adapt since the demise of deciduous woods. Although traditionally a forest dweller you will rarely see deer in the sterile environment of mature conifer plantations. In summer they often move onto windy high ground to avoid midges while in winter they come down into the valley bottoms to find better food. You are most likely to see them on the high ground above Loch Ness.

Male deer (stags) grow beautiful antlers every year. They are discarded in April or May and will be fully regrown by July or August ready for the rut in late September. At this time of year you may hear stags roaring at each other across the glens, the beginning of the competition for mating rights with a harem of hinds (females). If a stag is out-roared he will usually back down and concede his harem to the challenger. Occasionally the competition will move on to the next stage where the stags lock antlers in a battle of strength until one of them submits. Calves are usually born the following June. If they survive their first precarious year, despite the dangers of bad weather and predators such as foxes and golden eagles, they can expect to live for up to 15 years.

Population estimates vary between 300,000 and 750,000; even if the lower figure is the correct one this still represents the highest it's ever been and is felt by many to be jeopardising the ecology of the Highlands. In particular, such high numbers prevent the natural regeneration of many important trees and flowers. This imbalance was caused by man through the eradication of their natural predators, the wolf (the last wolf was killed in 1743), lynx and brown bear, and by maintaining high deer numbers for stalking on sporting estates (see p52). Today's marksmen are trying harder to emulate natural predators by weeding out the old, weak and young and by culling more hinds (as opposed to the traditional target of large healthy stags for trophies) in an attempt to redress the balance.

Roe deer (*Capreolus capreolus*) are a much smaller native species, mainly to be seen in woodland and they can sometimes be identified by their loud bark made when running away. They tend not to congregate in large herds as red deer do; you are more likely to see them alone or in pairs.

Other common and familiar mammals include **foxes** (*Vulpes vulpes*), **badgers** (*Meles meles*), **mountain hares** (*Lepus timidus*), **stoats** (*Mustela erminea*), and their smaller relation, the **weasel** (*Mustela nivalis*), **hedgehogs** (*Erinaceus europaeus*), **voles**, **mice** and **shrews**. More unusual are the **feral goats** (*Capra hircus*) which you may see around Loch Ness. These are descendants of goats which escaped and became feral during the Highland clearances in the 18th and 19th centuries.

The Highlands, being relatively unpopulated, are a vital refuge for some key British species which elsewhere have either disappeared altogether or are nearing extinction. The woods and forests, for example, are the last stronghold of Britain's only native squirrel, the **red squirrel** (*Sciurus vulgaris*). Their numbers have fluctuated dramatically over the years, disappearing almost entirely by the mid 1700s due to the clearing of ancient pine forests and epidemics of disease, and then establishing themselves once again in the new conifer plantations. Here this delightful creature exists in moderate numbers and has so far avoided the recent catastrophic decline experienced in much of England.

The introduction of the American **grey squirrel** (*Sciurus carolinensis*) at the end of the 19th century is blamed for this demise south of the border and it is only by keeping this species out of Scotland's red squirrel habitats that a similar fate can be avoided. It is one of those conservation paradoxes that the commendable attempts to increase the amount of deciduous woodland in the Highlands may also be aiding the spread of the grey squirrel. Coniferous forests

❑ **Forestry & Land Scotland**
There is no escaping the fact that the Great Glen Way passes through a lot of forestry plantations. These commercial stands of trees are essentially a crop of non-native species such as Sitka spruce and Douglas fir that are grown for timber and paper products. Forestry & Land Scotland (🖳 forestryandland.gov.scot), a government agency, own and manage the majority of these forests.

The history of Forestry & Land Scotland, formerly the Forestry Commission, dates back to WWI when forest cover in Britain had fallen to just 5%. With war looming the government recognised the need for a timber resource, particularly for wooden trenches. The Forestry Commission was set up in 1919 with the sole purpose of planting millions of trees for timber. The then chairman, Lord Lovat, planted some of the first trees near Fort Augustus. Today those trees are some of the highest in Scotland; the Great Glen Way passes directly below them as the Way follows the low route north out of Fort Augustus.

While those particular trees are an impressive sight, many of the plantations that the Way passes through are not always the most beautiful or ecologically diverse; many of the forests are virtual mono-cultures and the trees are planted very close together to maximise productivity. But things have been changing. Towards the end of the 20th century Forestry Commission Scotland, developed a new remit. Where they were once purely a commercial operation, they now have a conservation arm. A lot of the commercial crop is now ripe for harvesting and large areas have been clear-felled which has given the commission an opportunity to restock with not just non-native species but a broader range of native broadleaves and Scots pine; this is much better for the native wildlife, and much nicer to walk through for anyone on the Great Glen Way.

And they haven't stopped there; the commission is also a key player in specific conservation projects and now employ conservation officers who actively improve habitat for species such as red squirrels, otters, ospreys and capercaillie. And despite the negative impact of some commercial forests, some species have benefited from them, notably the aforementioned capercaillie as well as crossbills and the white-tailed eagle which will often use the branches of a Sitka spruce as a nest site.

The other big improvement in the way Forestry & Land Scotland operates is in outdoor access for the public, through the construction of footpaths and offering opportunities to explore the forests and see the wildlife. Indeed, the government agency was a partner in the creation of the Great Glen Way and is still involved in its management; something worth remembering as you walk those many miles through stands of conifers.

are now having to be managed specifically for red squirrels in order to keep this alien invader out.

The **pine marten** (*Martes martes*) is another woodland species which has all but disappeared from England and Wales but is doing very well in Scotland. In the 19th and early 20th centuries it suffered relentless persecution from gamekeepers which along with habitat loss and the demise of its favourite food, the red squirrel, took it to the brink of extinction. With more enlightened management on sporting estates and the increased spread of woodland this protected species is now able to re-colonise some of its former territory, and there are plenty of them along the Great Glen Way. However, you would be very lucky indeed to catch a glimpse of this elusive creature.

An equally shy and similarly persecuted animal is the **wildcat** (*Felis silvestris*), which is superficially similar in appearance to its domestic cousin. It became extinct from southern England as far back as the 16th century and nearly disappeared altogether from Britain in the early 1900s. Reduced harassment from gamekeepers and increased forestry have allowed it to re-colonise much of Scotland north of the central industrial belt. However, the wildcat is still threatened with extinction in Scotland due to hybridisation with domestic and feral cats. **Scottish Wildcat Action** (💻 scottishwildcat action.org), a conservation group supported by a number of conservation organisations including SNH, Forestry & Land Scotland and the Royal Zoological Society of Scotland (RZSS), is trying to reverse the trend and bring the wildcat back from the brink by neutering domestic cats and operating a breeding programme.

The **otter** (*Lutra lutra*), that great symbol of clean water and a healthy environment, is also now thriving in the Western Highlands after a sudden decline in the 1950s and '60s which was caused by a combination of water pollution (in particular by organochlorine pesticides), loss of well-vegetated river banks and hunting by otter hounds. In the Highlands they inhabit river banks and sea lochs as fish are their primary food.

Highland cattle

These domesticated wild-looking shaggy beasts fit perfectly into the dramatic scenery of the Highlands and are uniquely native to Scotland. They are descended from the wild ox, which was living in Scotland before humans, and from the Celtic Shorthorn which was brought to Britain about 5000 years ago. As a result they are well suited to the harsh environment and meagre grazing of the hills. The wealth of the Highlands was based on these cattle until the 17th century. At that time they would have been predominantly black in colour; today the toffee-coloured coat is preferred. You can tell the difference between cows and bulls by the horns: cows' horns are upturned while bulls' turn downwards.

REPTILES

The **adder** (*Vipera berus*) is the only common snake in Scotland and, of the three species which exist in Britain, the only poisonous one. They pose very little risk to walkers and will not bite unless provoked, doing their best to hide. Their venom is designed to kill small mammals such as mice, voles and shrews so deaths in humans are very rare, but a bite can be extremely unpleasant and occasionally dangerous particularly to children and the elderly. You are most likely to encounter them in spring when they come out of hibernation and during the summer when pregnant females warm themselves in the sun. They are easily identified by the striking zigzag pattern on their back. Should you be lucky enough to encounter one of these beautiful creatures enjoy it and leave it undisturbed. See also p56.

BUTTERFLIES

With around 33% of the land but only 10% of the human population, Scotland is ideal country for Britain's butterfly and moth population. A lepidopterist could spend many a happy hour here finding and identifying such seldom-seen species as the **pearl-bordered fritillary**, which is threatened by habitat loss elsewhere in the UK. Other species prevalent in the Highlands include the **large heath butterfly**, **mountain ringlet** and **mountain burnet**.

Despite the wide range of species, Scotland's butterflies are still under pressure from habitat loss and the intensive use of farmland. Thankfully, bodies such as Butterfly Conservation Scotland (see p60) work to preserve habitats for butterflies, moths and other species. To find out more about their work, visit their website where you can also learn how to help with their conservation efforts: they often run surveys on certain species, asking for reports of sightings.

BIRDS

Streams, rivers and lochs

Along lochs and wooded rivers look out for the striking **goosander** (*Mergus merganser*), a sawbill duck which hunts for fish, and the well-known **mallard** (*Anas platyrhynchos*), the ancestor of the farmyard duck. If you are walking in autumn you may catch the evocative sight of **white-fronted** (*Anser albifrons*) and **greylag** (*Anser anser*) **geese** flying in from Greenland. The white-fronted goose is distinguished by the white on the front of its head at the base of the bill. They return north again at the start of spring.

The **grey wagtail** (*Motacilla cinerea*) and the **dipper** (*Cinclus cinclus*) are two delightful birds which can be seen year-round bobbing up and down on boulders along loch shores or in the middle of fast-flowing streams. With its blue-grey head and back and bright-yellow underparts the grey wagtail is the most striking of all the wagtails. The dipper is unmistakable with its dinner-jacket plumage (black back and white bib) and can perform the amazing feat of walking underwater along the bed of streams. They are joined in summer by **common sandpipers** (*Tringa hypoleucos*), a tame long-legged, long-billed wader easily identified by its wagtail-like dipping action.

Look out for **sand martins** (*Riparia riparia*) on banks of sandy soil where they nest in burrows, often found by rivers but not exclusively so. Related to the house martin, these fast flyers are usually seen in flocks, zipping about catching insects.

STONECHAT
L: 135MM/5.25"

Woodland

The familiar woodland residents of chaffinches, robins, tits, songthrushes, blackbirds and tawny owls are joined by spring and summer visitors. Tropically bright **redstarts** (*Phoenicurus phoenicurus*), relatives of the robin, spend much time on the ground looking for food, often motionless before suddenly pouncing on insects or worms; acrobatic **pied flycatchers** (*Ficedula hypoleuca*) dart after insects in mid air; rather nondescript brown **tree pipits** (*Anthus trivialis*) perform song flights while darting from one high perch to another; yellow and green **wood warblers** (*Phylloscopus sibilatrix*) restlessly flit around in the woodland canopy along with tiny **willow warblers** (*Phylloscopus trochilus*), those miracles of bird migration who travel 2000 miles at a never-faltering speed of 25mph to spend the winter in central Africa.

In hilly woodland these species may be joined by the increasingly rare **black grouse** (*Lyrurus tetrix*). The male blackcock is unmistakable with his blue-black plumage but the female could be confused with the red grouse, though they rarely share the same habitat.

In pine forests you will find seed-eating finches such as **siskins** (*Serinus serinus*), **red crossbills** (*Loxia curvirostra*) and **Scottish crossbills** (*Loxia scotica*). The latter is very special indeed as it is found nowhere else but Scotland, the only bird with this distinction. This canary-like bird uses its powerful crossover bill to prise open the tough cones of the Scots pine to extract the seed, its principal food. With few remnants of Caledonian pinewood left in Scotland this unique bird is considered a threatened species with a population of only 1500 birds.

BLACK GROUSE
L: 580MM/23"

The **capercaillie** (*Tetrao urogallus*), the largest game-bird in Britain, is another casualty of scant pinewood habitat. This turkey-like member of the grouse family has suffered a significant decline over the last 30 years from about 40,000 birds down to about 5000. This is not the first time this species has come under attack. In the 18th century the bird was hunted to extinction and those seen in

Scotland today originate from Swedish capercaillie used to reintroduce the species in 1837. The capercaillie is regarded as an accurate indicator species, its low numbers alerting us to the decline of mature, varied forests. Some forward-thinking people are well aware of this bleak situation and are already working to restore Scotland's beautiful pinewoods (see box p61). This should bring a brighter future not only for these birds but also for the whole ecology of the Highlands.

Open hillside and moorland

Golden plovers (*Pluvialis apricaria*), **meadow pipits** (*Anthus pratensis*) and **stonechats** (*Saxicola torquata*) are joined in summer by **whinchats** (*Saxicola rubetra*) and **wheatears** (*Oenanthe oenanthe*) out on the open hills. Another summer visitor is the **curlew** (*Numenius arquata)*, a wader with a distinctive, long, curved bill. They over-winter on the coast, returning to the moors in summer to breed. In autumn huge flocks of **redwings** (*Turdus iliacus*) and **fieldfares** (*Turdus pilaris*) fly over from Scandinavia to feed on ripe berries.

Walkers on heather moorland often put up a covey of **red grouse** (*Lagopus lagopus*) which will speed downwind gliding and whirring just above the ground. This plump copper-coloured bird is highly valued for its sporting potential and is probably best known for its association with the 'Glorious Twelfth', the start of the grouse-shooting season in August, one of those over-hyped British rituals.

CURLEW
L: 600MM/24"

Birds of prey likely to be seen on moorland include **kestrels** (*Falco tinnunculus*), a small falcon often seen hovering in search of beetles or mice, the much less common **merlin** (*Falco columbarius*), the smallest falcon, which swoops low over the moors twisting and banking as it flies after meadow pipits, and **buzzards** (*Buteo buteo*) which fly in slow wide circles looking for small mammals. Although a large bird, the buzzard is significantly smaller than a golden eagle (see below) and can be distinguished by its drawn-out mewing cry.

High mountain

The **golden eagle** (*Aquila chrysaetos*), Britain's largest and most majestic bird of prey, is synonymous with Scotland's mountains and touches the essence of wilderness. Spiralling upwards on the thermals this huge bird, with its 7ft (2m) wingspan and long open primary feathers, couldn't be confused with any other. It feeds mainly on grouse, ptarmigan and mountain hares but won't turn down dead sheep or other carrion. For many years the number of breeding pairs was estimated to be around 450 but, in 2016, a study by RSPB Scotland and the

Scottish Raptor Study Group showed a population of 508 pairs, a rise of 15% in 13 years. This success is largely down to the efforts of conservationists who monitor breeding territories to protect them from persecution and disturbance. Studies have shown a direct correlation between eagles persecuted (usually shot or poisoned) and moorland managed for grouse-shooting. There is strong evidence to show that the number of breeding pairs is much lower than they should be in the Eastern Highlands where the habitat for the birds is perfect but the land is heavily managed for grouse-shooting interests. All of Britains's breeding pairs of golden eagle live in Scotland.

GOLDEN EAGLE
L: 910MM/36"

GOLDEN EAGLE (SILHOUETTE)

As thrilling a sight as the golden eagle is the **peregrine falcon** (*Falco peregrinus*) in flight. This king of the air can reach speeds of 50mph (80km/h) in level flight with swift shallow beats of its long pointed wings interspersed by long glides. But it shows off its true talents when diving after pigeon or grouse, its principal prey, sometimes reaching an incredible 180mph (290km/h). In the 1950s the population of peregrines dropped suddenly and disastrously. During this crisis Scotland held the only healthy population of peregrines in the world. The species was probably saved by the RSPB's and British Trust for Ornithology's painstaking research which linked the decline to the use of pesticides, in particular dieldrin and DDT. These chemicals were being used by farmers to treat their grain which was then ingested by seed-eating birds who in turn were eaten by peregrines. The revival of the species is one of the great success stories of modern conservation.

Above 2000ft (600m) you are likely to see fearless **ptarmigan** (*Lagopus mutus*), a cousin of the red grouse, scurrying across the ground in front of you. In winter its grey speckled plumage turns to pure white except for a black tail. **Snow buntings** (*Plectrophenax nivalis*), looking like pale sparrows, occasionally nest in the high mountains but most arrive in the winter migration from the Arctic.

Also haunting these heights are jet black **ravens** (*Corvus corax*), a massive crow with a powerful beak that soars at great speed across the sky, occasionally rolling onto its back with half-folded wings as if to prove its mastery of flight.

RAVEN
L: 650MM/25"

4 ROUTE GUIDE & MAPS

Using this guide

This route guide has been divided according to logical start and stop points. However, these are not intended to be strict daily stages since people walk at different speeds and have different interests. The maps can be used to plan how far to walk each day. The route summaries describe the trail between significant places and are written as if walking the path from south to north.

To enable you to plan your own itinerary, practical information is presented clearly on the trail maps. This includes walking times for both directions, all places to stay, camp and eat, as well as shops where you can buy supplies. Further service details are given in the text under the entry for each place.

For an overview of this information see Itineraries, pp29-34.

TRAIL MAPS

Scale and walking times
The trail maps are to a scale of 1:20,000 (1cm = 200m; $3^1/_8$ inches = one mile). Walking times are given along the side of each map and the arrow shows the direction to which the time refers. Black triangles indicate the points between which the times have been taken. **See box below about walking times**.

The time-bars are a tool and are not there to judge your walking ability. There are so many variables that affect walking speed, from the weather conditions to how many beers you drank the previous evening. After the first hour or two of walking you will be able to see how your speed relates to the timings on the maps.

Up or down?
Other than when on a track or bridleway the trail is shown as a **red dotted line**. An arrow across the trail indicates the slope; two arrows

---

❏ **Important note – walking times**
Unless otherwise specified, **all times in this book refer only to the time spent walking**. You will need to add 20-30% to allow for rests, photography, checking the map, drinking water etc. When planning the day's hike count on 5-7 hours' actual walking.

show that it is steep. Note that the arrow points towards the higher part of the trail. If, for example, you are walking from A (at 80m) to B (at 200m) and the trail between the two is short and steep it would be shown thus: A — — — >> — — — B. Reversed arrow heads indicate a downward gradient.

Accommodation

Apart from in large towns where some selection of places has been necessary, almost everywhere to stay that is within easy reach of the trail is marked. Details of each place are given in the accompanying text. The number and type of rooms is given after each entry: **S** = Single, **T** = Twin room, **D** = Double room, **Tr** = Triple room and **Qd** = Quad. Note that most of the triple/quad rooms have a double bed and one/two single beds (or bunk beds); thus for a group of three or four, two people would have to share the double bed, but it also means that the room can be used as a double or twin. See also pp18-20.

Rates quoted for B&B-style accommodation are **per person (pp) based on two people sharing a room** for a one-night stay; rates may well be discounted for longer stays. Where a **single room (sgl)** is available, the rate for that is quoted if different from the rate per person. The rate for **single occupancy (sgl occ)** of a double/twin may be higher and the per person rate for three/four sharing a triple/quad may be lower.

Unless specified, rates are for bed and breakfast. At some places the only option is a **room rate**, ie the price is the same whether one or two people (or more if permissible) use the room. In tourist towns, particularly, you can expect to pay extra at weekends (whereas in the few places on this route that cater to business people the rate is likely to be higher during the week). Note that a few places accept only a two-night stay, particularly at weekends and in the main season.

Rooms are either **en suite** (with a bath or shower in the room) or have **private** or **shared** facilities – a bathroom, or shower room, often (just) outside the bedroom. The text notes if a bath (☛) is available in at least one room for those who prefer a relaxed soak at the end of the day.

The text also indicates whether the premises have: **wi-fi** (WI-FI); if a **packed lunch** (Ⓛ) can be prepared, subject to prior arrangement (this is not noted for towns/cities where getting food is easy); and if **dogs** (🐾 – see also p50 and pp155-6) are welcome, again subject to prior arrangement, either in at least one room (many places have only one room suitable for dogs), or at campsites. The policy on charging for dogs varies; some places make an additional charge per day or per stay, while others may require a refundable deposit against any potential damage or mess.

If a place posts **current opening times** on their Facebook page rather than on a website this is indicated by the **fb** symbol.

Other features

Other features are marked on the map only when they are pertinent to navigation. To avoid clutter, not all features are marked all the time.

The route guide

FORT WILLIAM

Fort William is frequently derided as being something of a blot on an otherwise beautiful landscape but there have been attempts over the years to beautify it. Certainly, the pedestrianised high street and the green in front of the Alexandra Hotel are not unpleasant places to hang out. Most walkers will be itching to get their boots on and hit the trail but should you feel tempted to indulge in some of the perks of civilisation, Fort William has plenty to keep you occupied.

If you do have some time here there are a few things to see. **West Highland Museum** (☎ 01397-702169, 🖳 westhighlandmuseum.org.uk; Cameron Sq; May-Sep Mon-Sat 10am-5pm, also Sun 11am-3pm in July & Aug, Jan-Apr & Oct-Dec 10am to 4pm; free) is a treasure trove of fascinating artefacts on the Highlands; it's well worth a visit. There's a secret portrait of Bonnie Prince Charlie, displays about the crofting life and lots of information on Ben Nevis (see pp160-4), including the story of Henry Alexander who drove his Model T Ford to the summit in 1911.

Also worth a visit is **Lochaber Geopark Visitor Centre** (☎ 01397-705314, 🖳 lochabergeopark.org.uk/thingstodo/visitor-centre; summer daily 10am-4pm, winter Mon, Fri & Sun 10am-4pm, Tue & Sat 10am-2pm, Wed 10.30am-5pm; free) on High St, Fort William; see also box p59. It is staffed by volunteers so the opening days and hours can vary.

By the roundabout on Achintore Rd is **Lime Tree An Ealdhain Gallery** (see also Where to stay) which exhibits contemporary art; entrance is free and the gallery is open daily 10am-10pm except November.

Out of town is **Ben Nevis Distillery** (☎ 01397-702476, 🖳 bennevisdistillery.com; **fb**), which has been producing whisky for nearly 200 years. A tour of the distillery with a tasting at the end costs £5; a tasting tour including three malt whiskies is £18.

For those who have walked the Way in reverse and have just arrived in Fort William, there are showers (£2) at **The Nevis Centre** (bookings ☎ 01397-700707, 🖳 neviscentre.co.uk; **fb**; daily 9am-10pm), behind Morrisons. It also houses a concert hall and a 10-pin bowling alley and plays host to a number of annual events, including Fort William Mountain Festival in February or March (see p14).

Bicycles can be rented from **Nevis Cycles** (Map 1; ☎ 01397-705555, 🖳 neviscycles.com; **fb**; £25/day; £120/week), at 4 Lochy Crescent, Inverlochy; see also p28.

While in Fort William you may want to take the opportunity to **climb Ben Nevis** (1344m), the highest mountain in Britain. The peak is a popular goal for thousands of visitors a year and commands an exceptional view across the Highlands. The start of the path to the summit is just a couple of miles from the town centre (see pp160-4).

Services
For tourist information **Visit Scotland's Fort William iCentre** (☎ 01397-701801, 🖳 visitscotland.com; Jul & Aug Mon-Wed & Fri-Sat 9am-6.30pm, Thur 10am-6.30pm, Sun 9.30am-6pm; early Sep Mon-Wed & Fri-Sat 9am-6pm, Thur 10am-6pm, Sun 10am-5pm; late Sep-Oct Mon-Wed & Fri-Sat 9am-5pm, Thur 10am-5pm, Sun 10am-4pm; Nov-Mar Mon-Wed & Fri-Sat 9am-5pm, Thur 10am-5pm, Sun 10am-3pm) is at 15 High St. The staff can also book accommodation (see box p38) and sell bus tickets for Citylink.

Another source of information is 🖳 visitfortwilliam.co.uk; **fb**.

For a **supermarket**, at the northern end of the High St there's a Tesco Metro (Mon-Sat 7am-9pm, Sun 10am-5pm) and over by the station a branch of Morrisons (Mon-Fri 8am-9pm, Sat 7am-9pm, Sun 8am-6pm).

Fort William

Loch Linnhe

Nevis Cycles, 500m;
Ben Nevis Distillery, 1 mile
& A82 to Inverness

North Rd

To Glen Nevis

Belford Rd

trailblazer

Remains of
Fort William fort
and start of
Great Glen Way

The
Nevis
Centre

Morrisons

Bus
station

Ellis Brigham

Railway station

Underpass

Nevisport

Library &
internet @

Tesco
Metro

WH Smith & PO

Visit Scotland
Fort William iCentre

Mountain
Warehouse

Toilet

Lochaber
Geopark
Visitor
Centre

West Highland
Museum

Lloyds
Pharmacy

Cotswold
Outdoor

Lime Tree
An Ealdhain
Art Gallery

Victoria Rd

Alma Rd

Fassifern Rd

Cameron Rd

High St

Union Rd

Argyll Rd

Achintore Rd

Lundavra Rd

Connochie Rd

0   100   200m

ROUTE GUIDE AND MAPS

Where to stay

1 The Brevins
2 Ben Nevis Guest House
3 Tigh na Drochaid
4 Nevis Bank Inn
5 Premier Inn
6 MacLean House
7 Guisachan House
8 Fort William Backpackers
10 The Alexandra Hotel
11 St Andrew's Guesthouse
12 Constantia House
13 Stobahn
14 Bank Street Lodge
26 Travelodge Fort William
27 Lime Tree An Ealdhain
28 Myrtle Bank
29 Calluna

Where to eat and drink

4 Browns Restaurant
9 Cobbs
14 The Stables
   Restaurant & Grill
15 The Crofter Bar
16 The Wildcat
18 Ben Nevis Bar
19 Grog & Gruel
20 The Geographer
21 Aroma
22 Hot Roast Company
23 Crannog Seafood Restaurant
24 Spice Tandoori
25 Pier Head Takeaway
26 The Great Glen
   (Wetherspoon)
27 Lime Tree An Ealdhain

There is an **ATM** in Tesco Metro and there are several **banks** (with ATMs) along the High St as well as some **chemists**, including a branch of Lloyds Pharmacy, a **post office** (Mon-Sat 9am-5.30pm, Sun 10am-4pm) in WH Smith and a **library** (Mon & Thur 10am-8pm, Tue & Fri 10am-6pm, Wed & Sat 10am-1pm) – the latter is a good place to while away the hours or surf the internet on a miserable day.

Another popular activity in the rain is gear shopping. Fort William has several large **outdoor equipment shops** all open daily, including Mountain Warehouse and Cotswold Outdoor on the High St; Nevisport, which also has a café, bar and wi-fi (see Where to eat); and Ellis Brigham Mountain Sports near the station. Up-to-date **weather forecasts** are posted at all of them.

There are **showers** at the aforementioned Nevis Centre and also at the train station.

Transport

[See also pp43-6] The **railway station**, for services to Mallaig and south to Glasgow (as well as the sleeper service via Edinburgh to London), is at the northern end of town. The station has left-luggage lockers and showers.

The **bus station** is across the road by Morrisons' supermarket. This is where all the bus/coach services depart for routes north up the Great Glen to Inverness (Scottish Citylink 919), north-west to Uig (Scottish Citylink 915 & 916) and south to Glasgow (Scottish Citylink 914, 915 & 916), as well as Shiel Buses' 500 service to Mallaig and West Coast Motors' 918 service to Oban.

For a **taxi** there's Greyhound (☎ 01397-705050) and Lochaber (☎ 01397-706070).

Where to stay

There's no **campsite** within Fort William so campers should head to the site at Glen Nevis (see p157), which is only a couple of miles away.

Hostels Right in the centre is *Bank Street Lodge* (☎ 01397-700070, 🖳 bankstreet-

lodge.co.uk; **fb**; WI-FI) with dorm rooms (3-7 beds; from £16pp) which share facilities. They also have some en suite rooms (sgl/sgl occ from £30, double or twin £45 per room, rooms with 3/4/6 beds from £62/80 /90). Bedding is provided but no meals. However, there are full cooking facilities.

On Alma Rd there's the busy *Fort William Backpackers* (☎ 01397-700711, 🖳 fortwilliambackpackers.com; **fb**; 38 beds; shared facilities; WI-FI in communal areas), a colourful independent hostel. A dorm bed costs £19.50-20.50pp (or it's £46-48 for a private twin room) and a continental breakfast costs £2, or you can just have a few slices of toast for 40p. The rate includes bedding and guests can use the kitchen and sitting room during the day. Note that you need photographic ID for check-in.

Apartments As long as you are happy to stay for a minimum of three nights and accept that a short booking may not be accepted months in advance, *Calluna* (☎ 01397-700451, 🖳 fortwilliamholiday.co.uk; **fb**; WI-FI; 🐾; Jan-end Oct), on Connochie Rd, has four self-contained apartments sleeping up to 4/6/8 people. Bedding is provided and there are full cooking facilities. Dorm beds are £21pp, twins £23pp and quads £21pp but rates vary widely so see their website or contact them for the latest.

B&Bs and guest houses The difference in price between hostels and some of the cheaper B&Bs/guest houses is negligible when you take the cost of breakfast into account. Some of the nicest places are located at the top of the road to Glen Nevis. *The Brevins* (☎ 01397-701412, 🖳 the brevins.co.uk; 1S/1D/5D or T, all en suite; WI-FI) is one of the best places in Fort William. All the rooms are clean and comfortable. B&B costs from £42.50pp (sgl occ from £45pp) They have a two-night minimum stay.

Just on from here is the smart *Ben Nevis Guest House* (☎ 01397-708817, 🖳 bennevisguesthouse.co.uk; **fb**; 2D/1T/1Tr/2Qd, all en suite; ☞; WI-FI). There's a nice conservatory to sit in and a drying room. B&B costs £35-60pp.

Next is tidy, comfortable *Tigh na Drochaid* (☎ 01397-704177, 🖳 glennevis bb.co.uk; 1D/1T, both en suite; WI-FI), which is excellent value (£35-45pp, sgl occ £40-50) and run by friendly people.

On Belford Rd there are several good B&Bs but since this is the main road it could be a little noisy. *MacLean House* (☎ 01397-703083, 🖳 macleanhouse.co.uk; 4D/1T/1Tr/2Qd, all en suite; WI-FI) has tidy rooms; B&B costs from £35 (sgl occ from £59).

Alma Rd is a good area as it's quiet, centrally located and has views overlooking the town. Here you'll find smart *Guisachan House* (pronounced Goosh-a-gan; ☎ 01397-703797, 🖳 guisachanguesthouse.co .uk; **fb**; 1S private shower facilities, 2S/5T/7D/ 2Tr/1Qd, all en suite, ☛; WI-FI; mid Jan-Oct), a guest house where B&B costs £42.50pp (sgl occ from £78).

Fassifern Rd is packed with B&Bs, a selection of which follows. Starting at the northern end is one of the most interesting buildings in town, *St Andrew's Guesthouse* (☎ 01397-703038, 🖳 standrewsguesthouse .co.uk; 3D/1Tr, all en suite, 1T private facil-ities, 1D/1T share facilities; WI-FI; Mar-Oct), a beautifully turreted stone house dat-ing back to 1880. B&B costs £30-40pp (sgl occ £50-65).

Constantia House (☎ 01397-702893, 🖳 airbnb.co.uk; 2S/1T share facilities, 2Tr both en suite; WI-FI; Mar-Oct) has nice clean rooms and charges £25-35pp (sgl £30-40, sgl occ £50-60) for B&B. Just up from here is *Stobahn* (☎ 01397-702790, 🖳 stobahnguesthouse.co.uk; 1T/2D/1Tr all en suite, 1S/1D share facilities; WI-FI), a guest house with comfortable rooms. Rates are £30-40pp.

Below here on Bank St is *Bank Street Lodge* (see Hostels) which has some en suite accommodation but does not provide breakfast.

On Achinore Rd, *Myrtle Bank Guest House* (☎ 01397-702034, 🖳 myrtlebank guesthouse.co.uk; 11D/4T, all en suite; WI-FI; Feb-Dec) offers B&B for £35-50pp (sgl occ rates on request). They serve Scottish, vegetarian and continental breakfasts and have drying facilities for wet gear.

Hotels Right beside the official end of the West Highland Way is *Travelodge Fort William* (Fort William ☎ 0871 984 6419, booking line ☎ 0871 984 8484 but £2.50 booking fee; 🖳 travelodge.co.uk; 60D, all en suite; WI-FI 30 mins free per 24hrs, £3 for 24hrs), on the High St. Rates depend on demand; if you book early (online) and pay at the time of booking you may get a room for £32 (Saver rate; non refundable) but if not expect to pay £60-130 and even up to £170 in the peak season (the rate is the same whether one or up to three people share). If you want to get an early start their breakfast box costs £4.95; porridge may be available for £1.95. For a full cooked breakfast go to The Great Glen (see Where to eat) below the Travelodge.

The other large hotel chain has a hotel near the railway station: *Premier Inn* (☎ 0871-527 8402, 🖳 premier inn.com; 42D/61D or T, all en suite, ☛; WI-FI). If you book online very far in advance you may be able to get a room for as little as £29.50/45 (Saver rate, non refundable, non amend-able/Flex rate). Otherwise, expect to pay around £60-135 for a room; the best rates are always online. The beds are very com-fortable. Breakfast (continental buffet/hot buffet £7.50/9.50pp) is available next door at Brewers Fayre Loch Iall (Mon-Fri 6.30-10.30am, Sat & Sun 7-11am).

On Belford Rd, by the noisy A82, there's *Nevis Bank Inn* (☎ 01397-705721, 🖳 nevisbankinn.co.uk; **fb**; 5S/2D/14D or T/3Qd, all en suite; ☛; WI-FI; 🐾). B&B starts from £70-90.50pp (sgl/sgl occ from £119); breakfast is served in Browns restaurant (see Where to eat).

The Alexandra Hotel (☎ 01397-702241, 🖳 strathmorehotels-thealexan dra.com; **fb**; 7S/78D or T/8Tr, all en suite; ☛; WI-FI; 🐾) is a large old hotel in the cen-tre. B&B costs £45-65pp (sgl/sgl occ from £69/ 79) but they sometimes have special packages so it's always worth contacting them.

If you're unlucky and everywhere is booked, try looking on Achintore Rd, the A82 south to Glencoe and Glasgow. Here are wall-to-wall guest houses overlooking Loch Linnhe, though it's an unnecessarily

ROUTE GUIDE AND MAPS

long way to walk if you don't have to. At the start of Achintore Rd, by the round-about, is *Lime Tree An Ealdhain Hotel, Restaurant & Art Gallery* (☎ 01397-701806, 🖥 limetreefortwilliam.co.uk; **fb**; 5D/ 2T/2Tr, all en suite; ✆; WI-FI; 🐾) which has luxurious rooms (£55-100pp, sgl occ £90-140), a restaurant (see Where to eat) and an art gallery (see p76). They have a map room (with historical maps) and a mountaineering library but perhaps of more practical use to walkers is their drying room. The triple rooms can sleep four people if it is two adults and two children but would be rather cramped for four adults.

Where to eat and drink
All along the High St there is a wide selection of take-away places including Indian, fish and chips, and burger bars as well as several pubs. There are now some coffee shops, too, including the usual big names.

For the perfect choice for a delicious quick breakfast or lunch, head straight to the *Hot Roast Company* (☎ 01397-700606; **fb**; Mon-Sat 9am-4pm, Sun 11.30am-3.30pm). They serve their eponymous signature dish – tasty and filling hot rolls such as beef and horseradish or ham and mustard, all for around £3.49 – from 11am. Breakfast rolls are served 9-11am.

Aroma (daily 10am-4pm) is a busy coffee shop on the High St serving soup and paninis as well as cakes.

There are numerous **pubs** to choose from. *Grog & Gruel* (☎ 01397-705078, 🖥 grogandgruel.co.uk; **fb**;), halfway along the High St, is a cosy traditional pub with a good range of local beers. Food is served in the pub (Mon-Sat noon-9pm, Sun 5-9pm or 12.30-9pm in the peak season) and in the restaurant (evenings 5-9pm). Dishes include their popular hot dogs from £6.50, quesadillas from £5.95 and venison burgers (£11.95). There's live music in summer, usually on Thursday nights, and an open music session on Friday nights.

Almost opposite is *Ben Nevis Bar* (☎ 01397-702295, 🖥 bennevisbarfortwilliam .com; **fb**; food in the bar daily noon-5pm and in the restaurant Easter to Oct daily

noon to 10pm), with good pub grub such as steak & ale pie for £7.99. Also on the High St, *The Crofter Bar* (☎ 01397-704899, 🖥 crofter bar.co.uk; **fb**; food served daily summer 9am-9pm, winter generally 9am-3pm & 6-9pm) is a popular, good-value pub with Sky Sports and tasty meals.

Open long hours and conveniently located below the Travelodge is a branch of the family-friendly (but dog unfriendly) pub chain, Wetherspoon – *The Great Glen*; they serve food here daily from 7am until 11pm, to 10pm sometimes in the winter months.

Browns Restaurant (food served daily noon-2.30pm & 5.30-9.15pm) is at Nevis Bank Inn (see Where to stay). They get great reviews, serving a range of food from steaks (£21.95) to seafood (local scallops £19.95).

Cobbs (☎ 01397-704790, 🖥 cobbs .info; Mon-Sat 9am-4.45pm, Sun 9.30am-4.15pm), the alpine-style **café/bistro** upstairs at Nevisport, is popular; the café menu includes sandwiches, paninis and baked potatoes; the bistro is in a separate area and its menu includes mains (from £7.95) as well as daily specials. There's a **bar** (daily noon-11pm) downstairs.

The Wildcat (☎ 01397-698856, 🖥 wild catcafe.co.uk; daily 8am-5.30pm) is halfway down the High Street. This ethical café and wholefoods shop prides itself on being organic, vegan and plastic free. It's a pleasant spot for coffee and guilt-free cake. *The Stables Restaurant & Grill* (☎ 01397-700730, **fb**) below Bank Street Lodge (see Where to stay) serves food in the evenings year-round (Tue-Sat 5-8.30/9pm, to 9.30pm in the main season) but may also open for lunch in the peak season. There's plenty on the menu from chicken fajitas for £14.50 to a rack of ribs for £17.95; they also do French onion soup for £5.45.

At the southern end of the High Street is *The Geographer* (☎ 01397-705011, 🖥 geographerrestaurant.co.uk; **fb**) which has vegan and gluten-free steaks and salads. They also do hot dog and fries for £10.95 and sandwiches from £4.50.

The glitzy *Spice Tandoori* (☎ 01397-705192, 🖥 spice-tandoori.com; **fb**; daily noon-2pm & 5pm to late) has great views over Loch Linnhe. Among the long list of dishes is chicken tikka tandoori for £9.95.

Pierhead Takeaway (☎ 01397-704666, 🖳 pierhead-takeaway.business.site; Sun-Thur noon-midnight, Fri & Sat to 1am) does fish & chips, kebabs and burgers – and you can try a deep-fried Mars Bar here for £3.50.

One of the best places for local food and a special meal is the perfectly located *Crannog Seafood Restaurant* (☎ 01397-705589, 🖳 crannog.net; **fb**; daily noon-2.30pm & 6-9.30pm, to 9pm in winter).

Freshly caught seafood such as Shetland salmon fillet (£17.50) is superbly cooked and reasonably priced. There is always one meat dish (such as lamb, venison or beef) on the menu. They also do a two-/three-course (£14.95/18.95) lunch menu.

Some of the finest dining in Fort William can be found at *Lime Tree Restaurant* (see Where to stay Lime Tree An Ealdhain Hotel; daily 6-9pm); main dishes cost around £19.95. If their *Isag Bree* (fish stew, £22.50) is on the menu try it as it is superb.

FORT WILLIAM TO GAIRLOCHY   [MAPS 1-6]

Starting at the **remains of the old Fort William fort** (see box below) by the roundabout, this first stretch of the Great Glen Way, covering **10 miles (16km; 3hrs 20mins-4hrs 5mins)**, begins in unassuming style as you follow the back streets of the town.

For the first half a mile the highlights include a branch of *McDonald's*, a petrol station and a housing estate but these give way to a pleasant stretch along the banks of the River Lochy, where it opens out into the sea at Loch Linnhe. The waters come down the Great Glen from Loch Lochy and also from the Grey Corries mountains east of Ben Nevis. It's a surprisingly wide and mighty river by Highland standards and despite the urban centres of Fort William and Caol on each side, the banks of the river are pleasingly undeveloped and wooded so you

ROUTE GUIDE AND MAPS

❏ **Fort William's fort**

The Great Glen Way begins at the site of the defensive fortification that gives Fort William its name. The main structure of the fort would have been where the railway station now stands but here at the start of the Way you can see part of the site. In truth, there is little to see today other than a grassy sward and a few low stone walls but there is a panel that outlines a brief history of the place and its history is significant.

The stone stronghold was built in 1698, following the orders of King William III – hence 'Fort William' – on the site of an earlier wooden fort built under the orders of Oliver Cromwell. It was one of three forts positioned along the length of the Great Glen – the others being Fort George at Ardersier, near Inverness, and Fort Augustus – that were constructed as part of an effort to quell the dissenting Jacobites, the clans loyal to the exiled Stuart king (Charles Edward Stuart). The unrest came to a head in the 1745 Jacobite Uprising when Charles, or 'Bonnie Prince Charlie' as he is more romantically known, attempted to regain the British crown.

The uprising led to the siege of the fort at Fort William in March 1746, but ultimately defeat for the Jacobite cause came at the Battle of Culloden one month later. The subsequent manhunt for Bonnie Prince Charlie lasted five months and covered much of the Western Highlands. The operation to find him was run from the fort, but he eventually escaped back to France.

can picture what this landscape may have looked like thousands of years ago.

Beyond the **rugby pitch** the trail crosses a couple of bridges by the railway, one of which is the attractive **Soldiers Bridge**, so-called because the army built it as a gift to the local community. Before you cross it take the two-minute detour to the right to see the ruins of **Old Inverlochy Castle** (see box below). After Soldiers Bridge there is some tarmac-whacking as the trail follows the road around the fringes of Lochyside to the outlying town of Caol.

CAOL

There is not much to do in Caol (*pro-nounced Cool*), and you will probably be itching to get away from the urban sprawl, but should you need them there is a good range of services.

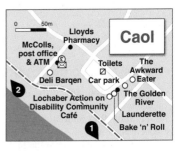

Services

In Caol everything is centred around the square where you'll find **McColls** (☎ 01397-704437; Mon-Sat 7am-8pm, Sun 8am-8pm); the shop is small but has a good range of groceries. There is an **ATM** inside as well as a **post office** (Mon-Sat 8am-8pm, Sun 10am-8pm).

In the unlikely event that your clothes are already too smelly to bear, there is a **launderette** (daily 10am-4pm) opposite McColls, and if you already have blisters head to the branch of **Lloyds pharmacy** (Mon-Fri 9am-6pm, Sat 9am-1pm).

Stagecoach's 46 & 47 **bus services** (see box p44) call here.

Where to eat and drink

In the square there are a few eateries to choose from including *Lochaber Action on Disability Community Café* (LAD Café; ☎ 01397-701171, 🖳 lad.org.uk; Mon-Fri 9.30am-3pm, closed Sat-Sun); the menu includes home-made soup and a roll/toastie for £4. Next door is *Bake 'n' Roll* (☎ 01397-704222; **fb**) where you can indulge in a full Scottish breakfast for £5.50 or baked potatoes for £4.20.

❑ Old Inverlochy Castle

It is a only a short detour from the path at Soldiers Bridge to the ruins of this fine castle. Inverlochy Castle dates back to 1280 when it was built for the well-heeled Comyn family who were of Norman origin and had little time for the native Celts. The property would change hands many times, usually through force and the Comyns lost their hold on the castle when Robert the Bruce was crowned King of Scotland in 1306.

In the 1500s it was used as a courthouse and in the 1700s as a storehouse for the nearby ironworks. But it really gained significance during the civil wars of the 1640s, when the Campbell clansmen, who then had control of it, were defeated by royalists who were loyal to Charles I and led by James Graham, First Marquis of Montrose. The battle was brutal and bloody with 1500 Campbell men put to the royalist swords. It was soon after this that the fort at Fort William (see box p81) was built, by order of Oliver Cromwell, to replace Inverlochy Castle and it ultimately fell into disrepair.

Considering the hundreds of years that have passed since then, it is remarkable that so much of the castle remains; more, ironically, than the more recent Fort William fort. For additional information see 🖳 inverlochycastle.co.uk.

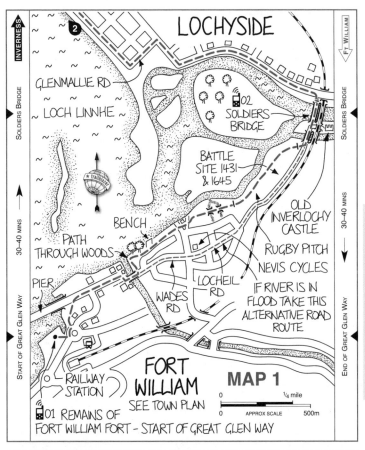

❏ **Gairlochy (see p91) – nowhere to sleep!**
Considering this is a popular tourist area it may come as a surprise to learn that accommodation is a bit of a problem at the end of this section. Apart from camping, the nearest places to stay are three miles away at Spean Bridge; there is no accommodation after Gairlochy until you get to Laggan. So the options are:
● **to camp** – there are free pitches near the Gairlochy locks and pitches at Gairlochy Holiday Park (see p91), about a mile along the road to Spean Bridge;
● **to walk** from Fort William right through **to Laggan** (23 miles/37km) or;
● at Gairlochy, **to leave** the Great Glen Way and walk the three miles along the road to **Spean Bridge** (see p91) where there is accommodation as well as buses to and from Fort William (see p78).

(Caol, *cont'd*) For **takeaways**, all the usual suspects are here with ***Deli Barqen*** (☎ 01397-702332; Sun Mon Thur 4-9.30pm, Fri, Sat 4-9.45pm, closed Tue & Wed) offering Chinese food, kebabs, burgers and fish & chips. There is more Chinese food at ***The Golden River*** (☎ 01397-703555; Wed-Mon 4-10pm) with dishes for around £5.30-8.

The Awkward Eater Takeaway (☎ 01397-706030, 🖳 theawkwardeater.co.uk; **fb**; Mon 5-8pm, Thur 5-9pm, Fri-Sun 4-9pm) has menus specifically designed to cater for a wide range of dietary preferences, offering vegan and gluten-free dishes starting from £5. Options include pizzas in two sizes as well as pastas, fajitas, nachos, burgers, salads and fish and chips.

The trail now continues along the shore of **Loch Linnhe** where it bends westwards to become **Loch Eil**. Here there are fine views down the length of Loch Linnhe towards the Atlantic. The loch is really a continuation of the Great Glen Fault (see box p59), once filled with a mighty glacier, now filled with sea water at its deeper, south-western end.

Beyond the **shinty fields** – shinty is a team game, unique to the Highlands, similar to hockey but where the ball can be played in the air – the path joins the start of the **Caledonian Canal** (see box below). If you need a bed or food already, the village of Corpach (see p86) is a 10-minute detour away. Follow the canal to the sea, and cross the lock to reach the village.

ROUTE GUIDE AND MAPS

❏ **The Caledonian Canal**

The Great Glen was the obvious place to construct a canal linking the Highlands' Atlantic coast with the North Sea at the Moray Firth. Nowhere else is there such a direct line through the mountains at such a low elevation. But why bother with such a mammoth construction project? The alternative for shipping was to negotiate the often treacherous waters around Cape Wrath and the Pentland Firth on the northern coast of Scotland. A canal through the Great Glen would provide safe passage, most notably for the British navy; this was a time when Napoleon was a significant threat to national security. It was also seen as an opportunity to provide employment and keep people in the Highlands at a time of high emigration from the area.

It was an extraordinary engineering challenge and the man who was tasked with getting the job done was Scottish civil engineer **Thomas Telford**. In 1803 he set about surveying the route after initial survey work by James Watt in 1773. The canal opened in 1822, although further work was carried out in the mid 1800s; it appears shortcuts had been taken in the original construction to lower costs.

The finished canal cost nearly £1,000,000 to build (which is almost £100 million in today's prices!), has 29 locks, is 22 miles in length and along with lochs Lochy, Oich and Ness, connects Corpach with Inverness, 60 miles away. It was closed for 10 years from 1995 for major repair works along its length. It's a testament to Telford, and all those who have worked on it since its inception, that the canal is so popular today both for commercial and leisure traffic.

The most famous feature on the Caledonian Canal, and the first you will see if you start your walk in Fort William, is **Neptune's Staircase**, a flight of eight locks that carries the canal from sea level to a height of 19 metres. It takes a boat about 1½ hours to get through all the locks and continue its journey. See also box p88.

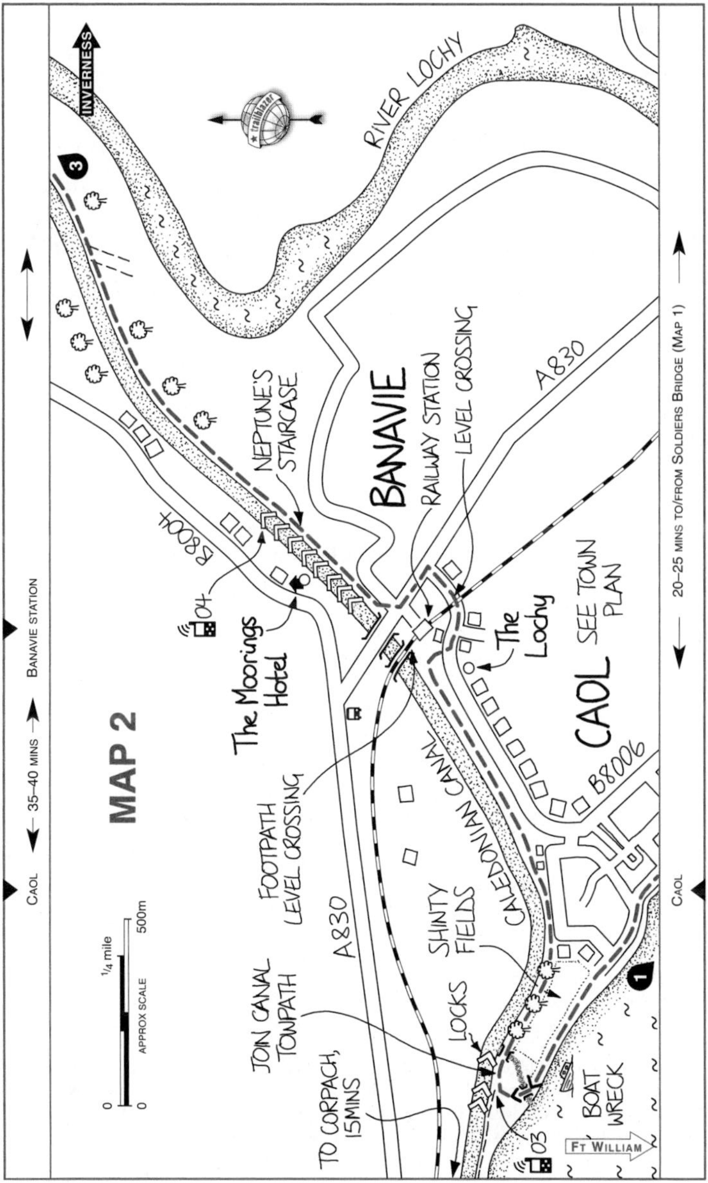

MAP 2

CAOL ← 35–40 MINS → BANAVIE STATION

¼ mile
500m
0
0
APPROX SCALE

INVERNESS

RIVER LOCHY

3

B8004

Neptune's Staircase

The Moorings Hotel

BANAVIE

RAILWAY STATION
LEVEL CROSSING

A830

FOOTPATH
LEVEL CROSSING

A830

JOIN CANAL TOWPATH

TO CORPACH, 15MINS

LOCKS

SHINTY FIELDS

CALEDONIAN CANAL

The Lochy

CAOL SEE TOWN PLAN

B8006

BOAT WRECK

FT WILLIAM

1

CAOL ← 20–25 MINS TO/FROM SOLDIERS BRIDGE (MAP 1) →

CORPACH

The village is not pretty in itself but the surroundings are beautiful. The mouth of the canal is one of the best places to admire mighty Ben Nevis towering over the head of Loch Linnhe. This is also where you will find **Corpach Sea Lock Office** (see box p19) which is where you need to pick up a key, if you want it, for access to the three compost toilets at the Trailblazer rest sites along the Way.

There is a **railway station** in Corpach for services to Mallaig, Banavie, Fort William and Glasgow and Stagecoach's 46 & 47 **bus services** call here; for details see pp43-6.

On the main road there is a small Co-op **supermarket** (daily 6am-11pm) with an **ATM** inside. This could prove invaluable if you have mis-calculated how much food you might need; unless you make the

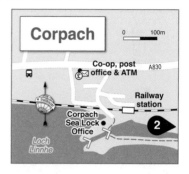

detour to Spean Bridge from Gairlochy this is the last shop you will see until the small shop at Well of the Seven Heads at Laggan Swing Bridge and the last supermarket until Fort Augustus. There is also a **post office** inside the Co-op.

The Caledonian Canal will be a constant companion to your left-hand side for the next 7½ miles (12km) to Gairlochy. Much of the canal is wooded on each side with beautiful native trees including some lovely stands of beech and Scots pine. At times the walking can be monotonous and the broad canal-side path can be hard on your feet but rest assured that this is just day one and the walking becomes more varied and interesting as you head north.

And there are points of interest along this stretch, notably the impressive flight of eight locks known as **Neptune's Staircase** (see box p84) at Banavie.

BANAVIE   [Map 2, p85]

The village of Banavie straddles the Caledonian Canal. The Great Glen Ultra Race (see p14) starts here in July.

If you want to avoid the mainly urban walking between Fort William and Banavie you can catch a train (the **railway station** is right on the trail by the main road) or take a bus; Stagecoach's 46 & 47 **bus services** call at Banavie (see pp43-6).

If you have walked from Fort William this could be a good spot for a pub lunch. *The Lochy* (☎ 01397-703587; **fb**; food Mon-Fri 11am-9pm, Sat & Sun noon-9pm), just before the railway station, has the usual bar meals for around £8-12. They also do sandwiches, toasties and fish & chips.

A more scenic spot for lunch, right next to the locks, is *The Moorings Hotel* (☎ 01397-772797, 🖳 moorings-fortwilliam.co .uk; **fb**). They have several options for eating and drinking and there are all sorts of things to choose from on the various menus. Their *café/bistro* (daily noon-4.30pm & 5-9.30pm), overlooking the canal, offers sandwiches and paninis from £5.95; the bistro menu includes steak and ale pie (£14.95) and chicken curry (£14.95).

They also have plenty of **beds** (8D/ 21D or T/2Tr/1Qd, all en suite; ✆; WI-FI; Ⓛ; 🐾) for the night. B&B costs from £45pp (sgl occ from £90).

ROUTE GUIDE AND MAPS

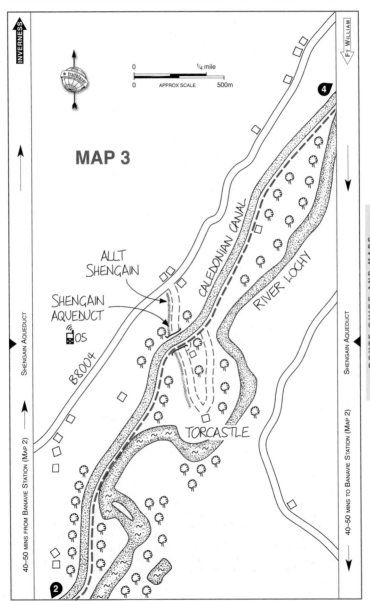

INVERNESS

FT WILLIAM

MAP 3

0   1/4 mile
APPROX SCALE
0   500m

ALLT SHENGAIN

SHENGAIN AQUEDUCT

05

B8004

CALEDONIAN CANAL

RIVER LOCHY

TORCASTLE

4

2

40–50 MINS FROM BANAVIE STATION (MAP 2)

40–50 MINS TO BANAVIE STATION (MAP 2)

ROUTE GUIDE AND MAPS

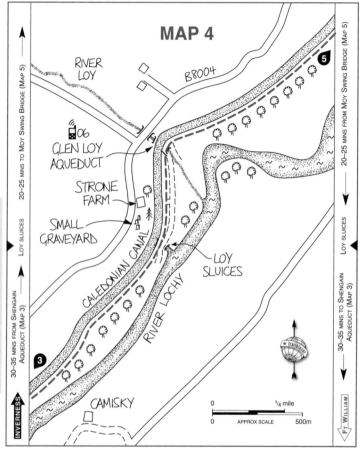

MAP 4

RIVER LOY

B8004

5

GLEN LOY AQUEDUCT

STRONE FARM

SMALL GRAVEYARD

CALEDONIAN CANAL

LOY SLUICES

RIVER LOCHY

3

CAMISKY

trailblazer

0   1/4 mile
0   APPROX SCALE   500m

ROUTE GUIDE AND MAPS

20–25 MINS TO MOY SWING BRIDGE (MAP 5)

LOY SLUICES

30–35 MINS TO SHENGAIN AQUEDUCT (MAP 3)

Ft WILLIAM

20–25 MINS FROM MOY SWING BRIDGE (MAP 5)

LOY SLUICES

30–35 MINS FROM SHENGAIN AQUEDUCT (MAP 3)

INVERNESS

❑ Gangoozling

In the course of researching this book I learned a new word: gangoozle. This is the act of standing on a towpath and watching the comings and goings on the canal. A favourite spot for a gangoozler is by the locks as there is always plenty going on with the raising and lowering of boats. Neptune's Staircase (see box p84), at Banavie, is probably the ultimate location for a spot of gangoozling since it takes so long for boats to get through the eight locks; plenty of free entertainment. As yet there is no verb to describe the act of staring at gangoozlers in bewilderment.

Less well-known sights are **Shengain Aqueduct** (Map 3), which carries the canal over the Allt Shengain, and the much bigger **Glen Loy Aqueduct** (Map 4) which takes the canal across the River Loy, a tributary of the River Lochy.

A further mile on is **Moy Swing Bridge** (Map 5) where the picnic benches will entice you to stop and have a rest. There is an official *wild camping spot* on the grass by the picnic benches with room for about four small tents. The swing bridge is the original cast-iron one, designed by Thomas Telford. It is operated by hand and despite its grand appearance its sole purpose is to provide access across the canal to the farmer's fields. From Moy it is just over a mile to the locks at Gairlochy.

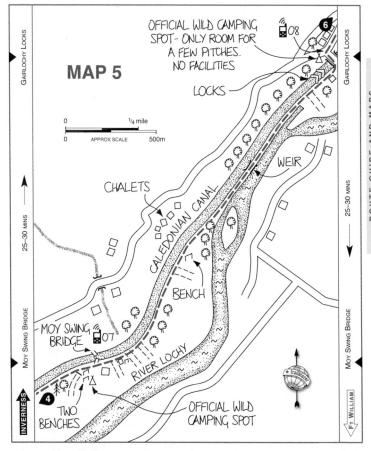

MAP 5

OFFICIAL WILD CAMPING SPOT- ONLY ROOM FOR A FEW PITCHES. NO FACILITIES

08

6

LOCKS

0   ¼ mile
0   APPROX SCALE   500m

WEIR

CHALETS

CALEDONIAN CANAL

BENCH

MOY SWING BRIDGE

07

RIVER LOCHY

4

TWO BENCHES

OFFICIAL WILD CAMPING SPOT

GAIRLOCHY LOCKS

GAIRLOCHY LOCKS

25–30 MINS

25–30 MINS

MOY SWING BRIDGE

MOY SWING BRIDGE

INVERNESS

FT WILLIAM

ROUTE GUIDE AND MAPS

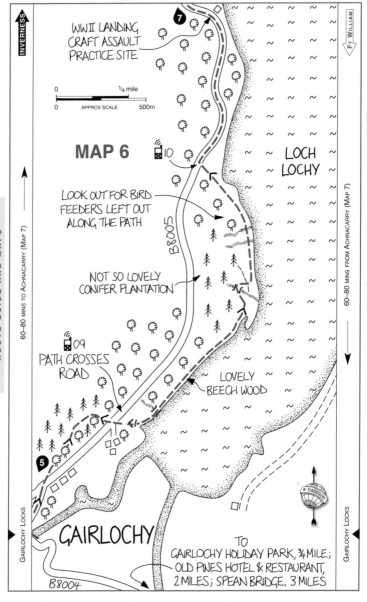

INVERNESS

Fᵀ WILLIAM

WWII LANDING CRAFT ASSAULT PRACTICE SITE

7

0   ¼ mile
0   APPROX SCALE   500m

MAP 6

10

LOCH LOCHY

LOOK OUT FOR BIRD FEEDERS LEFT OUT ALONG THE PATH

B8005

NOT SO LOVELY CONIFER PLANTATION

09 PATH CROSSES ROAD

LOVELY BEECH WOOD

5

GAIRLOCHY

TO GAIRLOCHY HOLIDAY PARK, ¾ MILE; OLD PINES HOTEL & RESTAURANT, 2 MILES; SPEAN BRIDGE, 3 MILES

B8004

ROUTE GUIDE AND MAPS

60–80 MINS TO ACHNACARRY (MAP 7)

60–80 MINS FROM ACHNACARRY (MAP 7)

GAIRLOCHY LOCKS

GAIRLOCHY LOCKS

GAIRLOCHY   **[Map 6]**

There are no facilities here (see box on p83) and no accommodation options other than an official **wild camping spot** with a handful of pitches (room for up to six tents) near the locks (see Map 5) so if you need a bed for the night, or want a formal campsite, you may have to head along the road towards Spean Bridge (see below).

SPEAN BRIDGE

The village is about three miles (5km) from Gairlochy. It is on the junction of the main A82 road heading north and the eastbound A86. Consequently it can be a busy rest stop for the large volumes of traffic in the summer but there are some quiet corners if you know where to look, plenty of accommodation and some good places to eat.

Services

The **Spar shop** (☎ 01397-712230; Mon-Sat 7am-9pm, Sun 8am-9pm) and **post office** (daily 8am-8pm) is right in the middle of the village. It's a reasonable size for a small village and should have most essentials. There is an **ATM** next to the shop and there is a **public toilet** in the car park behind the shop.

Transport

[See pp43-6] The **railway station** for trains to Fort William, Mallaig and Glasgow is tucked down a back street behind Spean Bridge Hotel. Just along the road from Spean Bridge Hotel is the stop for Scottish Citylink's 19, 915, 916 & 919 and Stagecoach's 19/19C **bus services**.

Where to stay

There are a few accommodation options before you reach the main part of Spean Bridge so you may not have to trudge all the way along the road (B8004) from Gairlochy.

Campers can stop at *Gairlochy Holiday Park* (off Map 6; ☎ 01397-712711, 🖳 theghp.co.uk; 🐾; Apr-Oct), about three-quarters of a mile along the road to Spean Bridge (B8004). A tent pitch here costs £7.50 for one person (£4.50 for an additional person) but you will have to share the site with caravans and house-sized tents.

Also on the B8004 from Gairlochy, and a couple of miles before Spean Bridge, is *Old Pines Hotel & Restaurant* (off Map 6; ☎ 01397-712324, 🖳 oldpines.co.uk; 2Tr, both en suite; WI-FI; ⓛ; 🐾; Easter to Oct). It's a plush spot set amongst the pine trees. They have camp beds so up to four people can sleep in a room. B&B costs £60-70pp (sgl occ rates on request); adding dinner to this costs £85-95pp based on two sharing.

The B8004 from Gairlochy joins the A82 and on that, as you walk into the village, is *Aonach Mor Hotel* (☎ 01397-712351, 🖳 aonachmorhotel.co.uk; 1S/2D/2T/1Tr, all en suite; 🛏; WI-FI; ⓛ), a simple hotel with B&B from £32.50pp (sgl £35, sgl occ £70); the restaurant here is open daily 6-8.30pm.

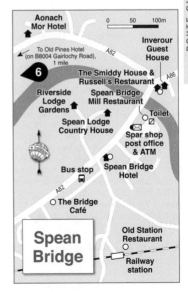

By the junction of the A82 and A86 is **The Smiddy House** (☎ 01397-712335, 🖳 smiddyhouse.com; **fb**; 3D/1T/1Qd, all en suite; WI-FI; Ⓛ), a restaurant with rooms that has an air of elegance about it. B&B costs £45-70pp (sgl occ £80-135, £195-250 per room for 2-4 sharing the Bryson Suite); dinner is also available (see Russell's Restaurant in Where to eat). Next door is **Inverour Guest House** (☎ 01397-712218, 🖳 inverour.co.uk; 1S/4D/1T/1Tr) with clean, comfortable rooms for around £50pp.

The centre of the village is dominated by the imposing **Spean Bridge Hotel** (☎ 01397-712250, 🖳 speanbridgehotel.co.uk; 2S/8D/5T/4Tr/1Qd, all en suite; ☞; WI-FI reception only; Ⓛ). B&B costs from £40pp (sgl occ from £70). Accommodation is either in the main hotel, an annex, or one of seven **chalets** (£76.50-101.50; 🐾 some chalets) each sleeping 2-5 people with a combination of double/single/bunk beds.

Away from the noisy road there are some very smart B&Bs down the leafy lane opposite Spean Bridge Hotel. The first is **Spean Lodge Country House** (☎ 01397-712004, 🖳 speanlodge.co.uk; **fb**; 1D/1T/1Tr, all en suite; WI-FI; Ⓛ), a beautiful 200-year-old Highland lodge set in perfectly manicured gardens, designed in the 19th century by a gardener from Kew Gardens in London. The rooms are also lovely and facilities include a drying room. For what you get, the rate is reasonable: £49.50-60pp (sgl occ £80-108).

At the end of the road, **Riverside Lodge Gardens** (☎ 01397-712702, 🖳 visitscotland-spean.co.uk; 2D or T/1T/1Tr, all en suite; ☞; WI-FI; Ⓛ; 🐾; May-Sep) is exactly where the name suggests, by the River Spean. It's probably the most peaceful place to lay your head in the village and although it is more modern than Spean Lodge, the rooms are still well presented. B&B here costs around £40pp (sgl occ from £50). If booked they are happy to pick guests up from Gairlochy and drop them off the next day.

Where to eat and drink
Spean Bridge is spoilt for good eateries.

First pick is **Russell's Restaurant** (see The Smiddy House, Where to stay; food served Apr-Oct Tue-Sun 6-9pm, Nov-Mar Thur-Sun 6-8.30pm); it offers a two/three-course menu for £29.50/35.

Old Station Restaurant (☎ 01397-712535, 🖳 oldstationrestaurant.co.uk; **fb**; mid Mar to late Oct restaurant Mon & Wed-Fri noon-9.30pm, Sat 9am-9.30pm, Sun noon-8pm, closed Tue) is also a good choice. It really is in the old station building and it has been tastefully preserved to feel like a 1940s' waiting room, complete with a roaring open fire in winter. Try the salmon fillet or venison casserole, both for £16.95. They also do light lunches; the toasties are £5.25. Booking is recommended, particularly at peak periods. However, you don't need to eat to visit; there is also a cosy **bar** (Mon & Wed 5-11pm, Thur-Sat to 1am, Sun to midnight) with real ales on tap including their own Old Station Commando from Cairngorm Brewery (see p23).

There are simpler, and cheaper, meals at **The Bridge Café** (☎ 01397-712957; **fb**; summer Mon-Sat 8am-7.30pm, Sun to 3pm, winter hours depend on demand); it is a popular place with tasty dishes located at the southern end of the village. Offering similar fare is the **Spean Bridge Mill Restaurant** (☎ 01397-712260; Mon-Sat 9am-5pm, Sun 10am-5pm) which is often busy with coach parties. They do cheap lunches; the haggis on toast is £2.95 and paninis and jacket potatoes will relieve you of £5.50. Note that it was temporarily closed at the time of research so call them for an update on reopening plans.

Spean Bridge Hotel (see Where to stay; food served daily 11am-2.30pm & 5-8.30pm) serves bar meals and the menu includes a wide choice of dishes such as curries and steaks; they also have a takeaway **fish & chips** window (**The Village Fryer**; same days & hours) on the side of the building.

As much as possible, the food at **Old Pines** (see Where to stay; Easter to Oct Tue-Sat noon-2.30pm, daily 6.30-8.45pm) is locally sourced and organic; booking is recommended for the evenings.

❏ **General Wade's roads**
Following the Jacobite uprising and the defeat of Bonnie Prince Charlie and his sympathisers, the British government set about fortifying the Highlands to prevent any further unrest. The forts of Fort William, Fort Augustus and Fort George (at Ardersier, near Inverness) were built in a strategic line up the Great Glen. To ease access to them, and to ensure that the locals were kept in check, plans were made to construct roads from the central lowlands to these forts.

The man appointed with leading this project was General George Wade, who designed and oversaw the construction of 250 miles (402.5km) of roads including the challenging route from Strath Spey over the 770-metre high Corrieyairack Pass to the Great Glen. The roads were constructed from stone and in places are remarkably well preserved. The road through the Great Glen was completed in 1727. It was aligned on the south side of the glen and at Loch Oich the Great Glen Way follows the same route.

GAIRLOCHY TO JUNCTION BY LAGGAN LOCKS   [MAPS 6-12]

The long walk along the forestry track by the shores of Loch Lochy can be quite a trudge at times but it is made easier by the wonderful views across the loch. But the highlight of this **13-mile (21km; 3hrs 50mins-4hrs 55mins)** section is not Loch Lochy, it is the first part of the day through the beautiful birch and beech woodland between Gairlochy and Clunes. There is modern history here too as this was where special forces were trained during WWII. Don't forget to look back over your shoulder; if the weather is clear there is a great panorama of the Grey Corries ridge and Ben Nevis on the far side of the Great Glen.

It is at Gairlochy that you finally leave the canal towpath and head uphill. The lane climbs up and out of the village through the woodland. Bear right at the two junctions and then turn almost immediately left into woods on the well-maintained path that runs parallel to the road. This is a purpose-built path for Great Glen Way walkers, which is much kinder to your feet than the tarmac.

After a few minutes the path crosses the road and heads down through beautiful broadleaved woodland to the shore of Loch Lochy.

The path hugs the shoreline, passing beneath the mighty boughs of beeches. This beautiful woodland walk is abruptly cut short when the beeches give way to the tightly packed spruces of a conifer plantation. Here the path winds inland, away from the shore, to a burn. If the water is low it's easy to cross but if it's in spate, head upstream a short way to a bridge and then head back downstream to join the path proper. Once again you are back in glorious native woodland, this time a birch forest.

Over the next mile or so there are several incongruous **bird feeders** placed by the path, some of them quite elaborate in design. They seem well-stocked up and popular with the chaffinches, suggesting that some kindly lad or lassie pays regular visits along this path to keep them maintained.

ROUTE GUIDE AND MAPS

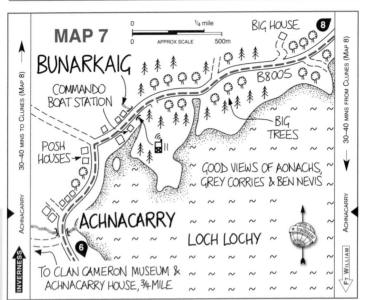

❑ WWII training at Loch Lochy

Anyone who has driven the A82 from Spean Bridge northwards will have had their eye drawn to the **WWII Commando Memorial** that stands prominently on a hill overlooking the glen. Between 1942 and 1945, 25,000 men used the area as a training ground, with Achnacarry House at Achnacarry, on the shores of Loch Lochy, acting as their base. Training exercises famously included running to the summit of Ben Nevis. Less well known are the exercises that were carried out on and around Loch Lochy at **Bunarkaig**. As you walk the Way, along the shores of the loch, look out for the concrete platform (Map 6) in the birchwoods by the road. This unassuming feature is a practice landing craft assault site; the men who trained here went to Normandy in the D-Day landings of 1944.

Further around the bay there is a commando boat station where the exercises were so realistic that, as the interpretation panel says, *'it was as close to battle conditions as they could get without actually slaughtering half the trainees'* (Donald Gilchrist). The soldiers would stage an offensive by heading out into the loch in rowing boats, where officers would fire upon them with live ammunition to make the experience as authentic as possible. The instructors who shot at them were said to be *'skilled in the Achnacarry art of shooting to miss, but not by very much'*.

The soldiers were also sent on gruelling exercise hikes between Clunes and Laggan, so if you find yourself complaining about sore feet on those seven miles, consider that you are following in the footsteps of WWII soldiers who had to march this route in 70 minutes. Oh, and when they got there they had to dig themselves a defensive bunker.

Eventually the path meets the lane (B8005) and you follow this all the way to Clunes. Shortly after joining the road there is a notable historic site on the right. An unassuming concrete platform set among the trees is in fact a WWII **landing craft assault practice site**. The special forces trained for the D-Day landings in this area. About half a mile further on, after Achnacarry you will also find a **commando boat station** (Map 7, see opposite).

Before that, at **Achnacarry** it's worth making a short detour to **Clan Cameron Museum** (☎ 01397-712090, 🖳 clancameronmuseum.co.uk; daily Apr-early Oct 11am-4.30pm, early Oct-Apr open by appointment; £4). Exhibits in this small museum take you all the way back through the history of the Cameron clan from the 14th century to the modern day. There is also more information about the WWII commando training that took place here.

There is a lovely spot for *wild camping* (Map 8) in a glade by the loch shore, just before you get to Clunes; see Map 8. At the Forestry cottages at **Clunes** bear right and follow the forestry track as it runs parallel to Loch Lochy. There are fine views up and down the loch, where breaks in the plantation allow, but you may find this section begins to get a little tedious, especially if the weather is bad.

There is rudimentary shelter towards the end, at the *Glas-dhoire Trailblazer rest site* (Map 11). This is one of a number of sites set up for canoeists but walkers are equally welcome to **camp** or rest here. There is space for eight tents, with fire sites set along the shore and a three-sided wooden shelter. There is a compost toilet too but you will need to have picked up a key from Corpach (see p86 and box p19).

Once you reach the farm at **Kilfinnan** (Map 12), the end of this section is within sight. Follow the farm track down to the head of the loch and to a junction. Here you will need to make a decision: do you head to Laggan for the Loch Oich route or take the alternative Invergarry link route (see pp104-5).

ROUTE GUIDE AND MAPS

❏ **Arkaig Community Forest**
Not far from Achnacarry (see Map 7), about 1½ miles from the Great Glen Way along the track past Clan Cameron Museum, is one of the finest remnants of ancient Caledonian pine forest in this part of Scotland.

A visit to this forest is a trip back in time to how much of the land in Scotland would have looked before it was slowly transformed by man over the years into the largely barren landscape it is today. The Arkaig pinewood, a mix of Scots pine, birch, ling and juniper on the southern shore of Loch Arkaig is known to have existed as far back as 1600 at least, and there may well have been a forest here for thousands of years. It is home to red squirrels, pine martens, wildcat and black grouse. Forestry & Land Scotland (see p61), who own the site, are in talks to sell it to Arkaig Community Forest Group, a local charity which was established with the aim of purchasing the forest. In doing so the group hopes to protect and expand it, and to develop forestry activities that benefit the local community and visitors. If you would like to learn more visit the website 🖳 arkaigforest.org.

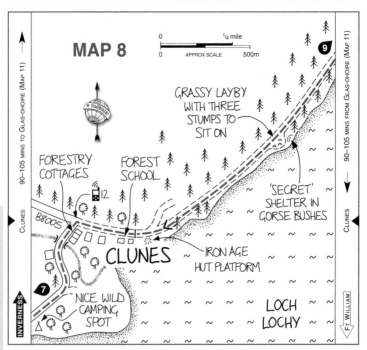

Side trip to the Loch Lochy munros

Other than Ben Nevis (see pp160-4) and its accompanying peaks, the only munros (peaks over 3000ft/914m) that grace the Great Glen are **Meall na Teanga** (918m) and **Sron a' Choire Gairbh** (937m). As they are almost equidistant between Fort William and Inverness they surely offer the best views of the length of the Great Glen.

Important note: You should only undertake this side trip if you are familiar with hillwalking in Scotland or can go with someone who is. These are isolated mountains and while the ascents are not technically difficult there is always a risk of exposure; the weather can change rapidly in the Highlands and particularly so up high. For details of the relevant maps see p38-40.

Those coming by car can park at the road end at Kilfinnan (see Map 12). From here the round trip takes about 7-10 hours. If you are coming from the south along the Great Glen Way you can join the path to the munros by taking the sharp left turn just before Kilfinnan (see Map 12). The problem with this is you end up heading back the way you came on a path running parallel and just above the one you were just walking along. To avoid this huge dog-leg you can bushwhack your way, for about 300 metres, up and through the conifer plantation above the Glas-dhoire Trailblazer rest site (see Map 11), to pick up the forestry track higher up the hill, thus saving yourself three unnecessary miles.

From the forestry track a hill path strikes off up the hill a couple of hundred metres east of the Glas-dhoire burn. Follow this up and onto the *bealach* (mountain pass) at 615m. This saddle sits between the two munros so take your pick as to which one you climb first. The smaller of the two, Meall na Teanga, is to the south. Pick your way across the rocky western shoulder of the satellite peak Meall Dubh to reach another saddle and then climb the northern ridge of Meall na Teanga to its summit.

Return the same way back to the 615m bealach and follow the zigzag path up the southern flank of the higher munro, Sron a' Choire Ghairbh. The zigzags peter out and you find yourself on the ridge looking over the northern cliffs into the spectacular Coire Garbh. The summit of Sron a' Choire Ghairbh is to the north-west.

The views from both peaks, but particularly from Meall na Teanga, are wonderful. It's a fantastic vantage point from which to appreciate the distance you have walked up the Great Glen, and how far you still have to go! Return the same way back to Glas-dhoire or Kilfinnan.

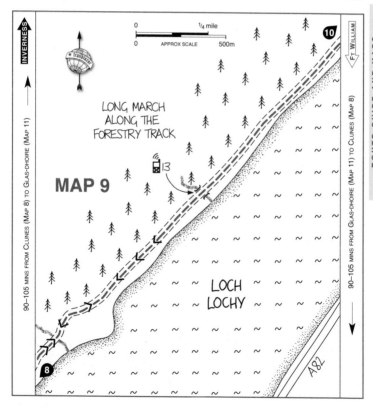

ROUTE GUIDE AND MAPS

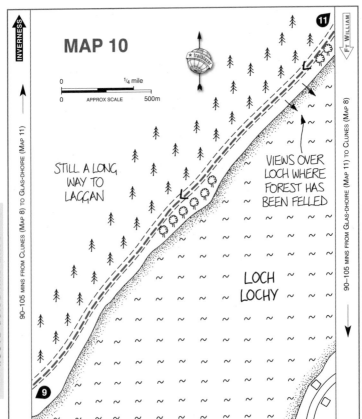

MAP 10

INVERNESS

FT WILLIAM

0   ¼ mile
0   APPROX SCALE   500m

STILL A LONG
WAY TO
LAGGAN

VIEWS OVER
LOCH WHERE
FOREST HAS
BEEN FELLED

LOCH
LOCHY

11

9

ROUTE GUIDE AND MAPS

90–105 MINS FROM CLUNES (MAP 8) TO GLAS-DHOIRE (MAP 11)

90–105 MINS FROM GLAS-DHOIRE (MAP 11) TO CLUNES (MAP 8)

❏ **Important note – walking times**
Unless otherwise specified, **all times in this book refer only to the time spent walking**. You will need to add 20-30% to allow for rests, photography, checking the map, drinking water etc. When planning the day's hike count on 5-7 hours' actual walking.

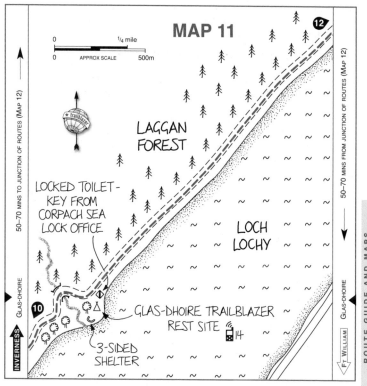

JUNCTION BY LAGGAN LOCKS TO FORT AUGUSTUS
[MAPS 12-19]

You have a choice of routes at the start of this stretch: the Invergarry route goes up the hill to the left; the route via Laggan and the east shore of Loch Oich is to the right. Both routes almost meet a couple of miles further on at Laggan swing bridge so you can take either now and then change your mind at the swing bridge and take the other route if you wish.

The **12-mile (19.5km; 3hrs 40mins-4hrs 50mins) Laggan route** is the gentler and less strenuous of the two and it follows a delightful and quiet loch-side path. It is also the most logical route between Laggan and Aberchalder but the powers that be have created an **8½-mile (13.5km; 3hrs 10mins-4hrs 20mins) alternative route** (Invergarry Link Route), presumably to filter some of the money from walkers' pockets into the local economy of Invergarry. Fair enough, I suppose, and the walk is a pleasant one boasting loftier viewpoints than the Loch Oich route. But it is more strenuous, climbing and descending in and out of Invergarry. One good reason to take this route is to stock up on supplies at Invergarry or get a bed and a beer for the night at Invergarry Hotel.

Junction by Laggan Locks to Aberchalder via Laggan & Loch Oich
[Maps 12-16]

From the junction bear right and head past the wigwams (for week-long breaks only) to the **locks at Laggan**. There is a lovely *wild camping* spot on the south shore here (Map 13) with space for up to five tents and fantastic views down the length of Loch Lochy. One of the Way's more curious pubs is on the top side of the locks: The Eagle (see p102) occupies an old barge. The Way is obvious now, once again following the towpath along a lovely stretch where the canal is wooded on both sides.

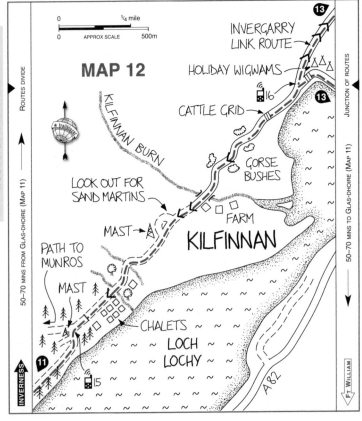

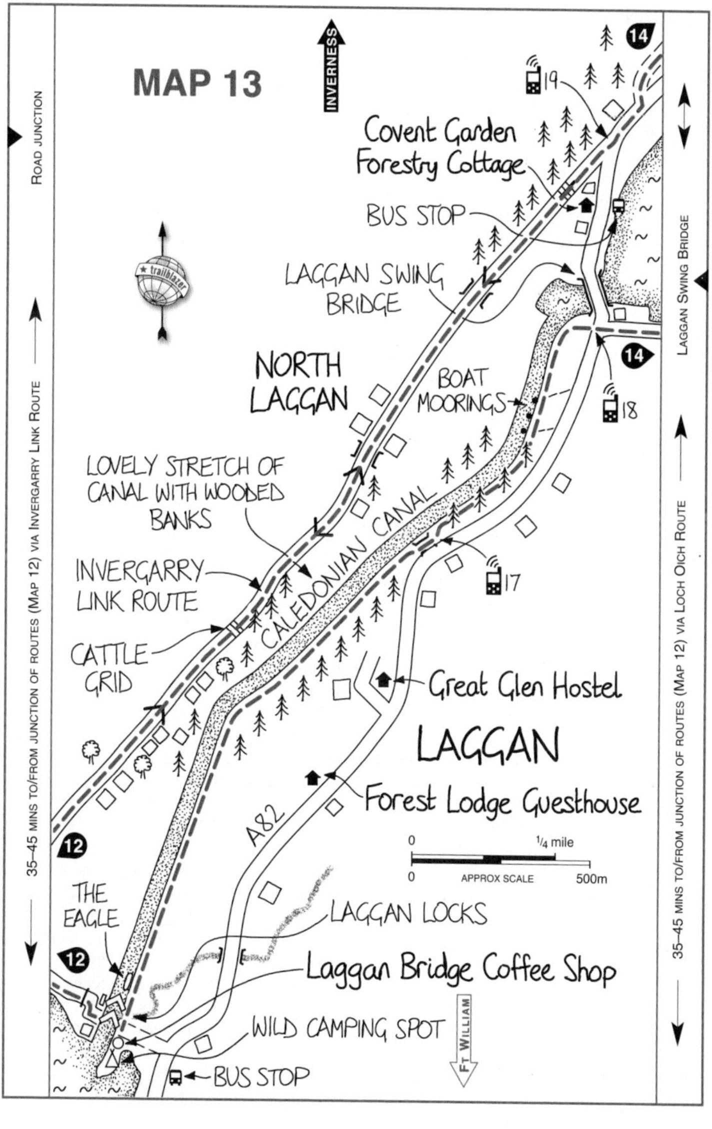

MAP 13

INVERNESS

ROAD JUNCTION

35-45 MINS TO/FROM JUNCTION OF ROUTES (MAP 12) VIA INVERGARRY LINK ROUTE

Covent Garden
Forestry Cottage

📱 19

14

BUS STOP

LAGGAN SWING
BRIDGE

LAGGAN SWING BRIDGE

NORTH
LAGGAN

BOAT
MOORINGS

14

📱 18

LOVELY STRETCH OF
CANAL WITH WOODED
BANKS

INVERGARRY
LINK ROUTE

CATTLE
GRID

CALEDONIAN CANAL

📱 17

Great Glen Hostel

LAGGAN

Forest Lodge Guesthouse

0   ¼ mile
0   APPROX SCALE   500m

A82

12

THE
EAGLE

12

LAGGAN LOCKS

Laggan Bridge Coffee Shop

WILD CAMPING SPOT

FT WILLIAM

🚌 ← BUS STOP

35-45 MINS TO/FROM JUNCTION OF ROUTES (MAP 12) VIA LOCH OICH ROUTE

ROUTE GUIDE AND MAPS

LAGGAN [Map 13, p101]

Laggan is spread out over a wide area from Laggan Locks in the south to the shores of Loch Oich at the Laggan swing bridge. There is no real focus to the village but there are a few places to stay and eat.

Services

There is a single shop at **Loch Oich Food Co** (Map 14; ☎ 01809-501246; **fb**; Mon-Fri 6am-2pm; WI-FI; ⓛ). It's a family-run place with groceries but they also cater well for Great Glen Way walkers with a good range of snacks (including breakfast baps from £2) to take away and lunch bags, though these need to be ordered 24hrs in advance. A look at the map shows the shop close to the trail but there is no way of going off-piste and cutting through the forest to the shop because the ground is too steep; the only option is walk half a mile up the main road from the swing bridge.

Scottish Citylink's 915, 916 & 919 **bus services** call at the bus stops on the main A82 road at Laggan Locks and also outside Covent Garden Forestry Cottage near Laggan swing bridge. See box p44 for service details.

Where to stay

There are a few places in the Laggan area, most of which are on the A82 main road between Laggan Locks and the swing bridge. By Laggan Locks itself is a small **wild campsite** with secluded pitches set amongst the pine trees and wonderful views down the length of Loch Lochy.

Starting at the southern end of the road is *Forest Lodge Guesthouse* (☎ 01809-501219, ⌨ forestlodgeguesthouse.co.uk; 3D/1T/3Tr, all en suite; WI-FI; ⓛ; late Mar to mid Oct), a modern detached house with drying facilities and great views down the glen. B&B costs £37.50pp (sgl occ £55).

Halfway up this stretch of road, and accessible from the point where the Way draws level with it, is *Great Glen Hostel* (☎ 01809-501430, ⌨ greatglenhostel.com; 3T/1Qd/4 x 5-beds, 2 x 6-bed & 1 x 8-bed dorms; most share facilities; WI-FI). The quad room and the rooms sleeping up to five people have a double bed and bunk bed(s), and one of the 5-bed rooms is en suite. Dormitory beds cost £20-22pp and private rooms £24-25pp (sgl occ from £30). Booking is recommended, particularly in the summer months, as the hostel is sometimes booked for sole occupancy. Facilities include a self-catering kitchen, grocery store (selling milk, bread, cereals, snacks, tinned foods, pasta and frozen ready meals), a drying room and laundry facilities (coin-operated machines). It's a beautiful building and is a convenient place to stay but bear in mind that unless self-catering the nearest evening meals are just under a mile away at The Eagle (barge).

Finally, close to the swing bridge is *Covent Garden Forestry Cottage*, a forestry cottage which operates through Airbnb (⌨ airbnb.co.uk; private bathroom; ☞; WI-FI). They have one small double room and charge from £25pp (sgl occ £50) for B&B. Check out their lovely wild and colourful front garden.

Where to eat and drink

Other than the takeaway snacks at *Loch Oich Food Co* (see Services), the only other places to eat are at *Laggan Bridge Coffee Shop* by Laggan Locks which is good for sandwiches (£2.50) and breakfast rolls (£2) to take away. And then, moored above Laggan Locks, is the most curious bar in the Great Glen: *The Eagle* (☎ 07789-858567, ⌨ eaglebargeinn.weebly.com; **fb**; Apr to Oct only, food served daily noon-3.30pm & 5.30-8.30pm) a pub on a barge. The barge still has plenty of historical features that date back to her time as a troop carrier during WWII. On board there is a bar and restaurant. Dishes include light bites such as soup and sandwiches as well as bar food such as sausage & chips (£7.50); some of the dishes on the evening menu, such as the shellfish platter, must be ordered by 3pm the day before you plan to go. They accept cash only.

At Laggan Swing Bridge you have the option of joining the Invergarry Link Route (see p105), but to continue on the Loch Oich route take the right turn down the lane before the swing bridge. The lane winds round more holiday chalets and the Great Glen Water Park to the **Old Invergarry Railway Station** (Map 14; see box p104). It's a fairly straightforward walk from here to the head of Loch Oich, simply following the broad track through more beautiful loch-side woodland. At times you may be tempted by the parallel path between you and the shore. Don't let it entice you! The path is blocked in places by fallen trees and sections of it are in a poor state. It's better to stick to the higher path

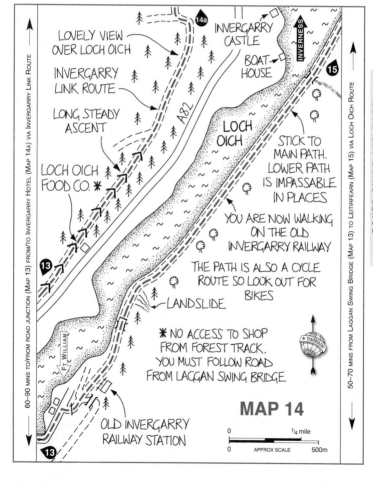

LOVELY VIEW OVER LOCH OICH

INVERGARRY LINK ROUTE

LONG STEADY ASCENT

LOCH OICH FOOD CO. ✱

INVERGARRY CASTLE

BOAT HOUSE

INVERNESS

LOCH OICH

STICK TO MAIN PATH. LOWER PATH IS IMPASSABLE IN PLACES

YOU ARE NOW WALKING ON THE OLD INVERGARRY RAILWAY

THE PATH IS ALSO A CYCLE ROUTE SO LOOK OUT FOR BIKES

LANDSLIDE

✱ NO ACCESS TO SHOP FROM FOREST TRACK. YOU MUST FOLLOW ROAD FROM LAGGAN SWING BRIDGE

60–90 MINS TO/FROM ROAD JUNCTION (MAP 13) FROM/TO INVERGARRY HOTEL (MAP 14A) VIA INVERGARRY LINK ROUTE

50–70 MINS FROM LAGGAN SWING BRIDGE (MAP 13) TO LEITIRFEARN (MAP 15) VIA LOCH OICH ROUTE

ROUTE GUIDE AND MAPS

Ft WILLIAM

13

13

14a

15

A82

MAP 14

0   ¼ mile

0   APPROX SCALE   500m

OLD INVERGARRY RAILWAY STATION

❏ **The Inverness to Invergarry Railway**
The 24-mile railway between Spean Bridge and Fort Augustus had a troubled and short life. Construction of the line began in 1896, following an application by the Invergarry and Fort Augustus Railway Company, and was completed in 1901. However, the company was left penniless having underestimated the cost of construction. Operation of the line passed to the Highland Railway Company who began running trains along it in 1903. The high operating costs and low passenger numbers left the line struggling for survival. It closed for two years between 1911 and 1913 and ownership of the railway changed hands twice. From 1933 passenger services ceased and the line was used solely for transporting coal. The railway was doomed and in 1947 the tracks fell silent once and for all. But that's not the end of the story. **Invergarry Station platform**, on the Great Glen Way at the southern end of Loch Oich, had lain hidden under thick vegetation for decades but in 2012 a group of railway enthusiasts set about bringing it back to life. The platform is now there for all to see, fresh track has been laid and an old locomotive and wagons are on display. The group have plans to lay more tracks and construct a replica signal cabin, station building and carriage shed. To follow progress check **Invergarry and Fort Augustus Railway Museum's** website (🖳 invergarrystation.org.uk).

which is well maintained and, in following the old route of the railway, is broad and straight.

There is a ***Trailblazer rest site*** (ie wild campsite) at **Leitirfearn** (Map 15), roughly halfway along the length of Loch Oich. It's a pretty spot, set under the trees on the water's edge, and is usually fairly quiet; there is space for eight tents and fire sites. The compost toilet here is usually locked so you will need to have picked up a key (see box p19) if you want to use it.

Navigation along the path is easy until it nears the northern end of the loch. Here you will need to wake up as you will most probably have gone into autopilot on the straight path. Look for the small **hydro-turbine house** (Map 16) and cross the bridge in front of it. Immediately after the bridge turn left through the gate and follow the path as it arcs around the field to the main road at **Aberchalder swing bridge**.

Those who walked the Invergarry route will have enjoyed a fine view of the old **Bridge of Oich**; if you would like to do the same you will need to make the short detour across the swing bridge and look up the River Oich.

For the route description from Aberchalder to Fort Augustus, see p107.

❏ **Important note – walking times**
Unless otherwise specified, **all times in this book refer only to the time spent walking**. You will need to add 20-30% to allow for rests, photography, checking the map, drinking water etc. When planning the day's hike count on 5-7 hours' actual walking.

**Junction by Laggan Locks to Aberchalder via Invergarry
(Invergarry link route)**   Maps 12-14, Map 14a & Maps 15-16

From the junction of tracks at the head of Loch Lochy, follow the steep track to the left. The short sharp ascent is worth it as the lane now follows an elevated and exposed route above the glen, giving much better views than the lower route. Slowly the road descends to join the main road just north of **Laggan Swing Bridge** (Map 13). For Covent Garden Forestry Cottage (see p102) turn right onto the A82 from the Invergarry Link Route. Should you wish to join the Loch Oich route, continue south along the A82 and cross Laggan Swing Bridge and then take the next minor road on the left.

Continuing on to Invergarry, there is the option to get supplies at the Loch Oich Food Co shop (see p102), a small detour along the main road. A glance at the map shows the path passes close by this shop but there is no access to the shop from the path: the ground is too steep. The only way is to walk along the road.

The way climbs relentlessly higher up a forestry track, eventually levelling out at a viewpoint where there is a gap in the trees. Here you can see Loch Oich and **Invergarry Castle** (see box below). The descent down to Invergarry is long and claustrophobic as it winds down through the dense conifer plantation. You will be pleased when you finally reach the main road and the village.

The path out of Invergarry is not obvious. You need to locate the **phone box** (Map 14a). Just beyond this a narrow path snakes its way steeply up through rhododendrons and tall trees. At the top of this steep slope the path joins a wide track which contours the forested hillside before dropping down close to the main road. Continue on, along a path that rises and falls all the way to the swing bridge at Aberchalder. The views are unremarkable but in places the forest has been clear-felled so you get some respite from the commercial forestry blocks. At **Aberchalder** there is a lovely view of the old **Bridge of Oich**. Just after the swing bridge the route hooks up with the Loch Oich route and the Way follows the towpath all the way to Fort Augustus. There is an *official wild camping spot* for three tents just south of the road bridge.

ROUTE GUIDE AND MAPS

❑ **Invergarry Castle**   [Map 14, p103]

The Great Glen Way does not pass directly by this ruined castle but there is a good view of it from up on the hill on the Way between Laggan and Invergarry. You can also see it from the other side of Loch Oich. The castle was the home of the MacDonnell clan of Glengarry and occupies a strategic spot at a junction of the Great Glen with Glen Garry. The original castle was built in 1610 but was destroyed in 1654, as was its successor in 1716. The third and final manifestation is the one you see today. In 1745 Bonnie Prince Charlie stayed at the castle, on his way to fight for the Scottish crown at the Battle of Culloden. Following his defeat there he took refuge at the castle the following year, before spending months as a fugitive. Five years later the castle was, for the third and final time, destroyed. Despite its ruinous appearance large sections of it remain intact and it is still an imposing landmark on the shore of the loch.

At present the structure is considered unsafe and there is no public access but there are plans to shore up the walls and allow visitors into the site. For further information visit 🖳 glengarry.net/castle.php.

INVERGARRY [Map 14a, opposite]

This small village, on the banks of the River Garry that gives it its name, lies at the junction of the Fort William to Inverness road (A82) and the road out west to Skye (A87). It's relatively busy with traffic but, despite this, it has not grown with the boom in tourism. It retains a laid-back charm, sheltered beneath the grand beech trees.

Services

There is a small **post office and shop** (Mon 9am-noon & 1-4pm, Tue-Fri 9am-noon) a little way along the A87 (Skye) road and another tiny **shop** within the **petrol station** (Mon-Fri 7am-9pm, Sat & Sun 7am-7pm) on the A82. Don't expect to do your weekly shop at either of these.

From the bus stop near the petrol station you can catch Scottish Citylink's 919 **bus service**. If you are on your way to Uig you will need to wait opposite Invergarry Hotel for Scottish Citylink's 915 & 916 services which head up the A87 road. For details see box p44.

If you need to get somewhere and there's no bus, contact **Great Glen Travel** (☎ 01809-501222, ☎ 07713 640990, ✉ greatglentravel.com); they will give you a **taxi** ride to wherever it is you need to go.

Where to stay

Saddle Mountain Hostel (☎ 01809-501412, ✉ saddlemountainhostel.scot; **fb**; 1 x 6-bed dorm, 1 x 4-bed dorm, 1Tr/1Qd, one room sleeping five, most share facilities; WI-FI; Easter to Oct, closed Nov, Dec to Easter Wed-Mon only) has the cheapest beds in Invergarry. It's in a convenient spot for Way walkers, just off the trail as you descend from the forest. A bed in a dorm costs from £20pp; the triple has a single and a double bed (from £70 per room), the quad has four singles and is en suite (from £85 per room), the room sleeping five has a double bed and three singles (from £90 per room). Facilities include a drying room and a self-catering kitchen; if requested in advance breakfasts are available (£5).

Taking pride of place in the centre of the village is the historic *Invergarry Hotel* (☎ 01809-501206, ✉ invergarryhotel.co.uk;

1S/8D/1T/1Tr/1Qd, all en suite; WI-FI; (L)) which has been a welcome stopping-off point for Highland travellers for well over a hundred years. The rates for its luxurious rooms vary wildly depending on which room you are in and the time of year you are in it, but expect to pay anything between £40pp and £100pp (sgl occ approx £60-80).

If the hostel and hotel are full, the only other beds are further north along the A82. *Nursery Cottages* (☎ 01809-501285; ✉ nurserycottageinvergarry.co.uk; 1D/1T, ✆; one self-contained chalet sleeping four; WI-FI), on the left soon after the road junction, charges from £35pp (sgl occ £50) for B&B; the self-catering chalet costs from £25pp for two to four sharing. The Grade 2 listed building is cosy and comfortable.

Another half mile along the road is *Glen Albyn Lodge* (Map 15; ☎ 01809-501348, ✉ glenbynlodge.co.uk; 2D/1T, some en suite, private facilities; ✆; WI-FI; (L)). They have a pool table and, most tempting of all for walkers with smarting feet, a hot tub cabin (free if booked in advance). B&B costs from £38pp (sgl occ from £70); evening meals are available if requested in advance.

Where to eat and drink

The only place to eat and drink in Invergarry is *Invergarry Hotel* (see Where to stay; food served daily 10am-9pm; 🐾). Thankfully they do very good meals in their Brasserie, although you will pay for the quality. The cheapest main is the beer-battered west coast haddock at £15.95 while the ribeye Scotch beef is £23.95. They also do a nice cut of venison for £18.95, which is a far more ecologically minded choice for dinner.

If you want something cheaper it may be worth calling a cab (see above) to take you to Fort Augustus (see pp113-6) although by the time you've forked out for the taxi you might as well have treated yourself to that hunk of meat in Invergarry Hotel. Be aware that some of the eateries in Fort Augustus stop accepting orders around 8.30pm.

Aberchalder to Fort Augustus

The Invergarry and Loch Oich routes meet at **Aberchalder swing bridge** (Map 16) and from here it's an easy jaunt along the towpath, first on the east side of the canal, before crossing over to the west side at **Cullochy Lock**. There are some fine examples of birch forest bordering the canal and river, which run almost parallel to each other. These forests would once have covered many of the lower mountain slopes all around, after the last glacial period.

Kytra Lock (Map 17) is a beautiful spot to pause and take in the scene. There is a *Trailblazer rest site* set among the pine trees; the wild campsite here has space for three tents and fire sites, and a **compost toilet** but, as before, for that you need to have collected a key in Corpach (see box p19).

Soon after Kytra Lock the towpath eases its way into the throng of Fort Augustus.

ROUTE GUIDE AND MAPS

Symbols used in text (see also p75)
🐕 Dogs allowed; if for accommodation this is subject to prior arrangement (see p155)
🛁 Bathtub in, or for, at least one room   WI-FI means wi-fi is available
Ⓛ packed lunch available if requested in advance
fb signifies places that post their current opening hours on their Facebook page

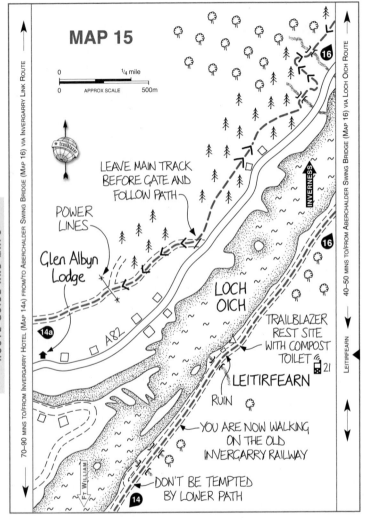

MAP 15

0   ¼ mile
0   500m
APPROX SCALE

LEAVE MAIN TRACK
BEFORE GATE AND
FOLLOW PATH

POWER
LINES

Glen Albyn
Lodge

A82

14a

INVERNESS

16

16

LOCH
OICH

TRAILBLAZER
REST SITE
WITH COMPOST
TOILET 📶
21

LEITIRFEARN

RUIN

YOU ARE NOW WALKING
ON THE OLD
INVERGARRY RAILWAY

FT WILLIAM

DON'T BE TEMPTED
BY LOWER PATH

14

trailblazer

70–90 MINS TO/FROM INVERGARRY HOTEL (MAP 14A) FROM/TO ABERCHALDER SWING BRIDGE (MAP 16) VIA INVERGARRY LINK ROUTE

40–50 MINS TO/FROM ABERCHALDER SWING BRIDGE (MAP 16) VIA LOCH OICH ROUTE

LEITIRFEARN

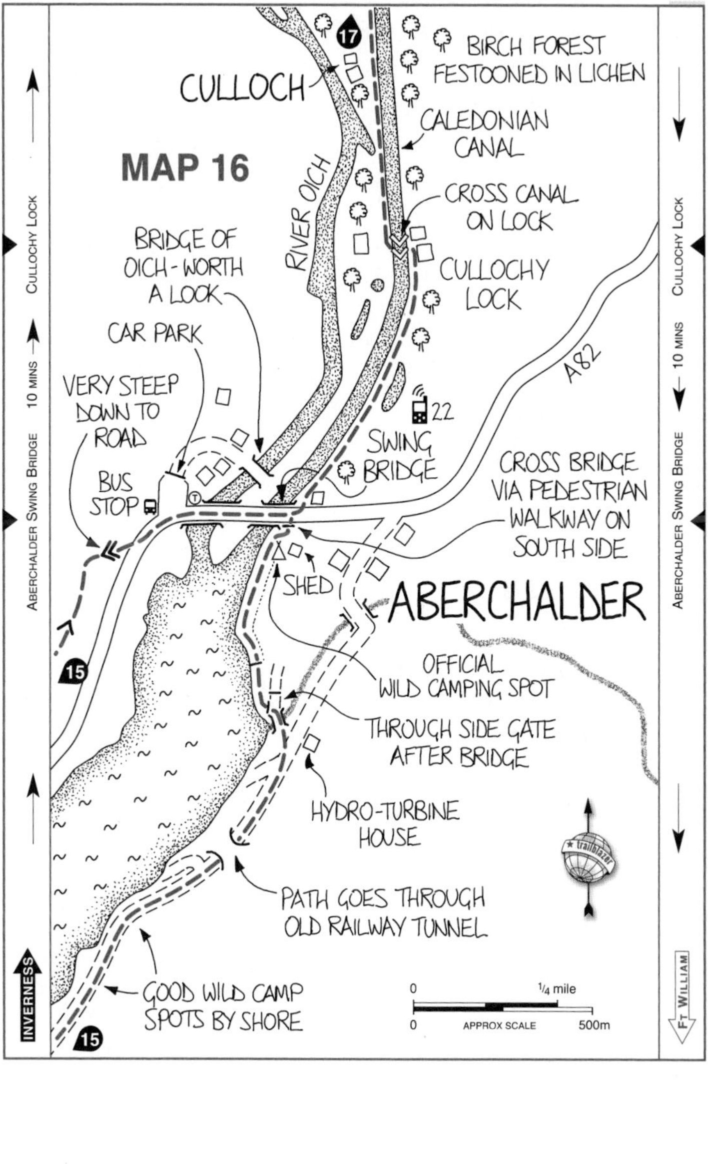
MAP 16
CULLOCH
BIRCH FOREST FESTOONED IN LICHEN
CALEDONIAN CANAL
RIVER OICH
CROSS CANAL ON LOCK
CULLOCHY LOCK
BRIDGE OF OICH - WORTH A LOOK
CAR PARK
VERY STEEP DOWN TO ROAD
BUS STOP
A82
22
SWING BRIDGE
CROSS BRIDGE VIA PEDESTRIAN WALKWAY ON SOUTH SIDE
SHED
ABERCHALDER
OFFICIAL WILD CAMPING SPOT
THROUGH SIDE GATE AFTER BRIDGE
HYDRO-TURBINE HOUSE
PATH GOES THROUGH OLD RAILWAY TUNNEL
GOOD WILD CAMP SPOTS BY SHORE
17
15
15
0
1/4 mile
0
APPROX SCALE
500m
CULLOCHY LOCK
10 MINS
ABERCHALDER SWING BRIDGE
INVERNESS
FT WILLIAM
trailblazer

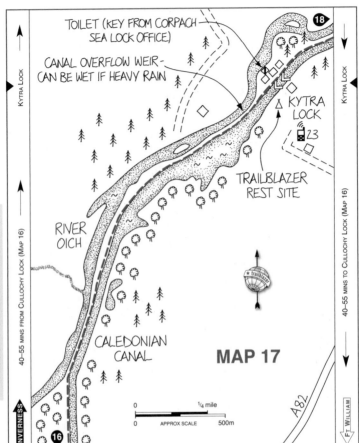

TOILET (KEY FROM CORPACH
SEA LOCK OFFICE)

CANAL OVERFLOW WEIR—
CAN BE WET IF HEAVY RAIN

KYTRA LOCK

KYTRA
LOCK

23

TRAILBLAZER
REST SITE

RIVER
OICH

CALEDONIAN
CANAL

MAP 17

0   1/4 mile
0   APPROX SCALE   500m

KYTRA LOCK

40–55 MINS TO CULLOCHY LOCK (MAP 16)

FT WILLIAM

A82

ROUTE GUIDE AND MAPS

40–55 MINS FROM CULLOCHY LOCK (MAP 16)

INVERNESS

16

18

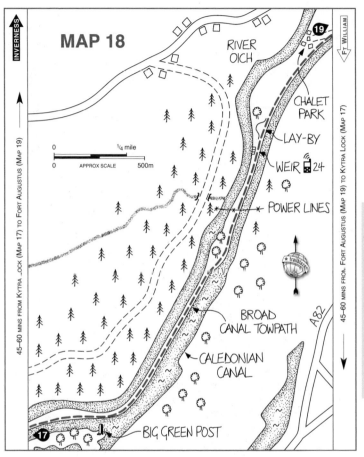

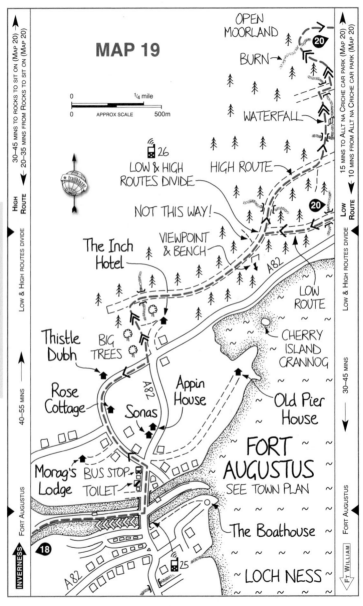

MAP 19

¼ mile

0   500m
APPROX SCALE

OPEN MOORLAND

BURN

WATERFALL

📱 26
LOW & HIGH ROUTES DIVIDE

HIGH ROUTE

NOT THIS WAY!

VIEWPOINT & BENCH

The Inch Hotel

A82

LOW ROUTE

CHERRY ISLAND CRANNOG

Thistle Dubh

BIG TREES

Rose Cottage

A82

Appin House

Sonas

Old Pier House

FORT AUGUSTUS
SEE TOWN PLAN

Morag's Lodge

BUS STOP
TOILET

The Boathouse

INVERNESS

A82

📱 25

LOCH NESS

30–45 MINS TO ROCKS TO SIT ON (MAP 20)
20–35 MINS FROM ROCKS TO SIT ON (MAP 20)

15 MINS TO ALLT NA CRICHE CAR PARK (MAP 20)
10 MINS FROM ALLT NA CRICHE CAR PARK (MAP 20)

HIGH ROUTE

LOW ROUTE

LOW & HIGH ROUTES DIVIDE

LOW & HIGH ROUTES DIVIDE

40–55 MINS

30–45 MINS

FORT AUGUSTUS

FORT AUGUSTUS

FT WILLIAM

ROUTE GUIDE AND MAPS

❑ **Cherry Island crannog**
A *crannog* is an ancient dwelling on a loch, often built on stilts over the water or on mounds of stone that formed small artificial islands, with a wooden bridge or cause-way linking it to the shore. The earliest known crannogs are around 5000 years old. Today Cherry Island crannog (see Map 19), in the south-west corner of Loch Ness, appears as a small wooded island, the only island in the loch. It is visible from the A82 main road near The Inch Hotel, outside Fort Augustus, and also through gaps in the trees on points along the Great Glen Way above the hotel. The island would have been a little larger than it appears today since the waters of Loch Ness rose 6ft with the construction of the Caledonian Canal.

If you have caught the crannog bug, perhaps, once you have finished the Great Glen Way, a visit to **The Crannog Centre** (🖳 crannog.co.uk) is in order. There, on Loch Tay at Kenmore, in Perthshire, they have reconstructed a complete crannog to how it would have looked 2500 years ago. It is about a 2½-hour drive from the Great Glen.

FORT AUGUSTUS   [see map p115]
This large village is very pretty and there-fore also very popular. Straddling the canal at the southern end of Loch Ness it was inevitable that it would become a focus of the Loch Ness monster tourism juggernaut. As a result there is a lot of accommodation, but it gets booked up fast and walkers have to compete with tourists from around the world coming to look for that mythical beast.

Despite the crowds, Fort Augustus, with its flight of canal locks, is a pleasant place to be and since it is roughly halfway along the Great Glen Way it is a good spot to have a rest day should you feel you need, or deserve, one.

Services
A good place to orientate yourself is by the bus stand on the north side of the bridge over the canal and river. From here Scottish Citylink's 919 **bus service** departs for Inverness and Fort William; for details see box p44.

All the services you are likely to need are concentrated in the petrol station build-ing by the river. Here you will find a large Londis grocery **shop** (summer Mon-Sat 8am-8pm, Sun 9am-8pm, limited hours in winter), a **post office**, **pharmacy** and **ATM**. There is another ATM near The Lock Inn.

Where to stay
For **campers**, *Loch Ness Highland Resort* (☎ 01320-366257, 🖳 lochnesshighland resort.com; **fb**), with its lodges and 'glamp-ing' pods, caters mainly for families on week-long holidays and not so much for Great Glen Way walkers. Should you pitch your tent here, be aware that you will be sleeping on ground that was used, in 1746, as a gathering point for the Duke of Cumberland and his men as they set about pursuing Bonnie Prince Charlie, who had just been defeated at the Battle of Culloden (see box p81).

Fort Augustus is crammed full of B&Bs, guest houses and hotels. The ones listed here are just a selection.

Tucked away up a side lane, which is conveniently where the Great Glen Way leaves the village, is *Morag's Lodge* (Map 19; ☎ 01320-366289, 🖳 moragslodge.com; **fb**; 80 beds in 6-bed & 4-bed mixed dorms/1Tr/2Qd in bunk beds, all rooms have private facilities; WI-FI in common areas; ⓛ; 🐾 private room only); it's a large **independent hostel** with dorms (from £25pp) and private rooms (from £32pp for two sharing, sgl occ full room rate). The hostel has plenty of 'chilling out' spaces and a bothy bar (generally daily 5pm-1am, but depends on demand) which can get quite lively with a young crowd in the sum-mer. Self-catering facilities are open 24

ROUTE GUIDE AND MAPS

hours; meals are available if requested by 4pm on your arrival day.

Continue along this lane for *Rose Cottage* (Map 19; ☎ 01320-366295, 🖳 rosecottagefortaugustus.co.uk; 1D/2D or T, all en suite; 🖤; WI-FI; Ⓛ) for a quiet place to stay. They offer B&B for £40pp (sgl occ from £60). Equally peaceful is *Thistle Dubh* (pronounced Thistle Doo; Map 19; ☎ 01320-366380, 🖳 thistle-dubh.co.uk; 2D/1T, all en suite; WI-FI) which has beds so comfortable you won't want to get out and walk the next day. For such a high standard their rates are very reasonable at £30-40pp (sgl occ £50).

By the canal, *The Holt* (☎ 01320-366202, 🖳 theholtfortaugustus.com; 1S/1D/1T, all en suite; WI-FI; Feb-Nov) overlooks the adjacent river and does B&B for £35pp (sgl £40, sgl occ rates on request).

At the southern end of the village on Fort William Rd is the all-round excellent *Loch Ness Guest House* (☎ 01320-366375, 🖳 lochnessguesthouse.com; 1S/1D/2Tr, all en suite; 🖤; WI-FI; Ⓛ; 🐾), a very friendly and homely Victorian granite house with sumptuous breakfasts. B&B costs £45-55pp (sgl occ £60-70).

Next along the road is *The Caledonian Hotel* (☎ 01320-366256, 🖳 caledonianhotel.co.uk; fb; 1S/6D/3T all en suite, 1T private facilities; 🖤; WI-FI; Ⓛ; Easter to end of Sep) with traditionally styled rooms from £47.55pp (sgl £70, sgl occ rates on request). A three-course evening meal (for residents only; £26) is available if booked in advance.

Across the road, *The Lovat* (☎ 01456-490000, 🖳 thelovat.com; 21D/6T/1Tr, all en suite; 🖤; WI-FI; Ⓛ; 🐾) dominates the top of the hill overlooking the village. This large and opulent hotel charges from £70pp.

In the shadow of The Lovat, on Station Rd, are two homely options: *Beaufort House B&B* (☎ 01320-366845, 🖳 beauforthouselochness.com; fb; 4D, all en suite; WI-FI) is a typical granite Edwardian townhouse with rates around £45-60pp; and *Kings Inn* (☎ 01320-366406; 2D, both en suite; WI-FI; 🐾), which charges from £40pp (sgl occ from £60) but accepts cash only. At over 300 years old it is believed to be the

oldest surviving building in Fort Augustus. Further along Station Rd adjoining the bank is the aptly named *Bank House B&B* (☎ 01320-366755, 🖳 visitlochness.co.uk; fb; 2D/1D or T en suite, 2S shared facilities), which was once the former bank manager's residence. Rates here are £40pp (cash or cheque only).

The most central place to stay is *Abbey Cottage* (☎ 01320-310524, 🖳 abbeycottagelochness.co.uk; 1S/3D, all en suite; WI-FI; Feb-Nov), a 250-year-old home with lovely views from their breakfast conservatory. B&B here costs from £40pp (sgl £66).

Across the road is *Richmond House Hotel* (☎ 01320-366719, 🖳 richmondhousehotel.com; 1S/3D/2T/3Tr, some en suite, some share facilities; 🖤; WI-FI; Ⓛ), a small hotel with rooms for £37.50-45pp (sgl from £40, sgl occ rates on request) above the bar. One of the triples (1S/1D) is in a self-contained flat.

At the northern end of town there is a collection of places, the most appealing of which is *Old Pier House* (Map 19, p112; ☎ 01320-366418, 🖳 oldpierhouse.com; 2D/1T/one self-contained suite sleeping up to five people, all en suite; 🖤; WI-FI; Apr to end Oct) in an enviable position on the shore of Loch Ness, well hidden from the hordes of Nessie hunters. The historic house sits next to the old pier that gives it its name, from where paddle steamers would transport timber up the loch to Inverness. The en suite facilities in the rooms are showers but there is a separate bathroom which is available to all B&B guests. In addition to **B&B** (£45pp, sgl occ 3/4/5 sharing rates on request) they have some **log cabins** (for 2, 4 or 5 people; 🐾) which are generally let on a weekly basis, but if available can be stayed in for a single night.

On the busy A82 road are two well-kept guest houses: *Sonas* (Map 19; ☎ 01320-366291, 🖳 airbnb.co.uk; 1D/1T/1Tr, all en suite; WI-FI) charges £37pp (sgl occ from £50, or it's £90 for three adults sharing) while *Appin House* (Map 19; ☎ 01320-366866, 🖳 booking.com/appin-house; 2D/1Tr; all en suite; 🖤; WI-FI; 🐾) has beds for £37.50pp (sgl occ from £50).

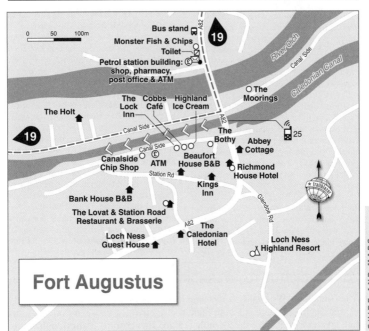

As you head up the woodland path out of the village look out for the sign pointing the way to **The Inch Hotel** (the official name is Inchnacardoch Country House Hotel; Map 19; ☎ 01456-450900, 🖳 inch hotel.com; **fb**; 13D/2D or T/2Qd, all en suite; ➼; WI-FI; 🐾; Apr-Oct); this is the place to stay for a traditional Scottish hunting lodge vibe. Tartan carpets and stags' heads on the walls are de rigueur here. Many of the rooms have fine views across the loch. Rates can vary daily depending on demand but expect to have to fork out £75pp (sgl occ from £90) for a standard room and as much as £120pp (sgl occ full room rate) for the suite with a four-poster bed.

Where to eat and drink
There is plenty of choice when it comes to finding something to eat in Fort Augustus but many of the establishments stop serving

food around 8.30/9pm. **The Lock Inn** (☎ 01320-366302; food daily noon-9pm), by the canal, is a lovely pub with a rustic edge, standard pub food such as burgers and steak pie both for £12.95 and real ales on tap. Don't be dismayed if all the tables in the bar are occupied: there are more tables upstairs.

The Bothy (☎ 01360-366710; food served daily noon-2.30pm & 5-8pm, summer to 8.30pm) is right by the locks on the canal. It's a popular bar with locals and has a pool table and sports on the telly. If you prefer some peace, there is a quieter restaurant area in the conservatory. The Balmoral chicken with haggis and whisky sauce is £14.90. If you are a whisky connoisseur, The Bothy is a good place to pull up a bar stool since they have a good choice of malts on their top shelf.

It would be hard to deny that **The Boathouse** (Map 19; ☎ 01320-366682,

⌨ lochnessboathouse.co.uk; **fb**; food summer daily noon-9pm, winter hours may vary) has the best location and views of any of the village's restaurants. Perched on a grassy sward where the canal opens into Loch Ness, if the weather is fine there is nowhere better to eat than on one of the tables by the shore.

Fine dining is on offer at *The Lovat* (see Where to stay). Their *Brasserie* (daily 7.30-9.30am, noon-2.30pm & 6-9pm, Fri & Sat to 9.30pm) is the place for a sumptuous meal in surroundings that they describe as 'shabby-chic'! The venison saddle is £24.50 and the veggie option – salt baked carrot with dumplings – is £19.50.

More affordable is the food on offer at *Richmond House Hotel* (see Where to stay; summer daily noon-9.30pm, rest of year depending on demand). They have a good range of bar meals such as burgers from £12.50 and haggis, neeps and tatties

from £12. All food is made on site and as much as possible from local produce.

Heading out of town, booking is recommended for the restaurant at *The Inch Hotel* (generally daily noon-2pm & 6.30-9pm) though food is available all day in their lounge.

For light bites, including vegan options, try *Cobbs Café* (☎ 01320-366824) by the canal. *The Moorings* (Restaurant & Takeaway; ☎ 01320-366484; daily summer 11am-10pm, winter to 9pm) does traditional fish & chips, as does the *Canalside Chip Shop* (☎ 01320-366456; daily noon-8pm). There is another excellent fish and chip shop by the bus stand, *Monster Fish & Chips* (daily noon-8pm), where you can get haddock and chips for £8.50. Finally, if you are lucky enough to be walking beneath a blazing sun, treat yourself to something at *Highland Ice Cream* (☎ 01320-366153; daily 9am-5pm) by the canal.

FORT AUGUSTUS TO INVERMORISTON   [MAPS 19-23]

The Great Glen Way really comes into its own north of Fort Augustus but only if you aim high! There is a high route and a low route between Fort Augustus and Invermoriston. Take the **9½-mile (15km; 2hrs 35mins-3¾hrs) high route**! Yes, it will make your calf muscles ache a bit more but you will spend the day high up on the open hill enjoying magnificent views across Loch Ness and the mountains to the north. By contrast the **low route** is a monotonous trudge through yet more commercial forestry plantations; it is, though, the same distance: **9½ miles (15km; 2hrs 20mins-3hrs 20mins)**.

Both routes out of Fort Augustus begin by following the back road past Morag's Lodge (Map 19). Don't be tempted by the more direct main road as a shortcut. It's fast, dangerous and there is no pavement/sidewalk. Leave the back road, just before the **road bridge**, and follow a narrow trail steeply up through a stand of enormous trees that make you feel quite small.

A level path then leads to a viewpoint where you can supposedly see **Cherry Island crannog** (see box p113) down on the loch, although I struggled to spot it when I was there, perhaps because of encroaching vegetation blocking the view. Just beyond this, it's decision time. Will you take **the high road or the low road**? For the latter see the route description on p118. As I've already said, the high route is hands-down the best choice.

High route from Fort Augustus to junction of routes
From the junction, the high route climbs steadily through the forestry, following tight zigzags past a **waterfall** and finally emerging onto the **open hill**. Finally, the views over Loch Ness begin to open up. It's a liberating feeling,

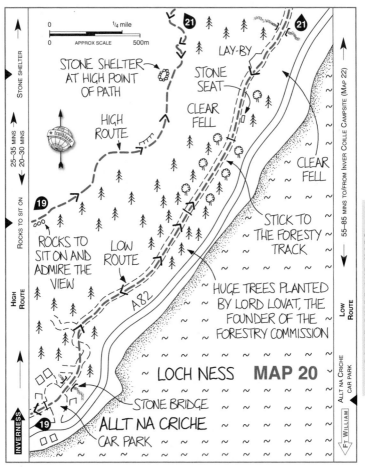

Map 20

ROUTE GUIDE AND MAPS

having been confined to the depths of the glen for much of the first half of the Way. The path constructors have left some large **rocks** (Map 20) by the trail; these are perfect for sitting on and getting your breath back after the climb up from Fort Augustus.

The going is comparatively easy now, as the trail winds its way towards the high point of the route. Here there is a rudimentary **stone shelter**. Don't get excited: it has no roof and is nothing more than a low circular wall, offering shelter from the prevailing wind. The next couple of miles continue in the same

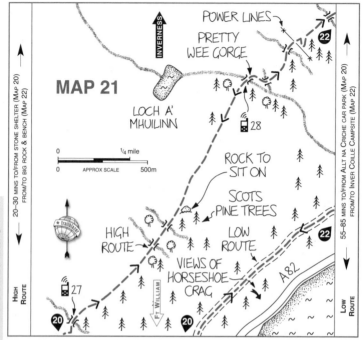

vein, across open moorland, punctuated by lone birch and pine trees. Look out for golden plover and wheatear. The **pretty, wee gorge** (Map 21) is a good spot for a lunch stop.

There is another opportunity for a sit down at a **bench by a big rock** (Map 22). This is the last view on this section. After this it's a knee-shattering descent down through the thick spruce forest.

Low route from Fort Augustus to junction of routes

This follows the high route as described on p116, as far as the path junction. From that point it's a fairly level walk through the forest on a broad track. This is a much less inspiring walk than the high route but there are moments of interest. Notably, about a mile past the **Allt na Criche** car park (Map 20) the way passes beneath the tallest trees you will encounter on the walk. And these are significant trees: they were planted by Lord Lovat, the founder, some say 'the father', of the Forestry Commission (see box p68). Indeed, this is the first land owned by the Forestry Commission in Scotland.

Continuing on, the track switches this way and that through the plantation. There are some large areas of clear-fell where the views open up across the loch. Look out for the famous **Horseshoe Crag** on the opposite side of the loch; a natural feature of scree and stone. Campers will find a few pitches at

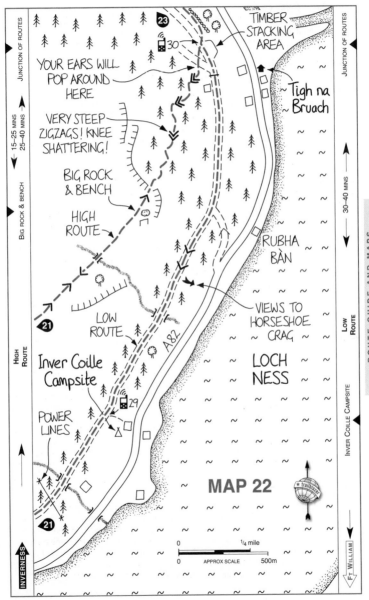

JUNCTION OF ROUTES

23

30

TIMBER STACKING AREA

YOUR EARS WILL POP AROUND HERE

~ Tigh na Bruach ~

VERY STEEP ZIGZAGS! KNEE SHATTERING!

BIG ROCK & BENCH

HIGH ROUTE

RUBHA BÀN

VIEWS TO HORSESHOE CRAG

LOW ROUTE

A82

Inver Coille Campsite

LOCH NESS

29

POWER LINES

21

MAP 22

21

INVERNESS

0   1/4 mile
0   APPROX SCALE   500m

Inver Coille Campsite (see below and Map 22); a sign points the way down a path that strikes off downhill from the Way. Beyond this, there is little of great interest and after mile after mile of forest track you eventually join up with the high route (see p116) for the final stretch into Invermoriston.

Junction of routes to Invermoriston

At the foot of the path the high route meets the low route and the trail follows an **old stone dyke**, running parallel to a forestry track. Irritatingly, the route goes further and further away from the destination of Invermoriston which lies a hop and a skip away across some fields. Eventually the path joins a broader track which doubles back and continues in the right direction, all the way to the beautiful **old stone bridge** (known as Telford's Bridge) at Invermoriston.

INVERMORISTON   [see map p122]

This little hamlet sits by the banks of the tumbling waters of the River Moriston. **Telford's Bridge** (see box below) dates back to 1813 and is well worth a look, as is the **waterfall**, best viewed from the **summerhouse** (Map 23), a short detour downstream.

Next to the main road, near the bridge is **St Columba's Well**, an unassuming pool of water set within a stone square. The water is said to have been blessed by St Columba in the 6th century AD and legend has it that it is the source of Loch Ness.

Services

The hamlet boasts the friendly, independent **Glenmoriston Stores** (☎ 01320-351212; Mon-Fri 6am-5pm, Sat 6am-1pm, Sun 8am-noon) selling the essentials. There are **public toilets** in the village hall.

The bus stop is by the village hall for Scottish Citylink's 919 **bus service**. For Scottish Citylink's 917 bus to Skye wait outside The Glenmoriston Arms Hotel. For further service details see box p44.

Where to stay

Accommodation is surprisingly plentiful for such a small settlement but much of it is spread out across the glen. Walkers on the low route to Invermoriston who want to **camp** or stay in a cabin should keep an eye out for the paths that lead from the Way down to *Inver Coille Campsite* (see Map 22; ☎ 01320-351224, 🖳 inver-coille.co.uk; **fb**; ✻), where you can **camp** for £10pp (inc use of shower/toilet facilities). Cabins are £55 per night for the whole cabin but there is a two-night minimum stay.

A short detour along the A82 is *Tigh-na-Bruach* (see Map 22; ☎ 01320-351349, 🖳 tighnabruach.com; **fb**; 3D, all en suite; WI-FI; ⓛ; mid Apr to Sep), a luxury guest house which comes at quite a price: £70pp.

Commanding the dominant position in the village is *The Glenmoriston Arms Hotel* (☎ 01320-351206, 🖳 glenmoristonarms.co.uk; 3D/8D or T, all en suite; WI-FI; Feb-Dec), a very grand hotel blending traditional and contemporary styles. Room rates start at around £70pp (sgl occ £95).

❏ **Telford's Bridge (also known as Invermoriston Old Bridge)**

The pretty stone bridge at Invermoriston was designed by Thomas Telford, he of Caledonian Canal fame (see box p84), as part of a drive to improve transport links in the Highlands. Constructed between 1805 and 1813, it is a twin-arched stone bridge, utilising a natural rock, in the centre of the river, as a pier. It has stood the test of time very well, although some stone is missing from the walls, and was used by traffic until the 1930s when it was usurped by the new and current road bridge.

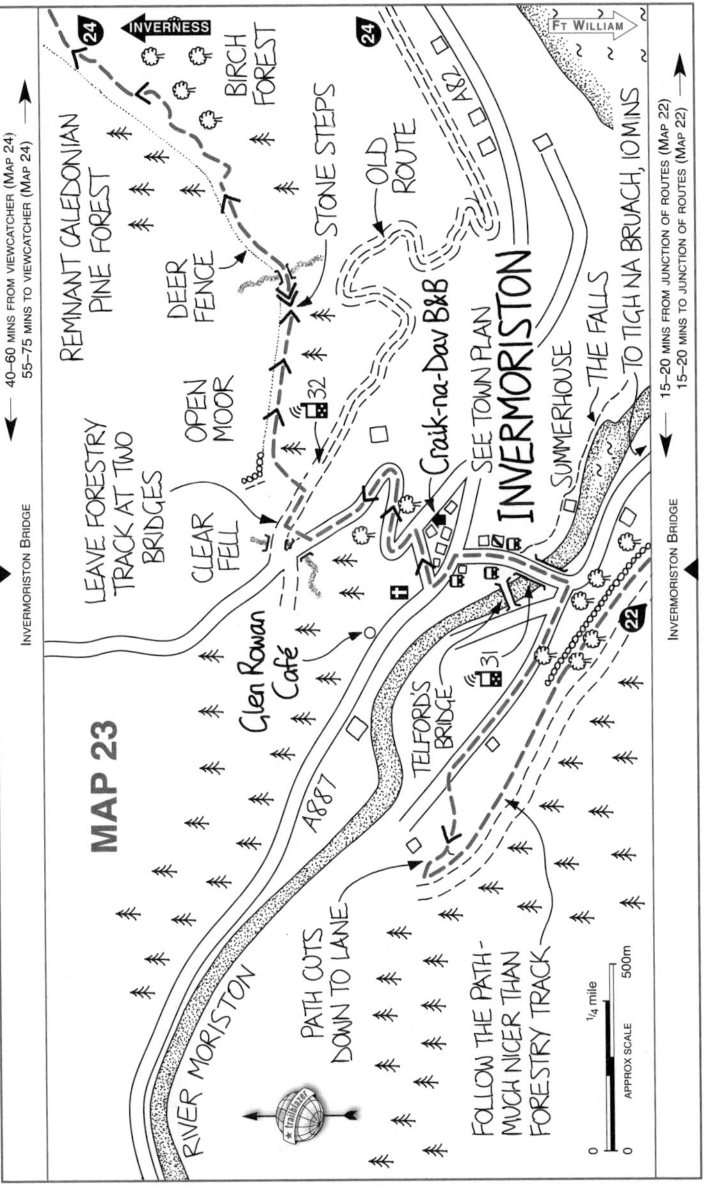

MAP 23

RIVER MORISTON

A887

PATH CUTS DOWN TO LANE

FOLLOW THE PATH - MUCH NICER THAN FORESTRY TRACK

Glen Rowan Café

TELFORDS BRIDGE

LEAVE FORESTRY TRACK AT TWO BRIDGES

CLEAR FELL

OPEN MOOR

REMNANT CALEDONIAN PINE FOREST

DEER FENCE

STONE STEPS

BIRCH FOREST

INVERNESS

FT WILLIAM

A82

OLD ROUTE

INVERMORISTON

SEE TOWN PLAN

Craik-na-Dav B&B

SUMMERHOUSE

THE FALLS

TO TIGH NA BRUACH, 10 MINS

INVERMORISTON BRIDGE

⌂32

⌂31

INVERMORISTON BRIDGE

40–60 MINS FROM VIEWCATCHER (MAP 24)
55–75 MINS TO VIEWCATCHER (MAP 24)

15–20 MINS FROM JUNCTION OF ROUTES (MAP 22)
15–20 MINS TO JUNCTION OF ROUTES (MAP 22)

¼ mile
500m
APPROX SCALE

ROUTE GUIDE AND MAPS

Next door is the more affordable ***Bracarina House*** (☎ 01320-351279, 🖥 bracarinahouse.co.uk; **fb**; 2D/3T/1Tr, all en suite; ☛; WI-FI; Ⓛ; 🐾) with B&B for £41pp (sgl occ £73).

Craik-na-Dav (☎ 01320-351277, 🖥 craik-na-dav.com; **fb**; 2D/1Tr, all en suite; WI-FI; Ⓛ; very 🐾 friendly) is a steep climb up the hill, but it is in the right direction for Way walkers. They charge around £40pp (sgl occ £75). A little further down the same lane is ***Darroch View B&B*** (☎ 01320-351388, 🖥 darrochviewbandb.com; 1D/1T, all en suite; WI-FI; Mar-Oct) with B&B for £35pp (sgl occ £55).

Where to eat and drink

The menu at *Glen Rowan Café* (Map 23; ☎ 01320-351208, 🖥 glen-rowan-cafe.co.uk; **fb**; Feb to end Oct Tue-Sat 9am-5pm, Sun 10am-4pm 10am-4pm), down the A887 road, includes such delights as sandwiches from £6 and fish & chips for £11.50.

The best place for an evening meal is *The Glenmoriston Arms Hotel* (see Where to stay; food available daily all day, last orders winter 8pm but in summer depends on demand). Their **restaurant** menu has a wide choice of tasty dishes. Highlights include the chicken stuffed with haggis

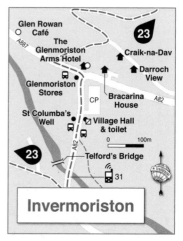

(£16.95) and the saddle of Highland venison (£25.95). Booking is recommended, particularly in the high season. There is also a **bar** where more typical pub grub is served such as fish & chips (£13.95) and veggie curry (£10.95). Even if you are not in the mood for food, the nearly 300-year-old bar is a great place to ease away the aches and pains of the walk and enjoy a dram or two.

INVERMORISTON TO DRUMNADROCHIT [MAPS 23-29]

This **14½-mile (23.5km; 4hrs 35mins-6¾hrs)** high traverse between Invermoriston and 'Drum' (as Drumnadrochit is known locally) was created by Forestry & Land Scotland as a means of improving the Way for walkers, offering greater views and taking walkers away from forestry operations on the old low route. It is possibly the standout day of the whole walk. It has a lot in common with the previous section's High Route from Fort Augustus, starting and finishing with steep ascents and descents with an airy traverse of open ground in between.

But this day's outing is possibly even more spectacular with wonderful views along the length of Loch Ness and some beautiful old native pine forest thrown in for good measure. On the whole it is a more varied walk than the Fort Augustus to Invermoriston section and if you have only one day to spare for your hike this would be the place to come and do it.

There's no avoiding it: it's another steep climb up to start the day. And the first mile or so is on tarmac as the Way follows a narrow lane that hairpins its way out of Invermoriston. The final haul is on a much more agreeable path through the woodland to the open hill above. There is an alternative route here but it has little to recommend it (see opposite).

Old route between Invermoriston and Drumnadrochit

If, for some reason, you want a less strenuous day between Invermoriston and Drumnadrochit, you can follow the **15¼-mile old route** (**24.5km; 4hrs 55mins-7hrs 5mins**) that passes through the forestry plantation. From the top of the switchback lane above Invermoriston simply follow the forestry track straight ahead rather than turning left up the steep path. It passes by Alltsigh (Map 23; see p121) and rejoins the main route a little over four miles after leaving Invermoriston (Map 25).

❑ The Loch Ness monster

Here it is: the bit about the Loch Ness monster. Without the monster it's probable that nobody outside Scotland would have heard of Loch Ness, although it does have some attributes in its own right. It is the largest loch in volume in Scotland and the largest lake in volume in the British Isles. It is also the second largest in surface area after Loch Lomond and the second deepest after Loch Morar. It is 22 miles long, around one to two miles wide and is said to contain 16.5 million gallons of water.

With such a huge volume of water for Nessie, as the monster is affectionately known, to hide in, it is no wonder that its existence has never been proved nor disproved. And that's a good thing for the local economy. The allure of Nessie never abates with hundreds of thousands of visitors from around the world flocking to the shores around Drumnadrochit and Fort Augustus every summer, hoping to spot the fabled beast. There are exhibitions (see p131), boat trips and souvenirs aplenty. Nessie brings in around £60 million per year to the Scottish coffers. But what exactly is, if anything, the Loch Ness monster and how did all this start?

The monster legend can be traced back as far as the 6th century AD when, in 565, St Columba recounts a scarcely believable tale of witnessing a large creature after it was alleged to have killed a man. There were infrequent sightings over the subsequent centuries but it would be a long time before Nessie became world famous. It all kicked off in 1933 when a couple in Drumnadrochit reported something strange in the water. The local newspaper, *The Inverness Courier*, took up the story of what they chose to call the 'Loch Ness Monster'. They could have had little idea of what they had just unleashed. It went, to coin a modern phrase, viral. Later that year, the first photograph purporting to show Nessie, taken by Hugh Gray, appeared in the papers, followed by a short, and difficult to interpret, film by Malcolm Irvine. It showed 'Nessie' swimming past Urquhart Castle. But the photograph that really set the cat among the pigeons was the now infamous 'Surgeon's Photograph' taken by R K Wilson in 1934 and published in the *Daily Mail*. It really was too good to be true, showing a dinosaur-like neck and head poking out of the water, but it captured the imagination of people around the world and the Nessie legend was truly born.

There have been over a thousand reported Nessie sightings to date, some of them accompanied with photographic evidence. Many of these have been debunked easily with most proven to be deliberate fakes but others have been taken by well-meaning people who have seen something they have been unable to identify in the water. It is often hard to judge the size and scale of an object some distance away in the water and it's quite probable that some of the sightings can be attributed to otters or even seals that have swum the short distance up the River Ness from the sea, as they are known to do. The most enticing explanation for Nessie is that it is a plesiosaur, an aquatic reptile. They are believed to have become extinct 65 million years ago but could a small population of them really have survived all this time? It seems unlikely.

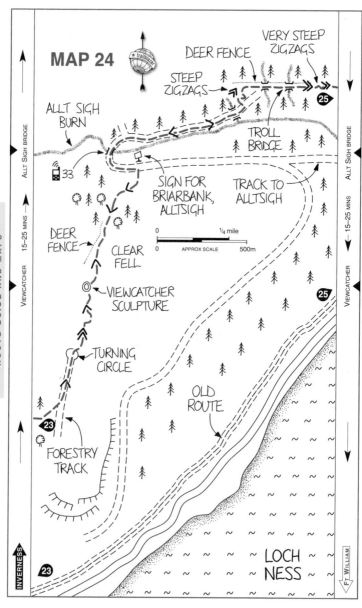

MAP 24

VERY STEEP ZIGZAGS

DEER FENCE

STEEP ZIGZAGS

ALLT SIGH BURN

TROLL BRIDGE

📱 33

SIGN FOR BRIARBANK, ALLTSIGH

TRACK TO ALLTSIGH

DEER FENCE

CLEAR FELL

0   ¼ mile
0   500m
APPROX SCALE

VIEWCATCHER SCULPTURE

TURNING CIRCLE

OLD ROUTE

23

FORESTRY TRACK

LOCH NESS

ALLT SIGH BRIDGE

15–25 MINS

VIEWCATCHER

ALLT SIGH BRIDGE

15–25 MINS

VIEWCATCHER

25

25

INVERNESS

FT WILLIAM

ROUTE GUIDE AND MAPS

Once again, the views come as a welcome reward for your efforts on the ascent. Look out for the **remnant Caledonian pine forest** (Map 23), a sight both magnificent for their gnarly beauty, and devastating for the knowledge that this is a pathetic remnant of the vast pine forests that once flourished in the Highlands (see box p61). And these particular specimens look like being the last of their kind; the ground beneath them is so heavily grazed that no regeneration can occur.

The next point of interest is a curious artwork high on the hill. A giant circular **viewcatcher** (Map 24) crafted from bent sticks entices you to stand and stare back down the Great Glen. It's certainly a good spot to contemplate how far you have walked. There are also fine views here over the mountains to the west.

The path undulates its way from the 'viewcatcher' through clearfelled forestry and down to a wide track that crosses the **Allt Sigh burn** at a hairpin. A track here leads down to the main road at Alltsigh where there are two places to stay but no other services.

Briar Bank (see Map 25; ☎ 01320-351381, 🖳 briarbanklochness.com; **fb**; 2D both en suite/1Qd private bathroom ☕; WI-FI; Ⓛ) is a friendly B&B on the shore of Loch Ness with beds from £35pp (sgl occ £60). The nearby *Lochside Hostel* (see Map 25; ☎ 01320-351274, 🖳 lochsidehostel.com; **fb**; 45 beds; WI-FI in public lounge), in the former Youth Hostel building, reopened in 2016 under the wing of the MacBackpackers coach tour outfit. They offer dormitory style accommodation with beds from £18pp in dorms of 4-8 beds. There is also a twin room with bunk bed for £22.50pp. Facilities include a shared kitchen, internet access and laundry facilities (coin-operated machines); a continental breakfast is available. Stagecoach's No 40 **bus service** (see box p44) stops here.

If you thought you had finished your climbing for the day, sadly you were wrong. There now follow some tight switchbacks up to a pretty little **bridge of bendy sticks** over a burn. This is **Troll Bridge** where local schoolchildren have left curious paintings and poems. Rest a while here because the next stretch of path is the steepest on the whole walk. Thankfully it doesn't last too long and there is a very welcome big **stone shelter** (no roof; see Map 25, p126) at the top of this climb which makes for an excellent spot for lunch – and the views are magnificent!

After refuelling, there is a nice stretch through pine trees down to another forestry track where you will find another **stone wall shelter** next to some old **granny pines**. The old (low) route (see p123) joins the new main trail another half mile further on. Follow the forestry track as it contours the steep hillside, winding this way and that, eventually coming to a dead end where a narrow trail (Map 26) leads you onwards. There is a lovely section through lichen-encrusted birch trees before the trail crosses rough pasture and climbs to a road.

A few hundred metres to your left are the remains of **Dun Scriben** (Map 27), a prehistoric fort, but you can't really see it from the Way and even if you manage to find your way to it there is little more to see than some old stones.

ROUTE GUIDE AND MAPS

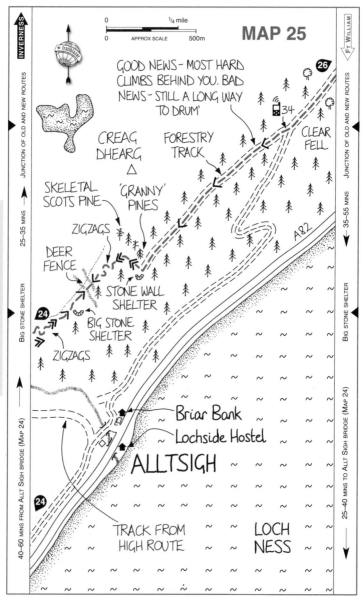

MAP 25

¼ mile

0

APPROX SCALE

500m

INVERNESS

Fᴛ Wɪʟʟɪᴀᴍ

JUNCTION OF OLD AND NEW ROUTES

25-35 MINS

35-55 MINS

BIG STONE SHELTER

BIG STONE SHELTER

40-60 MINS FROM ALLT SIGH BRIDGE (MAP 24)

25-40 MINS TO ALLT SIGH BRIDGE (MAP 24)

GOOD NEWS - MOST HARD CLIMBS BEHIND YOU. BAD NEWS - STILL A LONG WAY TO DRUM'

26

34

CREAG DHEARG △

FORESTRY TRACK

CLEAR FELL

SKELETAL SCOTS PINE

'GRANNY' PINES

ZIGZAGS

DEER FENCE

STONE WALL SHELTER

BIG STONE SHELTER

A82

ZIGZAGS

24

Briar Bank

Lochside Hostel

ALLTSIGH

24

TRACK FROM HIGH ROUTE

LOCH NESS

The Way joins the road at its end at **Grotaig**. ***Loch Ness Clay Works, Pottery and Café*** (☎ 01456-450217, 🖥 lochnessclayworks.moonfruit.com; **fb**; daily 10am-6pm, check in advance in Jan/Feb as they may be closed) is about 200 metres off route to the left. They serve light lunches, cakes and hot drinks and will also do out-of-hours breakfast and evening meals, subject to prior arrangement.

The Way follows the road relentlessly for nearly three miles (5km). It's quite hard on your feet but there are nice views across the moors. Listen out for the mournful cry of the curlew. *(cont'd on p130)*

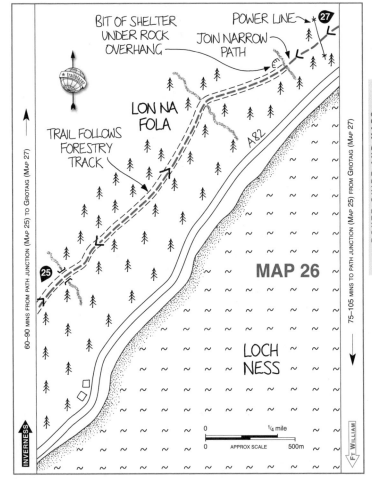

ROUTE GUIDE AND MAPS

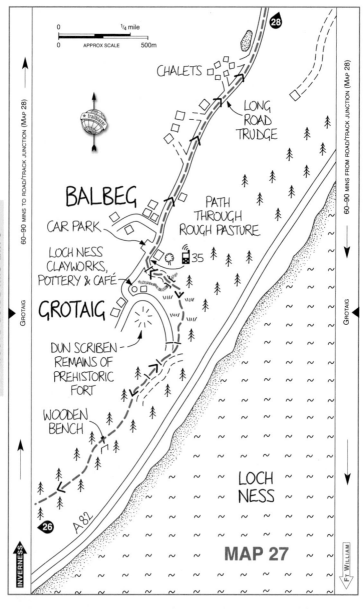

0   ¼ mile

0   APPROX SCALE   500m

★ trailblazer

28

CHALETS

LONG ROAD TRUDGE

60–90 MINS FROM ROAD/TRACK JUNCTION (MAP 28)

GROTAIG

Ft WILLIAM

BALBEG

CAR PARK

PATH THROUGH ROUGH PASTURE

LOCH NESS CLAYWORKS, POTTERY & CAFÉ

35

GROTAIG

DUN SCRIBEN REMAINS OF PREHISTORIC FORT

WOODEN BENCH

A 82

26

LOCH NESS

MAP 27

60–90 MINS TO ROAD/TRACK JUNCTION (MAP 28)

GROTAIG

INVERNESS

ROUTE GUIDE AND MAPS

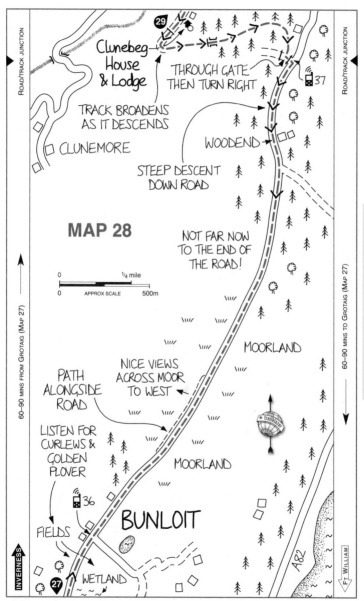

29

Clunebeg
House
& Lodge

THROUGH GATE
THEN TURN RIGHT

📱37

TRACK BROADENS
AS IT DESCENDS

CLUNEMORE

WOODEND

STEEP DESCENT
DOWN ROAD

MAP 28

NOT FAR NOW
TO THE END OF
THE ROAD!

0   1/4 mile
0   APPROX SCALE   500m

MOORLAND

NICE VIEWS
ACROSS MOOR
TO WEST

PATH
ALONGSIDE
ROAD

LISTEN FOR
CURLEWS &
GOLDEN
PLOVER

MOORLAND

📱36

FIELDS

BUNLOIT

27

WETLAND

A82

ROAD/TRACK JUNCTION

ROAD/TRACK JUNCTION

60–90 MINS FROM GROTAIG (MAP 27)

60–90 MINS TO GROTAIG (MAP 27)

ROUTE GUIDE AND MAPS

INVERNESS

FT WILLIAM

(cont'd from p127)   After pounding the asphalt it comes as some relief to join the track (Map 28) that drops down to the River Coiltie. There is a smart place offering accommodation and food near the foot of the hill: ***Clunebeg House & Lodge*** (Map 28; ☎ 01456-450097, 🖥 clunebeglodge.com; Easter to late Oct). Accommodation is available in the Lodge and the House. In the **Lodge** (2D/4T, all en suite; WI-FI; Ⓛ), one of the double rooms has a 4-poster bed and B&B costs from £32.50pp (sgl occ full room rate). In the **House**, next door, there are three suites sleeping 4-6 people (from £90-100 for three sharing, £110-120 for six sharing; breakfast not included). Evening meals can be eaten at the lodge if arranged in advance. Reservations are recommended for the ***restaurant*** (food served daily 6-9pm); there is a varied menu with burgers for £11.95, pasta for £11.50, and lamb shank for £14.50; their meal deal with a choice of six mains and four puddings costs £20. There is also a **bar**, open the same hours as the restaurant.

Drumnadrochit is now tantalisingly close; simply follow the track alongside the river (Map 29) to join the lane you left earlier. It very quickly meets the main road which leads into town.

DRUMNADROCHIT [see map p132]

Drumnadrochit, or 'Drum' as the locals call it, sits by sheltered Urquhart Bay, where the rivers Enrick and Coiltie flow through riparian forest (see box below) into Loch Ness. The village unashamedly styles itself as the capital of all things 'Nessie'.

There is an, almost, official **Loch Ness Centre & Exhibition** (☎ 01456-450573, 🖳 lochness.com; daily Easter to June & Sep-Oct 9.30am-5pm, July & Aug 9.30am-6pm, Nov to Easter 10am-3.30pm – note that the hours can vary so it is best to check in advance; £8.45, 10% discount for members of English Heritage, Historic Environment Scotland and the National Trust/National Trust for Scotland) which was opened by explorer Sir Ranulph Fiennes and has been endorsed by Scottish Natural Heritage. There are seven themed areas, each taking you through a different aspect of the loch's history from its prehistoric period to the modern day search for the monster.

Nearby is **Nessieland** (☎ 01456-450342, 🖳 nessieland.co.uk; daily summer 9am-7pm, winter 11am-3pm; from £7pp, family tickets about £20) which has its own exhibition set in some mock caves. They also run boat trips on the loch so you can look for the mythical beast yourself. And if that's inspired you there are plenty of Loch Ness monster-themed goods for sale in their gift shop. Note that it was temporarily closed at the time of research so call them for an update on plans for reopening.

❑ URQUHART CASTLE AND URQUHART BAY WOODS

Urquhart Castle

The history of Urquhart Castle can be traced back to AD580 when a Pictish Fort is said to have stood on the same site. At that time St Columba is believed to have rested here on his way from Iona to Inverness. The ruins that can be seen today date back to at least the 13th century when, in 1296, it was captured by the English King, Edward I, but was later recaptured by the Scots under the newly crowned King of Scotland, Robert the Bruce, in 1306. But that wasn't the end of the turmoil; there were frequent battles over the castle between the English and Scots and also the Clan MacDonald and the Scottish crown. The castle came to an untimely end during the first of the Jacobite uprisings, whereby the Catholic Stuarts tried to regain the Scottish crown. Government troops, who had been using the castle as a garrison, destroyed much of it in 1692, once they had no more use of it. Historic Environment Scotland (see p61; daily Apr, May & Sep 9.30am-6pm, Oct to 5pm, Jun-Aug to 8pm, Nov-Mar to 4.30pm; £12) now looks after the ruins.

Scottish Citylink's **bus services** Nos 917 & 919 call here and link the castle with Drumnadrochit; see box p44 for details.

Urquhart Bay Woods

The woodland of ash, alder and willow to the east of Drumnadrochit, bordering the shores of Urquhart Bay, is owned and managed by the Woodland Trust (see p60). They describe it as 'one of the best examples of surviving ancient wet woodland in Europe'. It is certainly worth taking a wander along the small network of paths and, if the hustle and bustle of the village is getting too much, there are worse places to bring a picnic lunch. There is plenty of birdlife here; look out for willow warblers in the branches and kingfishers along the river. Access to the woods is along Kilmore Rd.

If some of the monster memorabilia seems too tacky, you'll find more meaningful culture by taking a trip to **Urquhart Castle** (see box p131) two miles south along the A82 main road; the city link **buses** 917 and 919 pass through Drumnadrochit and make a stop at the castle (see public transport p44). But even the castle can't escape the monster: despite its fascinating history it is almost more famous now as a good vantage point from which to look for Nessie. Indeed the castle even features in one of the many dubious photographs that purportedly show the monster; the castle was also prominent in the Hollywood movie *Loch Ness*.

Glenurquhart Highland Gathering (see p14) is held here in August.

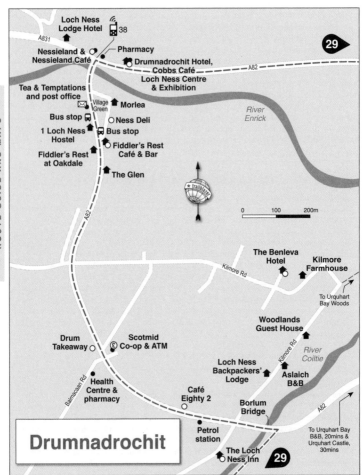

Services

Tea & Temptations (☎ 01456-450800; **fb**; open daily: shop 6am-6pm, tearoom 8.30am-6pm but hours can vary), formerly the village post office, is in the centre of the village. The **shop** sells basic essentials, newspapers, Capaldi's ice cream – and a fine bacon roll and Lavazza coffee to take away. Their pies are also recommended. The tearoom serves breakfasts, lunches and teas (see p134). They can also make up packed lunches.

If you prefer a chain store there is a **Scotmid Co-op supermarket** (☎ 01456-450206; daily 6am-10pm) at the southern end of the village.

Drumnadrochit is the last place you can get money out before Inverness, not that you'll have much opportunity to spend any of it between here and the end of the walk. There is an **ATM** outside Scotmid.

Should you be suffering any ailments this is a good place to get checked out; the **health centre**, incorporating a **pharmacy** (☎ 01456-450577; Mon-Fri 8.30am-6pm) is at the southern end of the village. There is another pharmacy (☎ 01456-450838; Mon-Sat 8.45am-6pm) near the main road junction by Nessieland.

Scottish Citylink's 917 & 919 **bus services** depart from the bus stop by the village green but they all also stop at Urquhart Castle; for service details see box p44.

Where to stay

For **camping**, *Borlum Caravan and Camping Park* (Map 29; ☎ 01456-450544, 🖥 borlum.co.uk/Camping/Campsite; WI-FI, 🐾; open all year) has plenty of space in their large field by the main road. A pitch costs £10.50pp including use of shower and toilet; facilities also include coin-operated washing/drying machines.

As the Way descends into Drumnadrochit it joins the main road where it crosses the River Coiltie. Immediately after the bridge take a left for *The Loch Ness Inn* (☎ 01456-450991, 🖥 stayloch ness.co.uk; **fb**; 6D/4T/1Tr/1Qd, all en suite; WI-FI available but not always reliable; Ⓛ; 🐾), a stylish and popular riverside pub with plenty of rooms; some are in

an attached cottage. Prices vary but start around the £50pp mark (sgl occ rates on request). Their new **bunkhouse** (contact details as above) has five dorms (from £30pp) – 3 x 4-bed, 1 x 5-bed and 1 x 6-bed – one of which is female-only, as well as three family rooms – one sleeping five people (from £150) and two sleeping six people (from £160). Each bed has its own reading light, plug socket and USB charging point. Bunkhouse guests have the use of two self-catering kitchens, a living-room, a coin-operated laundry and a bike store.

A short walk down Kilmore Rd is *Loch Ness Backpackers' Lodge* (☎ 01456-450807, 🖥 lochness-backpackers.com; **fb**; 3 x 6-bed & 2 x7-bed dorms; 1D/1T, two rooms sleeping 4-5 people; all share facilities; WI-FI; Ⓛ; 🐾) an independent **hostel** in an old farmhouse. A dorm bed costs £20pp (£50 for one/two sharing a room, four/five sharing £85/100 but there is a discount for children); they always try to keep one dorm for women only. Facilities include a self-catering kitchen, a licensed bar (stocked with local drinks, particularly beers and whiskies), a sitting room and a laundry service (£7).

A **B&B** with possibly the best views of Loch Ness is *Urquhart Bay* (☎ 01456-459136, 🖥 urquhartbay.com; 2D, both en suite; 🛏; WI-FI; Ⓛ); however, it is about a mile down the A82 towards Urquhart Castle. The rooms have fantastic views across Loch Ness and a Z-bed can be put in both but these are only suitable for a child. Subject to prior arrangement they can pick you up from the village (though it is not a difficult walk) and will provide an evening meal and a packed lunch. B&B costs £37.50pp (sgl occ £50-60).

Back in Drumnadrochit, on Kilmore Rd, *Aslaich B&B* (☎ 01456-459466, 🖥 aslaich.co.uk; **fb**; 2D en suite/1Tr private facilities; WI-FI; Ⓛ) has beds for around £40pp (sgl occ £40-60); facilities include a drying room.

Next door is *Woodlands Guest House* (☎ 01456-450356, 🖥 woodlands-lochness .co.uk; 3D/1T/1Tr, all en suite; 🛏; WI-FI; Ⓛ) which has very swish and spacious rooms. Rates start at £40pp (sgl occ £50-65). If requested in advance they are happy to take guests to **Cobbs** (see Where to eat).

Kilmore Rd continues in a loop back to the main road. Continue along it for *Kilmore Farmhouse* (☎ 01456-450524, ▭ kilmorefarmhouse.co.uk; **fb**; 3D/1T/1Tr, all en suite; WI-FI; ⑮; Easter to end Oct), which has clean, comfy rooms in a peaceful setting for £45pp (sgl occ £65). The owner is a keen walker and also a qualified acupuncturist and is happy to sort out the aching feet and shoulders of weary Great Glen Way walkers. Special diets are catered for if requested in advance.

The last place to stay on Kilmore Rd is *The Benleva Hotel* (☎ 01456-450080, ▭ benleva.co.uk; 3D/3T/1Qd, all en suite; ▼; WI-FI; ⑮; 🐾), a delightful 300-year old former manse which offers B&B from £55pp (sgl occ from £65, three/four sharing from £130).

Back on the main drag is *The Glen* (☎ 01456-450279, ▭ lochness-theglen.com; 2D en suite, 2Tr private facilities; WI-FI) where B&B (with a continental breakfast) is very reasonably priced at £22.50-35pp (sgl occ £40-60). Next door is *Fiddler's Rest* (☎ 01456-450678, ▭ fiddledrum .co.uk; **fb**; 1D/1T both en suite, 1Tr private bathroom; ▼; WI-FI; ⑮; Mar-Nov/Dec); see also Where to eat. On the other side of the road and owned by the same people is *Fiddler's Rest at Oakdale* (▭ oakdale-rooms.co.uk; 1D/1D or T both en suite, 1D/1T share bathroom; ▼; WI-FI; ⑮; Mar-Nov/Dec), a large Victorian villa which has been tastefully refurbished. Rates at both, including a continental breakfast, range from £30 to 40pp (sgl occ from £50).

Overlooking the village green is *Morlea* (☎ 01456-450410, ▭ morleabed andbreakfast.co.uk; **fb**; 1S/4D/1T, some en suite; WI-FI) a comfortable B&B with a very friendly welcome which charges around £40pp (sgl occ full room rate).

Opposite the green is *1 Loch Ness Hostel* (☎ 07773-160260, ▭ 1lochness hostel.co.uk; 2D/1T/1Tr/1Qd, one room sleeping up to five, as well as garden rooms sleeping up to four people; all en suite; WI-FI) which is a bit of a mis-nomer as it is more a B&B than a hostel, though it has a kitchen so

guests can prepare their own meals. Prices vary but are generally around £30pp (sgl occ £40-60, three/four/five sharing from £50/60/70); breakfast costs £3pp. Some of the beds in the garden rooms are bunk beds.

Over near Nessieland, the 18th-century *Loch Ness Lodge Hotel* (☎ 01456-450342, ▭ lochness-hotel.com; 50D or T, all en suite; ▼; WI-FI; ⑮; Mar-Oct) with its roaring fire and leather sofas, offers classy accommodation in a woodland setting. Some of the rooms can sleep an additional child. It's a big hotel and prices range from £47.50pp to £60pp (sgl occ full room rate). Note that it was temporarily closed at the time of research; contact them for an update.

The last hotel before you leave the village is the more modern *OYO Loch Ness Drumnadrochit Hotel* (☎ 01456 450218, ▭ lochnessdrumnadrochit.cobbshotels.com; 3S/11D/8T/2Tr/4Qd, all en suite; WI-FI; Mar to end Oct) another large hotel offering B&B from around £40pp (sgl occ is an eye-watering and inexplicable £200pp or more).

Where to eat and drink
There is plenty of choice for hungry tums. First off, as you enter the village from the south, is *The Loch Ness Inn* (see Where to stay; daily 8-10am & noon-9pm). It's often busy which is testament to its lovely riverside position and good food. Dishes vary in price from the Highland beef burger for £12 to the salmon fillet for £17.

As you head along the main road towards the village look out for the unassuming but delightful *Café Eighty2* (☎ 01456-450400; **fb**; Mar-Dec Mon-Sat 9am-5pm, Sun 11am-5pm), a 'proper' café where everything is home-made and made well. Try the sumptuous Scottish breakfast (£8.95) or one of the tasty toasties or salads. They also do a fine line in cakes.

Providing good competition and at the northern end of the village, family-run **Tea & Temptations** (☎ 01456-450800; **fb**; food 8.30am-6pm but hours can vary), is also a shop (see p133). The tearoom serves full Scottish breakfasts, brunches, lunches and teas. There's home-made soup, excellent coffee and a tempting range of freshly baked cakes and pastries.

The Benleva Hotel (see Where to stay; summer daily 6-9pm, Sun also 12.30-2.30pm), down Kilmore Rd, is a good choice for an evening meal; they are sometimes also open for lunch during the week but check in advance. The food is tasty and not too expensive, with the steak and Loch Ness ale pie at £13.95. It is also good for beer lovers as it serves a range of local beers.

In the centre of the village is another good ale house and also a fine spot for lunch or dinner: *Fiddler's Rest Café and Bar* (see Where to stay; restaurant Mar-Nov/Dec daily 12.30-2.30pm & 6-8.30pm) makes the most of Scottish tradition with salmon, venison and lamb on the menu. It's one of the most popular places in the village and for good reason. Mains, including Loch Ness cider and onion pork belly, are around £16.95.

For lighter bites, *Ness Deli* (☎ 01456-450282, 🖳 nessdeli.co.uk; **fb**; summer Mon-Sat 9am-8pm, Sun from 10am; winter hours variable), on the village green, is a no-nonsense café; their sandwiches and toasties have imaginative fillings such as brie, black pudding & cranberry.

Cobbs Café (☎ 01456-450573; daily 8am-5pm, winter hours variable) at Drumnadrochit Hotel does some excellent cakes and light lunches; the hotel also has a *restaurant* (daily 5-11pm). The *café* at Nessieland (see p131) was temporarily closed at the time of research so call them for an update on reopening plans.

For fish & chips, *Drum Takeaway* (☎ 01456-450123; daily noon-2pm & 4-10pm, all day in main season) does what you would expect for around £6.

DRUMNADROCHIT TO INVERNESS   [MAPS 29-37]

And so to the final stage and it's a long one: **20 miles (32.5km; 6¼hrs-8hrs 40mins)** and a few of those are on the road. The trail leads away from Loch Ness and the Great Glen on this final day and across low hills and moorland in this rarely visited part of Scotland. There is yet more forest too, both the less attractive commercial type and the more appealing Caledonian pine and birch woodland.

It's a long haul and there is really very little in the way of food, drink or services between Drumnadrochit and Inverness, apart from one B&B (Rivoulich Lodge, see p139). If you are lucky the makeshift – and highly eccentric – café in the woods at Abriachan may be open but don't rely on it (see p139). It's **essential that you have plenty of sustenance with you**. The picnic benches at Abriachan Community Woodland, which is roughly halfway, are as good a place as any to rest those weary feet for a spell.

The day starts in wearisome fashion, following the thundering traffic along the main road for over a mile. The narrow pavement feels far too close to the lorries and buses that roar past at 60mph. When you finally reach the path near **Temple Pier** (see below; Map 30) – where the world water-speed record was attempted – it feels as if you may have dodged an untimely end. *(cont'd on p139)*

(cont'd on p139)

❏ **Temple Pier and the world water speed record**
Just outside Drumnadrochit is Temple Pier. There is nothing much to see here but this is where, in 1952, John Cobb attempted to break the world water-speed record, on Loch Ness. He arrived at the pier with his jet-propelled *Crusader* boat. After many test runs Cobb went for the record on 29th September. Although he became the first man to pass 200mph on water, it ended in tragedy. The *Crusader* flipped at high speed, breaking apart as it did so and John Cobb died. Sadly the world-record attempt did not count because he did not complete the necessary distance.

ROUTE GUIDE AND MAPS

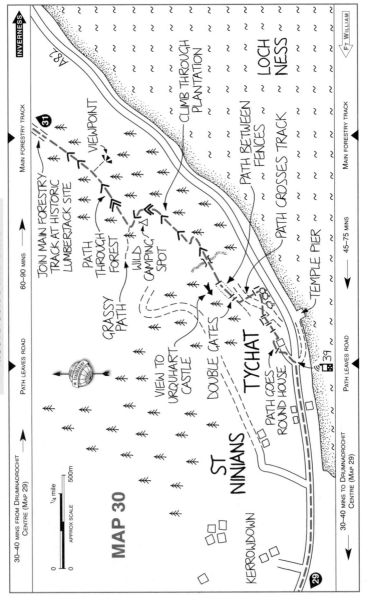

MAP 30

INVERNESS

A82

MAIN FORESTRY TRACK

31

JOIN MAIN FORESTRY
TRACK AT HISTORIC
LUMBERJACK SITE

VIEWPOINT

CLIMB THROUGH
PLANTATION

LOCH
NESS

PATH BETWEEN
FENCES

PATH
THROUGH
FOREST

WILD
CAMPING
SPOT

PATH CROSSES TRACK

GRASSY PATH

DOUBLE GATES

VIEW TO
URQUHART
CASTLE

TYCHAT

TEMPLE PIER

PATH GOES
ROUND HOUSE

39

ST
NINIANS

KERROWDOWN

29

FT WILLIAM

MAIN FORESTRY TRACK

PATH LEAVES ROAD

45–75 MINS

30–40 MINS TO DRUMNADROCHIT
CENTRE (MAP 29)

30–40 MINS FROM DRUMNADROCHIT
CENTRE (MAP 29)

PATH LEAVES ROAD

60–90 MINS

¼ mile

APPROX SCALE

0   500m
0

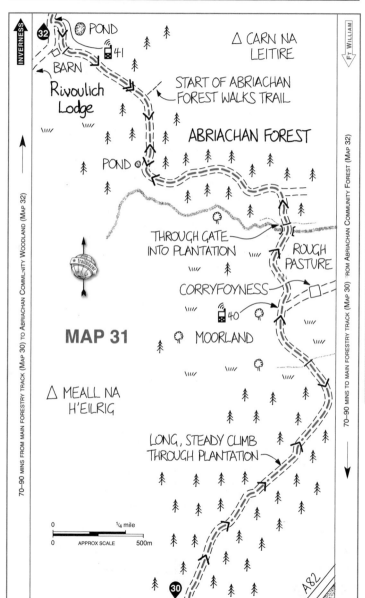

INVERNESS

FT WILLIAM

32
POND
41
BARN
Rivoulich
Lodge

△ CARN NA
LEITIRE

START OF ABRIACHAN
FOREST WALKS TRAIL

ABRIACHAN FOREST

POND

THROUGH GATE
INTO PLANTATION

ROUGH
PASTURE

CORRYFOYNESS

40

MOORLAND

MAP 31

△ MEALL NA
H'EILRIG

LONG, STEADY CLIMB
THROUGH PLANTATION

0   ¼ mile

0   500m
APPROX SCALE

30

A82

70–90 MINS FROM MAIN FORESTRY TRACK (MAP 30) TO ABRIACHAN COMMUNITY WOODLAND (MAP 32)

70–90 MINS TO MAIN FORESTRY TRACK (MAP 30) FROM ABRIACHAN COMMUNITY FOREST (MAP 32)

ROUTE GUIDE AND MAPS

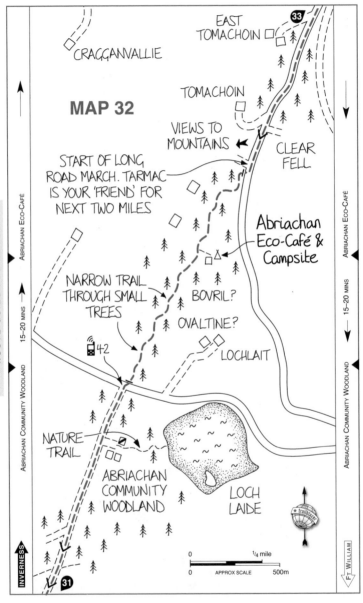

CRAGGANVALLIE

EAST
TOMACHOIN

33

MAP 32

TOMACHOIN

VIEWS TO
MOUNTAINS

START OF LONG
ROAD MARCH. TARMAC
IS YOUR 'FRIEND' FOR
NEXT TWO MILES

CLEAR
FELL

Abriachan
Eco-Café &
Campsite

NARROW TRAIL
THROUGH SMALL
TREES

BOVRIL?

OVALTINE?

LOCHLAIT

42

NATURE
TRAIL

ABRIACHAN
COMMUNITY
WOODLAND

LOCH
LAIDE

0   ¼ mile

0   APPROX SCALE   500m

ABRIACHAN ECO-CAFÉ

15-20 MINS

ABRIACHAN COMMUNITY WOODLAND

INVERNESS

31

ROUTE GUIDE AND MAPS

ABRIACHAN ECO-CAFÉ

15-20 MINS

ABRIACHAN COMMUNITY WOODLAND

FT WILLIAM

(cont'd from p135) The path takes you through some beautiful ancient oak trees and slowly climbs away from the road into the forest. You will stay in this forest for about the next two miles (3km) before crossing moorland to once again follow the track through a plantation. There's a nice *wild camping* spot in the woods but only enough room for one or two tents. It's not an official wild campsite so this is a proper out of the way spot.

Rivoulich Lodge (off Map 31; ☎ 01456-284868, 🖳 www.rivoulichlodge .co.uk; **fb**; 3D/1D or T all ensuite; WI-FI; Ⓛ) is a six-mile, three-hour hike from Drumnadrochit and 200m off the trail. Opened in 2019, it's already attracting excellent reviews for the warm welcome and their comfortable rooms which cost from £60-100 (for two people sharing). Breakfast is £4.50-8.50pp and evening meals are available if booked in advance.

At the end of this track is the welcome sight of the wooden buildings of **Abriachan Community Woodland** (Map 32; 🖳 abriachan.org.uk). There is a very pleasant nature trail here. It may seem absurd to suggest a short walk while in the middle of a very long one, but it really is a delight, taking you to the shore of Loch Laide, where, depending on the time of year, you may see dragonflies or whooper swans. If you want to explore the woods even more, there's an extensive network of paths with the Abriachan Forest Walks Trails (see Map 31). Abriachan also has public toilets and there are picnic benches. Lunch? Oh, go on then.

The kettle's on and it's time for tea at Abriachan Eco Café

After crossing the lane it's just under a mile to *Abriachan Eco Café & Campsite* (☎ 01463-861462; **fb**; daily all year but no fixed hours) set very much among the birch trees on what is 'the highest inhabited croft in Scotland'. In a homogenous world of sterile blandness, this café is a shining light. Despite the signs you will see on the path don't rely on the café being open or having enough food to see you all the way to Inverness but, if it is open, do stop here for at least tea and biscuits. You will either be baffled or delighted, but probably both. I don't want to spoil the surprise but expect chickens, pigs and a be-wellied waitress walking out of the woods with a tray. You can also **camp** here for £5pp (solar shower additional cost; compost toilets available). Note that if you are walking with a dog this is private land so your dog must be kept on a lead.

❏ **Important note – walking times**
Unless otherwise specified, **all times in this book refer only to the time spent walking**. You will need to add 20-30% to allow for rests, photography, checking the map, drinking water etc. When planning the day's hike count on 5-7 hours' actual walking.

ROUTE GUIDE AND MAPS

After the eccentricity of the café, the very narrow path twists and turns through the bushes to emerge on a deserted country lane in what feels like the back of nowhere. This road will be your guiding friend for two miles (3km) across bog and moor.

By the time you reach the lonely house at **Altourie** (Map 34) you may not want to be its friend any more but that's fine because you join a nice solid path through lots of gorgeous Caledonian pine forest. It's still a long hike, though, and the views you had back on the road are long gone. You are now on the march towards Inverness, following an **old drovers' road** (Map 35) where the cattle were led from the Highlands to the market in Inverness.

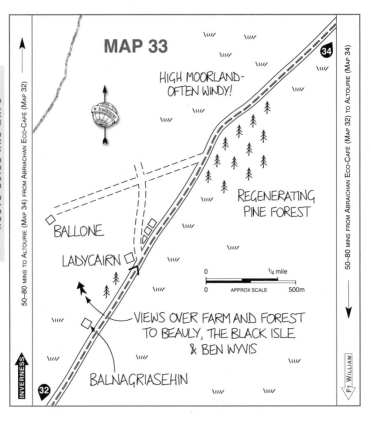

MAP 33

HIGH MOORLAND-
OFTEN WINDY!

★ trailhead

REGENERATING
PINE FOREST

BALLONE

LADYCAIRN

0   ¼ mile

0   APPROX SCALE   500m

VIEWS OVER FARM AND FOREST
TO BEAULY, THE BLACK ISLE
& BEN WYVIS

BALNAGRIASEHIN

50-80 MINS TO ALTOURIE (MAP 34) FROM ABRIACHAN ECO-CAFÉ (MAP 32)

50-80 MINS FROM ABRIACHAN ECO-CAFÉ (MAP 32) TO ALTOURIE (MAP 34)

INVERNESS

Ft WILLIAM

32

34

ROUTE GUIDE AND MAPS

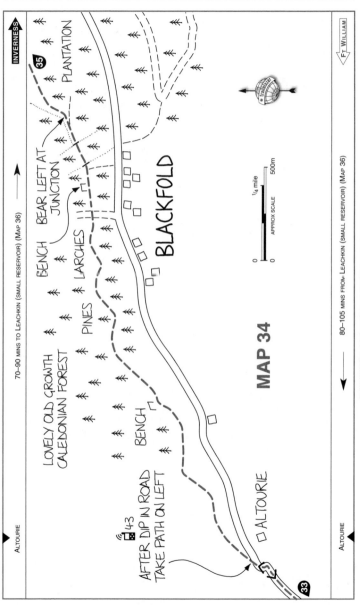

INVERNESS

35

PLANTATION

BEAR LEFT AT JUNCTION

BENCH

LARCHES

BLACKFOLD

PINES

LONELY OLD GROWTH CALEDONIAN FOREST

BENCH

MAP 34

ALTOURIE

AFTER DIP IN ROAD TAKE PATH ON LEFT

43

33

ALTOURIE

Fᴛ WILLIAM

APPROX SCALE

0   ¼ mile

0   500m

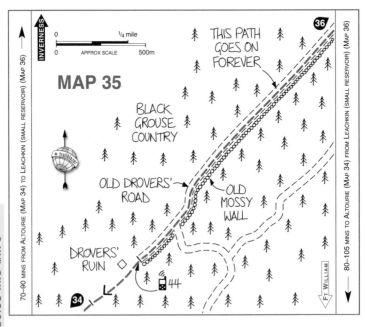

Finally there are glimpses of Beauly Firth (Map 36) in the distance and the realisation sinks in that you have nearly crossed from one side of Scotland to the other. All that remains is the steady descent into Inverness. The views over the city are surprisingly good from the open slopes on the edge of **Dunain Hill** (Map 36).

Once you have negotiated the backstreets, and passed the Scottish Natural Heritage building, you will find yourself back by the canal for the final time and then it's a short hop over the wooded **Ness Islands** (Map 37) in the River Ness and the 'finish line' at **Inverness Castle**. You've walked the length of the Great Glen. It's time for a celebratory drink.

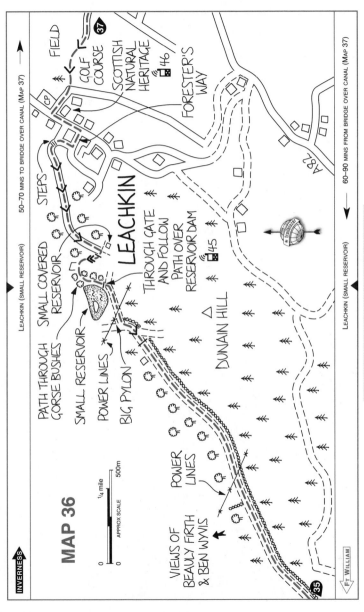

MAP 36

INVERNESS

¼ mile

0   500m
0
APPROX SCALE

VIEWS OF
BEAUTY FIRTH
& BEN WYVIS

POWER
LINES

FT WILLIAM

PATH THROUGH
GORSE BUSHES

SMALL RESERVOIR

POWER LINES

BIG PYLON

SMALL COVERED
RESERVOIR

STEPS

LEACHKIN

THROUGH GATE
AND FOLLOW
PATH OVER
RESERVOIR DAM

45

DUNAIN HILL

FIELD

GOLF
COURSE

37

CP

SCOTTISH
NATURAL
HERITAGE

46

FORESTER'S
WAY

A82

50–70 MINS TO BRIDGE OVER CANAL (MAP 37)

LEACHKIN (SMALL RESERVOIR)

LEACHKIN (SMALL RESERVOIR)

60–90 MINS FROM BRIDGE OVER CANAL (MAP 37)

ROUTE GUIDE AND MAPS

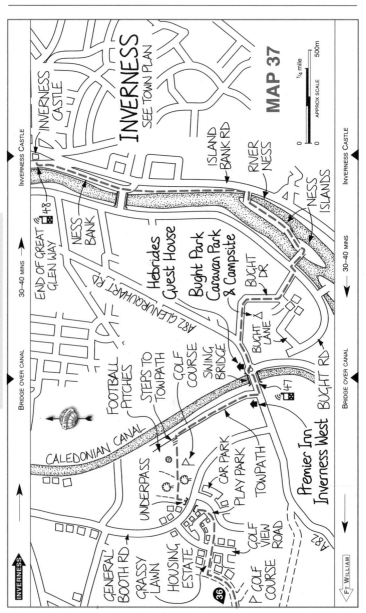

MAP 37

INVERNESS
SEE TOWN PLAN

¼ mile

APPROX SCALE

500m

INVERNESS CASTLE

INVERNESS CASTLE

ISLAND BANK RD

RIVER NESS

NESS ISLANDS

END OF GREAT GLEN WAY

NESS BANK

Hebrides Guest House

Bught Park Caravan Park & Campsite

BUGHT DR

BUGHT LANE

A82 GLENURQUHART RD

FOOTBALL PITCHES

STEPS TO TOWPATH

GOLF COURSE

SWING BRIDGE

CALEDONIAN CANAL

BRIDGE OVER CANAL

30–40 MINS

30–40 MINS

UNDERPASS

CAR PARK

PLAY PARK

TOWPATH

Premier Inn Inverness West

BUGHT RD

BRIDGE OVER CANAL

GENERAL BOOTH RD

GRASSY LAWN

HOUSING ESTATE

GOLF VIEW ROAD

GOLF COURSE

36

A82

ROUTE GUIDE AND MAPS

INVERNESS

FT WILLIAM

INVERNESS [see map p147]

The capital of the Highlands, as it is commonly known, is a thriving city occupying a prominent position on the **River Ness** – the name Inverness means 'Mouth of the Ness' – with Loch Ness to the south-west and Moray Firth to the north-east. Inverness has a long history, dating back to the 6th century when King Brude built a Pictish fort here. Modern-day Inverness owes its success to the ship-building that began during the 17th century. Through the 20th century the population doubled and to mark the millennium Inverness was officially declared a city. Today it thrives on tourism.

The city's charm lies in its lovely riverside setting with tree-lined avenues on each bank and the elegant **Greig Street Bridge**, a suspension footbridge, connecting one to the other. The most beautiful part of the river is at **Ness Islands** (Map 37); the islands are connected by footbridges from either bank and they are managed as a city park with the Great Glen Way passing through the middle.

Above the river, and dominating the skyline from every corner of the city, is **Inverness Castle** (⌨ highlifehighland.com/invernesscastleviewpoint/castle-viewpoint-2/; Apr-May & Sep-Oct daily 11am-6pm, Jun daily 10am-7pm, Jul-Aug daily 9am-8pm, Nov-Mar Fri-Mon 11.30am-4pm). It is not as dramatic as the castles of Edinburgh or Stirling, nor as old – the latest incarnation dating back to 1835 – but it has a long history; there has been a castle in the same location since 1056. Today it is a courthouse but for £5 you can climb the 94 steps to the viewpoint at the top and while you are there you can learn more about the castle's history.

At **Inverness Museum and Art Gallery** (⌨ 01463-237114, ⌨ highlifehighland.com; Apr-Oct Tue-Sat 10am-5pm, Nov-Mar Tue-Thur noon-4pm, Fri & Sat 11am-4pm) there are galleries and exhibits that tell the story of Highland life through the centuries.

For film, music and theatre buffs **Eden Court Theatre** (⌨ 01463-234234, ⌨ edencourt.co.uk) is well worth a visit. It is the cultural hub of the Highland region and has regular concerts, art-house films and plays and also hosts Inverness Film Festival (see p14). See their website for event details.

Inverness is the only city on the Great Glen Way and, after days of hard walking, you will most likely want to take advantage of the home comforts that 'Invernecky', as the locals like to call it, has to offer. And there is plenty to sate one's appetite.

Services

Visit Scotland Inverness iCentre (⌨ 01463-252401; Jul-Aug Mon & Wed-Sat 9am-7pm, Tue 10am-7pm, Sun 9.30am-5pm, times vary at other times of year) is at the end of the High St below the castle. In addition to providing tourist information the staff can book accommodation (£4 booking fee; plus 10% deposit).

At the **library** (⌨ 01349-781370; Mon-Tue & Fri 9am-6.30pm, Wed 10am-6.30pm, Thur 9am-8pm, Sat 9am-5pm) you can get free **wi-fi**, and **internet** access on their own computers.

There are plenty of **ATMs** around the centre of Inverness. Most of them are along the High St and on Academy St.

Shops on the High St include a Superdrug **pharmacy** and there are more household retail names in **Eastgate Shopping Centre** at the eastern end of the High St. The **post office** (Mon & Wed-Sat 9am-5.30pm, Tue 9.30am-5.30pm) is on Queensgate, just off Academy St.

The largest **supermarket** is Morrisons (Mon-Sat 7am-10pm, Sun 8am-8pm) on Millburn Road. There's also a Tesco Metro (Mon 7am-8pm, Tue-Sat 7am-10pm, Sun 8am-8pm) on Tomnahurich Street and a Co-op (daily 6am-10pm) on Church Street. If you are starting the walk in Inverness and need some last minute **outdoor gear** head for either Craigdon Mountain Sports or Blacks Outdoor at either end of Academy St.

Should you need medical help there is a doctor's surgery, on Crown Avenue, close to the city centre: **Crown Medical Practice** (⌨ 01463-214450, ⌨ crownmedicalpractice.co.uk; Mon-Fri 8am-6pm).

Bookworms cannot leave Inverness without paying a visit to **Leakey's** (⌨

01463-239947; **fb**; Mon-Sat 10am-5.30pm) which occupies the old Gaelic church building. That rarest of things, an independent bookshop, Leakey's is the largest second-hand bookshop in Scotland and something of an Inverness institution.

If you have a compost toilet key, or if wanting one because you will be walking from north to south (see box p19), you will need to go to **Seaport Marina Office**, on Telford St; see also Where to stay.

Bicycles can be hired from **Inverness Bike Hire** (☎ 01463-710664, 🖥 inverness bikehire.co.uk) for £20 per day (see also p28).

Transport
[See also pp43-6] For onward travel the **railway station** is on Academy St; from here there are services to Glasgow, Edinburgh, Kyle of Lochalsh (for Skye), Wick and Aberdeen.

The **bus station** is tucked behind the railway station. Scottish Citylink's 917, 919, 961, M90 & G10 **bus services** depart from here.

Where to stay
The Great Glen Way descends into the city to arrive at a swing bridge where Glenurquhart Rd crosses the canal. Just off

Bught Drive there is a **campsite**; *Bught Park Caravan Park and Campsite* (Map 37; ☎ 01463-236920, 🖥 invernesscaravan-park.com; **fb**; WI-FI £2 per 24hrs; late Mar to late Sep) is a large site in the middle of the houses. There is a dedicated area for backpackers, away from the caravans and motorhomes; note no camp fires and no dogs are allowed in this area. A pitch costs £10pp inc shower/toilet facilities; laundry and drying facilities are also available (£3 for each).

There is also an official *wild camping* spot at Seaport Marina for those returning their compost toilet key. There are no toilets or showers but there is space for four tents.

For a **hostel**, *Inverness Youth Hostel* (☎ 01463-231771, 🖥 hostellingscotland.org.uk/hostels/inverness; 163 beds; 4S/8T/1Tr/4Qd/one 6-bed room, all en suite; also 12Qd, 2 x 5-bed & 10 x 6-bed dorms share facilities; WI-FI ground floor only; open all year) is on Victoria Drive about 10 minutes' walk east from the city centre. A dorm bed costs £16-24pp; room rates are from £39.50 for a single up to £102 for five sharing an en suite room. The hostel also has internet access, laundry and drying facilities, meals, and a self-catering kitchen.

INVERNESS – MAP KEY

Where to stay
3 Fraser House B&B
13 The Waverley Guest House
18 Inverness Youth Hostel
24 Premier Inn
27 MacDonald Guest House
28 Glen Mhor Hotel
29 The Waterside Hotel
30 Glenmoriston Townhouse
31 Talisker B&B
32 Bannerman
33 Heathcote
34 Avalon Guest House

35 Bazpackers
36 Eildan Guest House
37 Atholdene House B&B
38 Dionard Guest House
39 The Gatehouse
40 Furan Guest House

Where to eat and drink
1 The Waterfront
4 River House Restaurant
5 Thai Dining
7 Wild Pancakes
8 Sam's Indian
9 McBains Restaurant by the River
10 The Mustard Seed

11 Aspendos Mediterranean Restaurant
12 George's Thai
14 Pizza Express
15 Little Italy
16 Velocity Café
17 Cinnamon Restaurant
19 Rendezvous Café
20 Number 27
21 Café 1
22 La Tortilla Asesina
23 The Castle Tavern
25 Urquhart's Restaurant
26 Rocpool

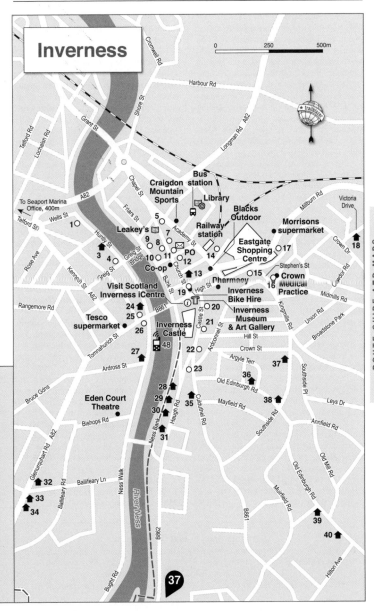

Inverness

To Seaport Marina Office, 400m

Craigdon Mountain Sports

Bus station

Library

Leakey's

Blacks Outdoor

Railway station

Morrisons supermarket

Eastgate Shopping Centre

PO

Co-op

Pharmacy

Stephen's St

Crown Medical Practice

Visit Scotland Inverness iCentre

Inverness Bike Hire

Inverness Museum & Art Gallery

Tesco supermarket

Inverness Castle

Eden Court Theatre

River Ness

Cromwell Rd

Harbour Rd

Shore St

Grant St

Longman Rd A82

Chapel St

Telford Rd

Lochalsh Rd

Wells St

Telford St

Friars St

Academy St

Millburn Rd

Victoria Drive

Crown Dr

Rose Ave

Huntly St

Greig St

Greig St

Bridge

Church St

Bank St

High St

Castle St

Ardconnel St

Kingsmills Rd

Castle Rd

Midmills Rd

Union Rd

Broadstone Park

Kenneth St A82

Rangemore Rd

Tomnahurich St

Ardross St

Bruce Gdns

Bishops Rd

Hill St

Crown St

Argyle Terr

Old Edinburgh Rd

Mayfield Rd

Southside Pl

Leys Dr

Annfield Rd

Glenurquhart Rd A82

Balliefary Rd

Balliefary Ln

Ness Walk

Ness Bank

Haugh Rd

Culduthel Rd

Southside Rd

Muirfield Rd

Old Edinburgh Rd

Old Mill Rd

Bught Rd

B862

B861

Hilton Ave

ROUTE GUIDE AND MAPS

0   250   500m

37

The independent ***Bazpackers*** (☎ 01463-717663, 🖳 bazpackershostel.co.uk; two mixed 6-bed dorms, female-only 4-bed dorm, 4-bed room, 3D/2T, shared facilities; WI-FI) **hostel**, right at the end of the Way on Culduthel Road, near the castle, is a popular sleepover spot for young travellers. A dorm bed costs £18-30pp and private rooms are £25-40pp based on two/three sharing (sgl occ full room rate). There is also a flat sleeping up to four people (in bunk beds) with a kitchen, sitting area and private bathroom from £99-160 a night.

There are lots of **guest houses** and **B&Bs** along Glenurquhart Rd; the first you will see is ***Hebrides Guest House*** (Map 37; ☎ 0800-054 9866; 2D both en suite/1Qd private facilities; 🛁; WI-FI; 🐕) a simple B&B with beds from £50pp. It's convenient, being right on the Way, but inconvenient in being some distance from downtown Inverness.

On the other side of the canal is a ***Premier Inn Inverness West*** (Map 37; ☎ 0871-527 9338, 🖳 premierinn.com; over 50 rooms, all en suite; 🛁; WI-FI), part of the nationwide chain. Despite the lack of character the beds are very comfortable indeed. Prices vary wildly, even on a daily basis. If you book online well in advance you may pay as little as £29.50 for a room sleeping up to two people, but the more general rate is £78 and the rate shoots up at busy times. There is another link in the chain, Premier Inn Inverness Centre River Ness, closer to the centre of town, by the river.

Continue north along Glenurquhart Rd, in the direction of the city centre, for plenty more places to stay including ***Avalon Guest House*** (☎ 01463-239075, 🖳 inverness-loch-ness.co.uk; 1D private facilities, 5D all en suite; WI-FI) with B&B for £35-60pp (sgl occ full room rate). The rate includes 'fluffy towels'.

Also on this road there's ***Heathcote*** (☎ 01463-236596, 🖳 heathcotebandb.co.uk; 3D, all en suite; WI-FI; 🐕) which charges £29-42pp (sgl occ £50-70) and is another very comfortable place to stay.

A little bit closer still to the city centre is ***Bannerman*** (☎ 01463-259199, 🖳 bannermanbandb.co.uk; 1S/2D/1T, all en suite; WI-FI) which borders on luxury with large, well turned-out rooms. B&B here costs £25-40pp (sgl £45-55, sgl occ full room rate).

On quiet Huntly Street is ***Fraser House*** (☎ 01463-716488, 🖳 fraserhouse.co.uk; 1S/1D/1T/1Qd, all en suite; WI-FI) with views over the river. Renowned for its big Scottish breakfast, the tariff here is around £40pp. They don't accept credit cards.

Macdonald Guest House (☎ 01463-232878, 🖳 macdonaldhouse.net; 1S/2D/2Tr/1Qd, all en suite; WI-FI) is a large establishment near the Eden Court Theatre. Prices vary from £30-80pp (sgl occ £60-130).

There is another cluster of B&Bs along Old Edinburgh Rd; it's not very central but it's a quiet and safe part of the city. One of the best here is ***Furan Guest House*** (☎ 01463-712094, 🖳 furan.co.uk; 1D en suite, 1Tr/one unit sleeping up to five people, both with private facilities; 🛁; WI-FI; 🐕) where the friendly owners will make you feel very welcome. They also do a mighty fine breakfast. B&B costs from £40pp (sgl occ from £60pp); the self-contained unit comprises a single and two double rooms as well as a small kitchen and costs from £160 per night including breakfast.

The Gatehouse (☎ 01463-234590, 🖳 gatehouseinverness.co.uk; 2D/1T, all en suite, 1D private shower facilities; WI-FI), an ivy-clad townhouse, offers B&B for £40-50pp (sgl occ £70-100).

At the northern end of Old Edinburgh Rd is ***Eildon Guest House*** (☎ 01463-231969, 🖳 eildonguesthouse.co.uk; 2D/1T/

Symbols used in text (see also p75)
🐕 Dogs allowed; if for accommodation this is subject to prior arrangement (see p155)
🛁 Bathtub in, or for, at least one room   **WI-FI** means wi-fi is available
Ⓛ packed lunch available if requested in advance
fb signifies places that post their current opening hours on their Facebook page

2Tr, all en suite; WI-FI) which is the most convenient, being close to the end of the Way and to the city centre. It's a smart place so remember to take your muddy boots off. The rate is from £30-50pp (sgl occ £65-90).

There is a plethora of guest houses along Southside Road. It's about a 15-minute walk to the city centre but it's a quiet place to rest your head. *Atholdene House B&B* (☎ 01463-233565, 🖳 atholdene .com; 1S/4D/4T/, all en suite; WI-FI) has very plush rooms with B&B from £47.50pp (sgl £69).

On the corner of Old Edinburgh Road and Southside Road is *Dionard Guest House* (☎ 01463-233557, 🖳 dionardguest-house.co.uk; 5D/ 1T, all en suite; WI-FI), a large town house with B&B from £47.50pp (sgl occ £75).

Another good B&B hunting ground is by the river, along Ness Bank. This is the very final stretch of the Way just before the finish at the castle. *Talisker B&B* (☎ 01463-236221, 🖳 scotland-inverness.co.uk/ talisker; 2S/4D, all en suite; WI-FI) has simple rooms from £37.50-45pp (sgl occ £40-55). If you feel you deserve a bit of luxury try the self-styled 'luxury boutique' *Glenmoriston Townhouse* (☎ 01463-223777, 🖳 glenmoristontownhouse.com; 3S/14D/14T, all en suite; ➤; WI-FI). Rooms come in three categories: Townhouse Comfort, Townhouse Club and Townhouse De Luxe River View, but they also have 1- and 2-bed apartments; some of the rooms have views over the River Ness and the tree-lined avenue below and the beds are made up with Egyptian cotton sheets and goose down pillows. Luxury comes at a price, however, with some room rates in the hundreds of pounds, but if you book early you might get lucky and bag one for around £40pp (sgl occ from £40).

Their neighbours at *Glen Mhor Hotel* (☎ 01463-234308, 🖳 glen-mhor.com; 10S/ 6D or T, all en suite; ➤; WI-FI) compete with the Glenmoriston for sophistication and they have equally good views from their riverside rooms. B&B here starts from £45pp (sgl/sgl occ from £60) but can be significantly higher depending on demand.

The Waterside at Glen Mohr (☎ 01463-233065, 🖳 glen-mhor.com; 5S/ 11D/17D or T/two rooms sleeping up to five people, all en suite; ➤; WI-FI), sandwiched between the two, is another rambling hotel with lots of rooms. It's owned by the Glen Mhor Hotel and has similar room rates.

For accommodation in the city centre, close to the nightlife and bus/railway stations, try *Waverley Guest House* (☎ 01463-716008, 🖳 waverleyinngroup.com; 8S/6D/ 11T/2Tr, most en suite; WI-FI; 🐾), a standard city-centre B&B with rates from £60pp (sgl £50, sgl occ rates on request).

Where to eat and drink

The best place for a drink to celebrate the conclusion of your walk is conveniently right at the end of the Walk, opposite the castle. *The Castle Tavern* (☎ 01463-718178, 🖳 castletavern.pub; **fb**; food served daily noon-10pm), 1 View Place, is just how a pub should be. It's friendly and full of chatter with a lovely terrace out front. And for real ale aficionados there is plenty on tap. They also do unpretentious bar meals.

Other cafés of note include the movie-themed *Rendezvous Café* (☎ 01463-718444, 🖳 rendezvous-cafe.co.uk; **fb**; Mon-Sat 8am-4pm, Sun 9am-4pm), 14a Church St, a local favourite that was, in the 18th century, a meeting room and later a '60s dance hall and record shop. In the summer they host classic film nights. It's a good spot for lunch with toasties/paninis for £5.50 and burgers for £6.50; gluten-free options available.

Velocity Café (☎ 01463-419956, 🖳 velocitylove.co.uk; **fb**; Mon, Tue, Fri 8am-6pm, Wed 8am-4pm, Thur 8am-9pm, Sat 9am-5pm, Sun 10am-5pm) on the corner of Stephen's St and Crown Avenue is part of a bicycle workshop so there is a heavy bike theme, from the Bicyclatte coffee to the Velocitea. It's a homely place to sit back and enjoy some quiet time. The soup is £3.95 and there are sandwiches for £4.20. Oh, and plenty of cake.

For tasty pancakes you could do a lot worse than *Wild Pancakes* (☎ 01463-232511, 🖳 wildpancakes.co.uk; **fb**; Wed-

Sun 9am-4pm) on Church Street. You can top your stack of pancakes with everything from bananas and chocolate to bacon and maple syrup.

Like most cities Inverness has restaurants offering cuisine from around the world. *Little Italy* (☎ 01463-712963; **fb**; Mon-Sat 11am-9pm) is a tiny, but delightful, independent Italian restaurant at the end of the High St. Its diminutiveness necessitates booking ahead and it's well-worth doing so; this is authentic Italian dining in the heart of the Highlands.

The branch of *Pizza Express* (☎ 01463-709700; Sun-Wed 11.30am-10pm, Thur-Fri to 10.30pm, Sat 11am-10.30pm) near the railway station does pretty fine pizzas too.

Moving across the Mediterranean, there are Spanish tapas at *La Tortilla Asesina* (☎ 01463-709809, 🖳 latortilla asesina.co.uk; **fb**; Mon-Fri noon-10pm, Sat & Sun noon to 10.30pm), 99 Castle St. The *patatas bravas* are £4.50 and the *calamares fritos* £5.95. There is more Mediterranean fare at *Aspendos Mediterranean Restaurant* (☎ 01463-711950, 🖳 highland aspendos.co.uk). They specialise in Turkish dishes which means plenty of lamb on offer. Try the lamb moussaka for £14.95.

There is fine dining to be had at *The Mustard Seed* (☎ 01463-220220, 🖳 mustard seedrestaurant.co.uk; **fb**; daily noon-3pm & 5.30-10pm) in an old church on Fraser St. The menu includes such delights as beetroot tortellini for £13.95 and Ardgay venison for £18.95.

The riverside *Rocpool* (☎ 01463-717274, 🖳 rocpoolrestaurant.com; Mon-Sat noon-2.30pm & 5.45-9.45pm), 1 Ness Walk, is another classy brasserie-style restaurant but the prices are correspondingly high-end with the Speyside venison dish making you £26.95 poorer. The linguine with grilled king prawns is £23.95.

There is a more intimate feel at *River House Restaurant* (☎ 01463-222033, 🖳 riverhouseinverness.co.uk; Tue-Sat 3pm-9.45pm), 1 Greig St; it has an à la carte menu specialising in seafood dishes such as sea bass (£23.75) and Shetland halibut (£25.75).

For Asian cuisine head to *Sam's Indian* (☎ 01463-713111, 🖳 samsindian

.com; **fb**; Mon-Wed noon-2pm & 5-10.30pm, Thur-Sun noon-10.30pm), 77-79 Church St, where mains are around the £11.95 mark. There's also Indian food at *Cinnamon Restaurant* (☎ 01463-716020; **fb**) on Millburn Road and Thai food at *George's Thai* (☎ 01463-226644; 🖳 georgesrestaurantinverness.co.uk; Mon-Sat noon-3pm, 5-10pm) in the centre of town opposite the post office where you can get a Thai curry for £8.95-11.95. *Thai Dining* (☎ 01463-220880, 🖳 invernessthai.com; **fb**; Tue-Wed 5-8.45pm, Thur-Sat 5-9.30pm) is a small Thai restaurant at the northern end of Academy St. The king prawn Thai green curry is £14.95.

Café 1 (☎ 01463-226200, 🖳 cafe1.net; **fb**; Mon-Fri noon-2.30pm & 5-9.30pm, Sat 12.30-3pm & 5.30-9.30pm), at 75 Castle St, is not cheap but the food is deservedly popular. The burger is the cheapest option at £15 with the Angus fillet steak coming in at £28.

Also on Castle St, and maintaining the numeral theme, is *Number 27* (☎ 01463-241999, 🖳 number27inverness.com; **fb**; food served Mon-Sat noon-9pm, Sun 12.30-9pm) for pasta, burgers and steaks. Mains cost around £12-24.

For riverside dining the aptly named *McBain's Restaurant by the River* (☎ 01463-714884; **fb**; Tue-Sat noon-2.30pm, 5.30-9.45pm), at 10 Bank St, is a good choice. It's small and intimate and, most importantly, the food is good.

Also by the river, but on the western side at 70-71 Huntly St, is *The Waterfront* (☎ 01463-233870, 🖳 thewaterfrontinverness.co.uk; **fb**; Mon-Sat noon-11pm, Sun to 10.30pm); it's a friendly bar and restaurant with a roaring open fire. They do seafood dishes and burgers (both from £12.95).

Urquhart's Restaurant (☎ 01463-233373, 🖳 urquharts-inverness.co.uk; **fb**; Tue-Sat noon-2.30pm & 5.30-9pm, Sun noon-9pm), at 2 Young St, has a lengthy menu with everything from venison sausages for £12.50 to penne pasta with chicken for £11.95. They also do a number of vegetarian dishes including veggie haggis, neeps & tatties for £11.50.

APPENDIX A: GAELIC

Gaelic was once spoken all over Scotland but there are now only about 80,000 Gaelic speakers, mainly in the north-west of Scotland. Gaelic names of geographical features are found all along the Great Glen Way; some of the most common words are listed below.

abhainn	river	*ciste*	chest
acarsaid	anchorage	*clach/clachan*	stone/hamlet
achadh/achaidh	field	*cnap*	lump/knob/small hill
adhar/adhair	sky	*cnoc*	hill
àite/àiteachan	place/places	*coille/choille*	wood/forest
Alba	Scotland	*coire/coireachan/*	corry/corries
Albannach/Albannaich	Scot	*choire*	(cirque)
allt/uillt	stream/burn	*crannog*	ancient dwelling on
aonach	ridge/moor		a loch,
àrd/àird	high	*craobh*	tree
		creag	rock/cliff/crag
bàgh/bàigh	bay	*crom*	crooked
baile	town	*cruach*	stack
bàn	white/fair	*cumain*	bucket
bàthach	byre		
beag	small	*dearg* or *dhearg*	red
bealach	mountain pass/col	*diallaid*	saddle
beinn/beinne/bheinn	mountain	*dobhran/dorain*	otter
bidean	pinnacle	*dorcha*	dark
bó/bà	cow	*dorus*	door
bodach/bodaich	old man	*drochaid*	bridge
bruthach	slope	*druim*	back/ridge
buachaille	herdsmen	*dubh*	black
buidhe/bhuidhe	yellow	*duinne*	brown
		dun	fortress/mound
cailleach	old woman		
caisteal	castle	*each*	horse
cala	harbour	*eag*	notch
calman/calmain	dove	*eaglais*	church
caol	narrows/strait	*earb*	roe deer
caora	sheep	*eilean*	island
càrn	cairn, or rounded rocky hill	*eòin*	bird
cas	steep	*fada*	long
cath	battle	*fasgadh*	shelter
cathair	chair	*feòla*	flesh
ceann	end/at the head of (often anglicised to kin)	*feur*	grass
		fiacaill	tooth
		fiadh	deer
cearc	hen	*fionn*	white/holy
ceum	step	*fithich*	raven
cìobair	shepherd	*fraoch*	heather

fuar	cold	*odhar*	dun-coloured
		òigh	maiden
gabhar	goat	*or*	gold
Gaidheal	Highlander		
Gaidhealtach	Highlands	*poca*	sack
gaoth	wind		
garbh	rough	*ràmh*	oar
geal	white	*rathad*	road
glas	grey/green	*ruadh*	red
gleann	glen/valley		
gorm	blue	*sàil*	heel
		sgor/sgorr/sgurr	peak
innis	meadow	*sionnach*	fox
iolair	eagle	*slat*	rod
		sneachda	snow
lach	duck	*spidean*	pinnacle
lairig	pass/col	*sròn*	nose
leathann	broad	*stac*	peak/point
liath	grey	*stob*	peak/point
linne	pool	*strath*	a long, wide valley
loch	lake or fjord		
lochan	small lake	*tigh/taigh*	house
		tioram	dry
machair	field	*toll*	hole
mam	hill	*tom*	hillock
meal/meall	round hill	*tràigh*	beach
monadh	moor		
mor/mhor	big	*uaine*	green
mullach	top	*uamh*	cave
		uiseag	lark
neul	cloud	*uisge*	water
nid	nest		

APPENDIX B: GPS WAYPOINTS

Each GPS waypoint below was taken on the route at the reference number marked on the map as below. This list of GPS waypoints is also available to download from the Trailblazer website – 🖵 trailblazer-guides.com.

Map	Ref	GPS waypoint	Description
1	01	N56° 49.286' W5° 06.425'	Start of GGW. Old Fort, Fort William
1	02	N56° 49.959' W5° 05.036'	Soldier's Bridge
2	03	N56° 50.508' W5° 07.118'	Junction of path and towpath near shinty fields
2	04	N56° 50.854' W5° 05.494'	Top (most northerly) lock on Neptune's Staircase

Map	Ref	GPS waypoint	Description
3	05	N56° 51.951' W5° 03.980'	Shengain Aqueduct
4	06	N56° 53.404' W5° 02.370'	Glen Loy aqueduct
5	07	N56° 53.902' W5° 01.133'	Moy Swing Bridge
5	08	N56° 54.792' W4° 59.861'	Road bridge above Gairlochy locks
6	09	N56° 55.155' W4° 59.351'	Path crosses B8005 road by 'no camping' sign
6	10	N56° 55.831' W4° 59.022'	Path joins B8005 road (after shore-side woodland path)
7	11	N56° 56.740' W4° 58.893'	Road bridge by commando boat station, Bunarkaig
8	12	N56° 57.261' W4° 57.598'	Junction of B8005 road with forest track at Clunes
9	13	N56° 58.019' W4° 55.720'	Bridge over burn
11	14	N56° 59.926' W4° 52.578'	Glas-dhoire Trailblazer Rest Site
12	15	N57° 00.843' W4° 51.095'	Junction of main track with track to munros
12	16	N57° 01.556' W4° 49.890'	Main route and Invergarry link route divide
13	17	N57° 02.231' W4° 48.709'	Bridge between canal and A82 road
13	18	N57° 02.599' W4° 48.230'	Junction of A82 and Loch Oich route, just south of Laggan Swing Bridge

● **Invergarry Link Route**

Map	Ref	GPS waypoint	Description
13	19	N57° 02.825' W4° 48.226'	Junction of A82 & Invergarry Link Route, just north of Covent Garden Forestry Cottage
14a	20	N57° 04.174' W4° 47.660'	Invergarry Hotel
15	21	N57° 04.390' W4° 45.723'	Trailblazer rest site & wild campsite, Leitirfearn
16	22	N57° 05.558' W4° 44.610'	Aberchalder Swing Bridge
17	23	N57° 07.347' W4° 43.318'	Kytra Lock
18	24	N57° 08.248' W4° 41.903'	Path passes by weir
19	25	N57° 08.700' W4° 40.838'	Bridge over canal in Fort Augustus
19	26	N57° 09.474' W4° 40.305'	High and low routes divide

● **High route**

Map	Ref	GPS waypoint	Description
21	27	N57° 10.921' W4° 39.036'	Footbridge over stream after stone shelter
21	28	N57° 11.478' W4° 38.308'	Bridge over Loch a' Mhuilinn burn

● **Low route**

Map	Ref	GPS waypoint	Description
22	29	N57° 11.459' W4° 37.384'	Junction of path down to Inver Coille Campsite
22	30	N57° 12.439' W4° 36.884'	Junction of high and low routes by timber stacking area
23	31	N57° 12.737' W4° 37.079'	Invermoriston road bridge
23	32	N57° 13.061' W4° 36.964'	New route leaves track; stay on track for old route
24	33	N57° 14.234' W4° 35.451'	Bridge over Alltsigh burn
25	34	N57° 15.090' W4° 32.639'	Junction of old and new routes
27	35	N57° 16.789' W4° 30.284'	Path joins lane at Grotaig

Map	Ref	GPS waypoint	Description
28	36	N57° 17.752' W4° 29.553'	Road passes lane to Bunloit
28	37	N57° 19.119' W4° 28.529'	Left turn through gate on to track and then right turn before second gate.
29	38	N57° 20.242' W4° 28.796'	Junction of A82 and A831 in Drumnadrochit
30	39	N57° 20.206' W4° 26.843'	Path leaves A82 road near Temple Pier
31	40	N57° 21.907' W4° 24.789'	Path passes track to Corryfoyness
31	41	N57° 22.630' W4° 26.141'	Junction of path and other track near barn
32	42	N57° 23.280' W4° 25.693'	Path crosses road north of Abriachan Community Woodland
34	43	N57° 25.620' W4° 23.058'	After dip in road take path on left
35	44	N57° 26.564' W4° 19.898'	Gate at start of stone wall
36	45	N57° 27.841' W4° 17.335'	Through gate and follow path over reservoir dam
36	46	N57° 28.001' W4° 16.334'	Scottish Natural Heritage building
37	47	N57° 27.889' W4° 14.643'	Over Caledonian Canal on outskirts of Inverness
37	48	N57° 28.453' W4° 13.568'	End of Great Glen Way by Inverness Castle

APPENDIX C: LANDSCAPE PHOTOGRAPHY

The art of landscape photography is in the ability to capture, in a two-dimensional image, the essence of these wild places; quite a challenge when one considers that the great outdoors is not just a visual treat but a stimulus to all our senses. The trick then is to use the visual element to convey the sounds, scents and overall mood.

Light is a key consideration in this. The best time for landscape photography is at dawn and dusk when the sun is low in the sky, casting a soft light that picks out the topography of the land. For the same reason, the autumn and spring often throw up some beautifully subtle light.

If you want to keep weight down in your rucksack you might opt for a pocket-sized point and shoot camera. The results from the latest models can be very impressive but, on the downside, there is less room for creativity with these cameras. If you are serious about your photography a digital SLR (Canon and Nikon lead the way here) or SLT (Sony) camera is the way to go and you will probably want a good wide angle lens and a telephoto zoom too. Whichever camera you choose there are a few ideas to bear in mind. Try different angles, different compositions and use bracketing (trying different exposures for the same subject).

Anyone who takes landscape photography seriously will use a tripod. These are essential for holding the camera steady in low-light conditions when a slow shutter speed is needed. There are some good lightweight ones available, from the likes of Manfrotto and Benbo, that are ideal for long-distance walkers.

Composing a picture is down to personal taste. Most photographers agree that the rule of thirds, having a background, middle and foreground, works best. Having something in the foreground, a rock or stream for example, complements the mountains in the background, while natural lines leading to a focal point also work well.

But sticking to rules is the way to stem creativity. There is nothing wrong with filling the frame with sky, if the sky is an interesting one, or shooting into the sun, to capture a dramatic silhouette, while shooting in the rain and cloud can capture that dark, brooding atmosphere.

APPENDIX D: TAKING A DOG

Many are the rewards that await those prepared to make the extra effort required to bring their best friend along the trail. You shouldn't underestimate the amount of work involved, though. Indeed, just about every decision you make will be influenced by the fact that you've got a dog: how you plan to travel to the start of the trail, where you're going to stay, how far you're going to walk each day, where you're going to rest and where you're going to eat in the evening etc.

If you're sure your dog can cope with (and will enjoy) walking 10 miles or so a day for several days in a row, you need to start preparing accordingly. Extra thought also needs to go into your itinerary. The best starting point is to study the town and village facilities table on pp30-1 (and the advice below), and plan where to stop and where to buy food.

Looking after your dog

To begin with, you need to make sure that your dog is **fully inoculated** against the usual doggy illnesses, and also up to date with regard to **worm pills** (eg Drontal) and **flea preventatives** such as Frontline – they are, after all, following in the pawprints of many a dog before them, some of whom may well have left fleas or other parasites on the trail that now lie in wait for their next meal to arrive.

Pet insurance is also a very good idea; if your dog is already insured, do check that it will cover a trip such as this.

On the subject of looking after your dog's health, perhaps the most important implement you can take is the **plastic tick remover**, available from vets for a couple of quid. These removers, while fiddly, help you to remove the tick safely (ie without leaving its head behind buried under a dog's skin).

Being in unfamiliar territory also makes it more likely that you and your dog could become separated. For this reason, make sure your dog has a **tag with your contact details** on it (a mobile phone number would be best if you have one with you); the fact that all dogs now have to be microchipped provides further security.

When to keep your dog on a lead

● **When crossing farmland**, particularly in the lambing season (around May) when your dog can scare the sheep, causing them to lose their young. Farmers are allowed by law to shoot at and kill any dogs that they consider are worrying their sheep. During lambing, most farmers would prefer it if you didn't bring your dog at all.

The exception to the dogs on leads rule is if your dog is being attacked by cows. Several years ago there were three deaths in one year in the UK caused by walkers being trampled as they tried to rescue their dogs from the attentions of cattle. The advice in this instance is to let go of the lead, head speedily to a position of safety (usually the other side of the field gate or stile) and call your dog to you.

● **Around ground-nesting birds** It's important to keep your dog under control when crossing an area where certain species of birds nest on the ground.

What to pack
You've probably already got a good idea of what to bring to keep your dog alive and happy, but the following is a checklist:
● **Food/water bowl** Foldable cloth bowls are popular with walkers, being light and taking up little room in the rucksack. You can also get a water-bottle-and-bowl combination, where the bottle folds into a 'trough' from which the dog can drink.
● **Lead and collar** An extendable one is probably preferable for this sort of trip. Make sure both lead and collar are in good condition – you don't want either to snap on the trail.
● **Medication** You'll know if you need to bring any lotions or potions.
● **Bedding** A simple blanket may suffice, or you can opt for something more elaborate if you aren't carrying your own luggage.
● **Poo bags** Essential.
● **Hygiene wipes** For cleaning your dog after it's rolled in stuff.
● **A favourite toy** Helps prevent your dog from pining for the entire walk.
● **Food/water** Remember to bring treats as well as regular food to keep up your mutt's morale. That said, the chances are they'll spend most of the walk dining on rabbit droppings anyway.
● **Corkscrew stake** Available from camping or pet shops, this will help keep your dog secure in one place while you set up camp/doze.
● **Tick remover** see p155.
● **Raingear** It can rain!
● **Old towels** For drying your dog.

When it comes to packing, leave an exterior pocket of your rucksack empty so you can put used poo bags in there (for depositing at the first bin). Keep all the dog's kit together and separate from the other luggage (usually inside a plastic bag inside your rucksack). Some dogs have their own 'doggy rucksack', so they can carry their own food, water, poo etc – which certainly reduces the burden on their owner!

Cleaning up after your dog
It is extremely important that dog owners behave in a responsible way when walking the path. Dog excrement should be cleaned up. In towns, villages and fields you need to pick up and bag the excrement and take it with you for disposal at the next possible opportunity.

Staying (and eating) with your dog
In this guide the symbol 🐾 denotes where a hotel, pub, or B&B welcomes dogs. However, this always needs to be arranged in advance – many places have only one or two rooms suitable for people with dogs. In some cases dogs need to sleep in a separate building. Some places make an additional charge (usually per night but occasionally per stay) while others may require a deposit which is refundable if the dog doesn't make a mess. Hostels (both YHA and, most of the time, independent) do not permit them unless they are an assistance (guide) dog. Smaller campsites tend to accept dogs, but some of the larger holiday parks do not; again look for the 🐾 symbol in the text.

When it comes to eating, most landlords allow dogs in at least a section of their pubs, though few cafés/restaurants do. Make sure you always ask first and ensure your dog doesn't run around the pub but is secured to your table or a radiator.

Henry Stedman

APPENDIX E: GLEN NEVIS & BEN NEVIS

Pastoral **Glen Nevis** (see below) is surrounded by some of the finest mountains in Britain and as a result has an excited buzz of activity year-round. It's not on the Great Glen Way but it's a much more beautiful place to spend your first night than in the streets of Fort William. The glen is just a couple of miles from town and there's a large campsite which is the only one in the area, a bunkhouse, a dedicated hostel and a B&B that also has hostel accommodation. And if you feel the urge to climb **Ben Nevis** (see pp160-4), Britain's highest mountain, this is the place to start.

GLEN NEVIS   [see maps pp158-9 & map p161]

Services
Glen Nevis Visitor Centre (☎ 01397-705922, 🖥 ben-nevis.com/visitor-center/visitor -center.php; daily Easter to May & Sep-Oct 9am-5pm, Jun-Aug 8.30am-6pm, Nov-Easter 9am-3pm), **Ioned Nibheis** in Gaelic, is well worth a look in if only to get an accurate **weather forecast** and **avalanche reports**. There is an excellent exhibition on the natural history and environment of the area, a bookshop and they stock outdoor gear; the staff also have a wealth of local knowledge. There are public toilets in the visitor centre.

Stagecoach's No 41B **bus** service runs from Roy Bridge via Spean Bridge and Fort William bus station to Glen Nevis Youth Hostel (year-round Mon-Sat 1/day each direction) and can be flagged down en route if it is safe to stop.

Where to stay
Glen Nevis Caravan and Camping Park (☎ 01397-702191, 🖥 glen-nevis.co.uk; **fb**; £10pp; 🐾; WI-FI; 15th Mar to 5th Nov) is a vast acreage of neatly cut grass and conifers sprawling over the bottom of the glen and it offers plenty of space for tents. They also have **camping pods** (£60-70 per night) sleeping up to two people (either double or twin) or three people, but bedding is not provided and dogs are only accepted in the pods by prior arrangement. The rate includes use of the shower and toilet facilities; the site also has a **laundry** (washing machine £2, drying machine 20p per 8 mins) and a well-stocked **shop** (daily 8am-7pm, till 9pm in July/Aug, low season Sun-Thur to 6pm).

Just up the glen from here is the popular *Glen Nevis Youth Hostel* (☎ 01397-702336, 🖥 hostellingscotland.org.uk/hostels/glen-nevis; 86 beds; 1S, 1D, 1x2-bed, 1x3-bed, 1x4-bed, 1x6-bed rooms, the rest are dorm rooms with up to 16 beds; 1x3-bed room en suite; WI-FI free on ground floor; ①), which is open all year. Rates are £17-27pp (twin/triple/quad room from £50/75/90). There is a self-catering kitchen and the hostel is licensed; breakfast (continental/cooked £5.95/7.50) is available if booked in advance. It has laundry facilities (£2 per wash, additional charge for drying machines) as well as a drying room. Note that the hostel can be booked for sole occupancy so advance booking is recommended, particularly in the main season.

Another good place to stay in a beautiful position at the start of the Ben Nevis path is *Ben Nevis Inn* (☎ 01397-701227, 🖥 ben-nevis-inn.co.uk; **fb**; WI-FI though it is not reliable), a carefully renovated barn which has a basic **bunkhouse** (24 beds; from £17pp) with kitchen facilities and a drying room; bedding is provided. Booking is recommended, particularly in the summer months. *(cont'd on p160)*

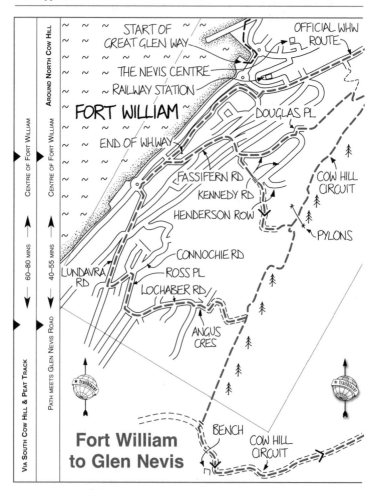

Fort William to Glen Nevis

START OF
GREAT GLEN WAY

OFFICIAL WHW
ROUTE

THE NEVIS CENTRE

RAILWAY STATION

FORT WILLIAM

DOUGLAS PL

END OF WH.WAY

FASSIFERN RD

KENNEDY RD

HENDERSON ROW

COW HILL
CIRCUIT

PYLONS

CONNOCHIE RD

LUNDAVRA
RD

ROSS PL

LOCHABER RD

ANGUS
CRES

BENCH

COW HILL
CIRCUIT

CENTRE OF FORT WILLIAM   60–80 MINS   VIA SOUTH COW HILL & PEAT TRACK

CENTRE OF FORT WILLIAM   40–55 MINS   PATH MEETS GLEN NEVIS ROAD

❏ **From Fort William to Glen Nevis for Ben Nevis**
There is currently only one bus a day from Fort William so if you plan to climb Ben Nevis (and aren't a B&B guest at Achintee Farm, see p160) the chances are you will need to walk to Glen Nevis from Fort William. There are three options and which you choose will probably depend on where you are staying in Fort William.
● **Road route option (West Highland Way)** – You can simply follow the signs for the West Highland Way which takes walkers along the busy A82 and then down Glen Nevis road. It takes 45-55 minutes.

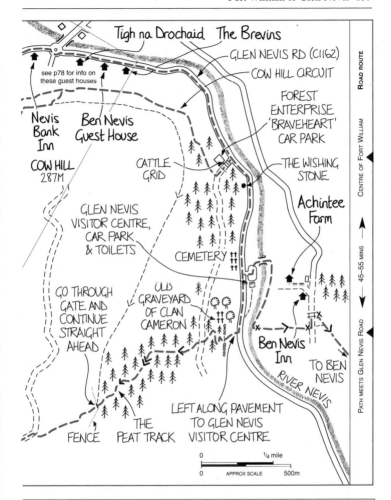

Tigh na Drochaid   The Brevins

GLEN NEVIS RD (C1162)

COW HILL CIRCUIT

ROAD ROUTE

FOREST ENTERPRISE 'BRAVEHEART' CAR PARK

see p78 for info on these guest houses

Nevis Bank Inn

Ben Nevis Guest House

CENTRE OF FORT WILLIAM

COW HILL 287M

CATTLE GRID

THE WISHING STONE

Achintee Farm

GLEN NEVIS VISITOR CENTRE, CAR PARK & TOILETS

45-55 MINS

CEMETERY

GO THROUGH GATE AND CONTINUE STRAIGHT AHEAD

OLD GRAVEYARD OF CLAN CAMERON

Ben Nevis Inn

TO BEN NEVIS

PATH MEETS GLEN NEVIS ROAD

RIVER NEVIS

FENCE

THE PEAT TRACK

LEFT ALONG PAVEMENT TO GLEN NEVIS VISITOR CENTRE

0   ¼ mile

0   APPROX SCALE   500m

● **South Cow Hill & Peat Track option** – Much more pleasant; there are great views back over Loch Linnhe as you rise out of Fort William but it's the longest option, taking 60-80 minutes.

● **Around North Cow Hill option** – This is easier than the South Cow Hill & Peat Track option. It's also far better than following the West Highland Way route as it's away from the road – as long as you **don't** go via the Leisure Centre. It takes 45-55 minutes.

(cont'd from p157) Next door, **Achintee Farm** (☎ 01397-702240, 🖳 achintee farm.com; WI-FI) offers a range of accommodation and **drying rooms** that everyone can use. They have a **hostel** with three separate units: one is self-contained with a double room, private shower and cooking facilities (from £45pp, sgl occ rates on request). Another unit has a twin room and a triple room; the third has a twin room. These units (£28pp, sgl occ rates on request) share a shower, toilet and cooking facilities. Bed linen is included; towels can be hired (£1). Note that unless you book a unit for sole occupancy you may have to share it with people you don't know.

They also offer **B&B** accommodation in the farmhouse (2D/1D or T, all en suite; 🖝; WI-FI; ⓛ; £55-65pp, sgl occ rates on request; Apr to early Oct). Booking is recommended and two-night bookings are preferred. Subject to prior arrangement B&B guests can be picked up in Fort William.

Where to eat and drink

At *Ben Nevis Inn* (see Where to stay) excellent food is available daily noon-9pm (Thur-Sun only in winter); the menu changes regularly but during the day may include filled wraps (from £7.25) and, in the evening, haddock & chips (£13.50) and chicken & haggis rumbledethumps (£13.95). There is also a vegan and gluten-free menu. It's the kind of place you could spend all day in, luxuriating in the glorious views up the glen and warming yourself by the woodburner. You can also listen to live music (usually on Tuesday evening in summer). It can get very busy, so best to book ahead for dinner.

Glen Nevis Restaurant and Lounge Bar (☎ 01397-705459; Mar/Apr to end Oct, daily 11am-11pm, food served 9am-11am and noon-9.30pm, May-Aug open from 7am for breakfasts) is a modern building with the air of a motorway service station but the food is good.

BEN NEVIS   [see map opposite]

You remember your first mountain in much the same way you remember having your first sexual experience, except that climbing doesn't make as much mess and you don't cry for a week if Ben Nevis forgets to phone next morning.
Muriel Gray *The First Fifty – Munro-bagging without a beard*

It is impossible to say who first climbed the highest mountain in Britain. Locals have been walking these hills since the beginning of time and would have been guides to the visitors who first left a record of their ascents in the 18th century. Although nowhere near the first to ascend the mountain, some credit must go to Clement Wragge who climbed the peak every day without fail for two years to take weather readings. Happy to set out in all conditions, he soon became known as 'inclement Wragge'. He was no doubt glad when a weather observatory was built on the summit in 1883 and a substantial path made to service it – it's now the 'Tourist route'. The observatory was abandoned in 1904.

❏ **Poor visibility navigation notes**
To get safely off the summit in severe conditions you must walk from the summit trig point on a **grid** bearing of 231° for 150 metres. Then follow a **grid** bearing of 281° to get off the plateau and onto the Tourist Route. **Remember** to add the number of degrees of magnetic variation to your compass to obtain the magnetic bearing you should follow.

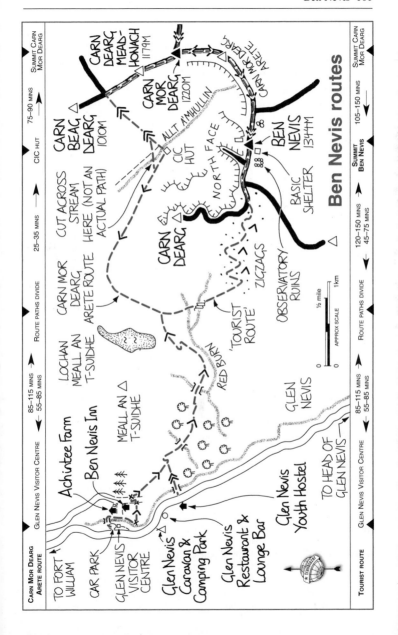

Ben Nevis routes

Today, 75,000 walkers a year attempt to reach the summit – and in the **Ben Race** (see p14) in September they run up – so don't think you'll get the place to yourself. Mass tourism has been a part of the Ben's life since the railway reached Fort William in 1894. Thankfully, the tacky idea of a summit hotel and pony rides to the top was abandoned soon after it was conceived.

Climbing Ben Nevis

Climbing the highest mountain in Britain is a spectacular way to begin your adventure and it offers a sumptuous view of the Great Glen that lies ahead of you. However, do not underestimate those 4406ft (1344 metres) to the summit. It may not sound that high in comparison with the highest peaks in other countries but it has a fearsome reputation for accidents and as with all mountains in the Highlands, you should not contemplate climbing it unless you are suitably equipped and knowledgeable (see p53).

There are several routes to the top. By far the most popular is the badly named

Tourist Route (significantly harder than its belittling name would suggest), ascending from Glen Nevis along the well-trodden line of the former pony track all the way to the summit. This route (see opposite) takes about 5½-6½ hours to reach the summit and get back. Some find it a relentless slog, particularly on the upper reaches of the mountain and especially when accompanied by scores of other walkers, as you will be on most days in summer. It is, however, the only option for those who would not class themselves experienced hillwalkers.

On the Tourist Route to the summit

For the latter category there is a superb route that provides a tough, long, but grand day out, befitting of Britain's highest mountain. The **Carn Mor Dearg Arête Route** (see p164) follows the Tourist route initially and then detours under the spectacular north face to climb Carn Mor Dearg (CMD), a significant mountain in its own right. From here it follows the narrow, rocky, crescent line of the Carn Mor Dearg Arête and then up the Ben's boulder-covered south-eastern slopes to the summit plateau. Descent is down the normal route. The whole trip takes about 8½-9½ hours.

Safety

The Tourist route is along a well-graded trail, easy to follow in good visibility, but a mountain path the none less. Expect loose rock and scree underfoot, patches of snow even late in the year and some steep sections. The alternative CMD route is largely on steep, rough ground with a fair bit of exposure in places. It is a long route, requiring stamina with some sections of easy scrambling. Neither route is suitable in snow or ice unless you are an accomplished winter mountaineer.

The main difficulties on Ben Nevis occur on the summit plateau in poor visibility. The plateau is broad, relatively featureless and fringed to the north by a wall of crags which drop precipitously into Coire Leis below. The gullies that cut into this rock wall have too frequently ensnared lost walkers and climbers wandering round the plateau in white-out conditions. The other real danger is that in an effort to avoid these gullies the walker aims too far south, missing the descent path and straying onto the dangerous ground at the top of the notorious Five Finger Gully on the west side of the plateau. In poor visibility – a frequent occurrence as the summit is in cloud an average of 300 days a year – your navigation must be spot on. Snow and cloud together can create a lethal formula. See the box on p160 about poor visibility navigation.

Maps
For either route you must take one of the following maps: OS Landranger Sheet 41 (1:50,000), OS Explorer 392 (1:25,000), Harvey's Walker's Map 'Ben Nevis' (1:40,000), or Harvey's Superwalker 'Ben Nevis' (1:25,000). If you have a choice, the last one is the best with its enlarged map of the summit of Ben Nevis; a real help in getting off the mountain in poor visibility.

Tourist route
The best place to start the ascent is from Glen Nevis Visitor Centre. Cross the River Nevis via the footbridge by the car park and follow the path to Ben Nevis Inn, another popular start point. From here the path climbs steadily and is soon joined by the steep path from Glen Nevis Youth Hostel.

If starting from the youth hostel, cross the footbridge over River Nevis and turn left over a ladder-stile. Take heed of any pertinent safety or weather information on the notice board here. The path climbs steeply to join the main trail from Glen Nevis Visitor Centre and Achintee Farm.

The trail climbs gently across the side of Meall an t-Suidhe, up two small zigzags and over three small bridges. Follow it into the ravine created by **Allt na h-Urchaire** (**Red Burn**) which falls off the western flanks of the Ben and then up onto a broad grassy pass on which **Lochan Meall an t-Suidhe** (Halfway Lochan) sits. Don't be tempted to cut across the zigzags as this causes further erosion on this intensively used path. South-east of the lochan the trail divides by a short, low stone wall. This is about 1½ hours' walking from the start including one or two essential stops. It's at least another 2-2½ hours from here to the summit. An indistinct trail continues straight ahead across the col above Lochan Meall an t-Suidhe. This is the start of the route via CMD (see p164).

The main trail doubles back on itself and climbs easily across the western slopes of Carn Dearg. Cross the Red Burn below a waterfall – you can fill up with water here: the water is fresh and many walkers happily drink it but, considering how many people walk this way, there is a small risk of picking up something unwanted, so it may be worth purifying it before drinking – and begin ascending the interminable zigzags up the severely eroded flank of the mountain. There are lots of short-cuts but they do not make the going easier or quicker either on the ascent or coming back down. They are steep, extremely slippery and best avoided.

As you ascend, the huge shoulder of Carn Dearg 4005ft (1221m) spreads out to your left. You may be able to make out the **orange emergency shelter** just west of its summit. Eventually the route crosses a rock band and at last you climb more gently

Emergency shelter at the summit

onto the vast **summit plateau** (3½-4hrs from the start). Among the boulder-strewn landscape are all manner of man-made structures: an emergency shelter, cairns, memorial plaques, the **ruins of an observatory** and the trig point. The summit is no place for quiet reflection. On most days you will be surrounded by the trappings of the modern world, crackling crisp packets, chirping mobile phones, the pervading smell of cigarette smoke, yet if the cloud is high the views are superb. The descent is back the way you came and takes about 2-2½ hours.

Carn Mor Dearg Arête Route

Follow the Tourist Route to Lochan Meall an t-Suidhe. Where the paths divide, continue straight on across the col. After five minutes there's a large cairn where a faint trail branches left towards the outflow of the lochan. Ignore this, keeping straight on along the main trail which climbs gently to another large cairn on the horizon. The trail begins to descend and turns sharply east (right) into **Coire Leis** under the impressive northern crags of Ben Nevis.

The **CIC hut** (🖳 smc.org.uk/huts/cic) is a famous Scottish climbing hut. Given its location below the sheer north-face cliffs it tends to be used almost exclusively by climbers but should you wish to stay here you will need to book well in advance. It is busy all year and some spaces are reserved for Scottish Mountaineering Club (SMC) members.

Leave the path after a few hundred metres picking your way down over the rough heather- and bilberry-covered slopes to the **Allt a' Mhuilinn**. This is the last reliable place for water until you descend off the Ben.

Choose a safe crossing point and head directly up the grassy, boulder-covered slopes ahead of you, climbing steeply to the ridge between Carn Beag Dearg and Carn Dearg Meadhonach. Continue climbing, more gently now, to the pink granite summit of **Carn Dearg Meadhonach** where there's a cairn and small stone windbreak. The views of the fearsome northern cliffs of Ben Nevis are awe-inspiring from here with snow lingering all year in shaded pockets. To the east the Nevis Range chairlift transports summer tourists and winter skiers up the northern slopes of Aonach Mor.

Descend south to a small col, then up and over the summit of **Carn Mor Dearg** 4002ft (1220m) and onto the spine of the arête. This sweeps round to the south-west dropping to a col. From here there are wonderful views south over the Mamores. Climb steeply up the grey south-east slopes of Ben Nevis on broken rock and boulders. The paths are indistinct. Take care in poor visibility not to stray too close to the corrie edge. Rejoin the mass of humanity on the summit. The trip time so far including a few short stops is about 6-7 hours. The descent is down the Tourist Route (see p163).

If the ascent of Ben Nevis inspires you to discover more of Scotland's hills take a look at Trailblazer's *Scottish Highlands Hillwalking Guide*.

Map key

- ♠ Where to stay
- ○ Where to eat & drink
- Λ Campsite
- ⊠ Post office
- ⓒ Bank/ATM
- □ Building

- ⓘ Tourist information
- 📖 Library/bookstore
- @ Internet
- ⊤ Museum/gallery
- 🏠 Church/cathedral
- ⊠ Public toilet

- 🚌 Bus stop/station
- —▭— Rail line & station
- ▭ Park
- CP Car park
- ● Other

Great Glen Way	Slope	Fence
Subsidiary path	Steep slope	River
(4WD) track	Stile	Trees/wood
Road	Gate	GPS waypoint
Steps	Bridge	12 Map continuation

	Fort William	Lochyside	Caol	Banavie	Gairlochy	Glas-dhoire	Laggan Locks junction	Laggan	Leitirfearn	Aberchalder
Lochyside	**2**									
	3									
Caol	**2.5**	0.5								
	4	*1*								
Banavie	**3.5**	1.5	1							
	5.5	*2.5*	*1.5*							
Gairlochy	**10**	8	7.5	6.5						
	16	*13*	*12*	*10.5*						
Glas-dhoire	**19.5**	17.5	17	16	9.5					
	31.5	*28.5*	*27.5*	*26*	*15.5*					
Laggan Locks junction	**22**	20	19.5	18.5	12	2.5				
	35.5	*32.5*	*31.5*	*30*	*19.5*	*4*				
Laggan	**23**	21	20.5	19.5	13	3.5	1			
	37	*34*	*33*	*31.5*	*21*	*5.5*	*1.5*			
Leitirfearn	**27**	25	24.5	23.5	17	7.5	5	4		
	43.5	*40.5*	*39.5*	*38*	*27.5*	*12*	*8*	*6.5*		
Aberchalder	**29**	27	26.5	25.5	19	9.5	7	6	2	
	46.5	*43.5*	*42.5*	*41*	*30.5*	*15*	*11*	*9.5*	*3*	
Kytra Lock	**32**	30	29.5	28.5	22	12.5	10	9	5	3
	51.5	*48.5*	*47.5*	*46*	*35.5*	*20*	*16*	*14.5*	*8*	*5*
Fort Augustus	**35**	33	32.5	31.5	25	15.5	13	12	8	6
	56.5	*53.5*	*52.5*	*51*	*40.5*	*25*	*21*	*19.5*	*13*	*10*
Invermoriston	**44.5**	42.5	42	41	34.5	25	22.5	21.5	17.5	15.5
	72	*69*	*68*	*66.5*	*56*	*40.5*	*36.5*	*35*	*28.5*	*25.5*
Grotaig	**54**	52	51.5	50.5	44	34.5	32	31	27	25
	87.5	*84.5*	*83.5*	*82*	*71.5*	*56*	*52*	*50.5*	*44*	*41*
Drumna-drochit	**59**	57	56.5	55.5	49	39.5	37	36	32	30
	95.5	*92.5*	*91.5*	*90*	*79.5*	*64*	*60*	*58.5*	*52*	*49*
Abriachan	**66**	64	63.5	62.5	56	46.5	44	43	39	37
	107	*104*	*103*	*101.5*	*91*	*75.5*	*71.5*	*70*	*63.5*	*60.5*
Inverness	**79**	77	76.5	75.5	69	59.5	57	56	52	50
	127	*125*	*124*	*122.5*	*112*	*96.5*	*92.5*	*91*	*84.5*	*81.5*

Great Glen Way
(Loch Oich route)

DISTANCE CHART 1

miles/*kilometres* (approx)

Kytra Lock	Fort Augustus	Invermoriston	Grotaig	Drumnadrochit	Abriachan	Inverness
3						
5						
12.5	9.5					
20.5	*15.5*					
22	19	9.5				
36	*31*	*15.5*				
27	24	14.5	5			
44	*39*	*23.5*	*8*			
34	31	21.5	12	7		
55.5	*50.5*	*35*	*19.5*	*11.5*		
47	44	34.5	25	20	13	
76.5	*71.5*	*56*	*40.5*	*32.5*	*21*	

	Fort William	Lochyside	Caol	Banavie	Gairlochy	Glas-dhoire	Laggan Locks junction	Invergarry	Aberchalder	Kytra Lock
Lochyside	**2** *3*									
Caol	**2.5** *4*	0.5 *1*								
Banavie	**3.5** *5.5*	1.5 *2.5*	1 *1.5*							
Gairlochy	**10** *16*	8 *13*	7.5 *12*	6.5 *10.5*						
Glas-dhoire	**19.5** *31.5*	17.5 *28.5*	17 *27.5*	16 *26*	9.5 *15.5*					
Laggan Locks junction	**22** *35.5*	20 *32.5*	19.5 *31.5*	18.5 *30*	12 *19.5*	2.5 *4*				
Invergarry	**27** *43.5*	25 *40.5*	24.5 *39.5*	23.5 *38*	17 *27.5*	7.5 *12*	5 *8*			
Aberchalder	**30** *48.5*	28 *45.5*	27.5 *44.5*	26.5 *43*	20 *32.5*	10.5 *17*	8 *13*	3 *5*		
Kytra Lock	**33** *53.5*	31 *50.5*	30.5 *49.5*	29.5 *48*	23 *37.5*	13.5 *22*	11 *18*	6 *10*	3 *5*	
Fort Augustus	**36** *58.5*	34 *55.5*	33.5 *54.5*	32.5 *53*	26 *42.5*	16.5 *27*	14 *23*	9 *15*	6 *10*	3 *5*
Invermoriston	**45.5** *74*	43.5 *71*	43 *70*	42 *68.5*	35.5 *58*	26 *42.5*	23.5 *38.5*	18.5 *30.5*	15.5 *25.5*	12.5 *20.5*
Grotaig	**55** *89.5*	53 *86.5*	52.5 *85.5*	51.5 *84*	45 *73.5*	35.5 *58*	33 *54*	28 *46*	25 *41*	22 *36*
Drumna-drochit	**60** *97.5*	58 *94.5*	57.5 *93.5*	56.5 *92*	50 *81.5*	40.5 *66*	38 *62*	33 *54*	30 *49*	27 *44*
Abriachan	**67** *109*	65 *106*	64.5 *105*	64.5 *103.5*	57 *93*	47.5 *77.5*	45 *73.5*	40 *65.5*	37 *60.5*	34 *55.5*
Inverness	**80** *129*	78 *127*	77.5 *126*	76.5 *124.5*	70 *114*	60.5 *98.5*	58 *94.5*	53 *86.5*	50 *81.5*	47 *76.5*

Great Glen Way
(Invergarry Link Route)

DISTANCE CHART 2

miles/*kilometres* (approx)

Fort Augustus	Invermoriston	Grotaig	Drumnadrochit	Abriachan	Inverness
9.5					
15.5					
19	9.5				
31	*15.5*				
24	14.5	5			
39	*23.5*	*8*			
31	21.5	12	7		
50.5	*35*	*19.5*	*11.5*		
44	34.5	25	20	13	
71.5	*56*	*40.5*	*32.5*	*21*	

INDEX

Page references in red type refer to maps

TRAILBLAZER TITLE LIST
see also overleaf for our
British Walking Guides

Adventure Cycle-Touring Handbook
Adventure Motorcycling Handbook
Australia by Rail
Cleveland Way (British Walking Guide)
Coast to Coast (British Walking Guide)
Cornwall Coast Path (British Walking Guide)
Cotswold Way (British Walking Guide)
The Cyclist's Anthology
Dales Way (British Walking Guide)
Dorset & Sth Devon Coast Path (British Walking Gde)
Exmoor & Nth Devon Coast Path (British Walking Gde)
Great Glen Way (British Walking Guide)
Hadrian's Wall Path (British Walking Guide)
Himalaya by Bike – a route and planning guide
Iceland Hiking – with Reykjavik City Guide
Inca Trail, Cusco & Machu Picchu
Japan by Rail
Kilimanjaro – the trekking guide (includes Mt Meru)
London Loop (British Walking Guide)
Madeira Walks – 37 selected day walks
Moroccan Atlas – The Trekking Guide
Morocco Overland (4x4/motorcycle/mountainbike)
Nepal Trekking & The Great Himalaya Trail
Norfolk Coast Path & Peddars Way (British Walking Gde)
North Downs Way (British Walking Guide)
Offa's Dyke Path (British Walking Guide)
Overlanders' Handbook – worldwide driving guide
Pembrokeshire Coast Path (British Walking Guide)
Pennine Way (British Walking Guide)
Peru's Cordilleras Blanca & Huayhuash – Hiking/Biking
Pilgrim Pathways: 1-2 day walks on Britain's sacred ways
The Railway Anthology
The Ridgeway (British Walking Guide)
Scottish Highlands – Hillwalking Guide
Siberian BAM Guide – rail, rivers & road
The Silk Roads – a route and planning guide
Sinai – the trekking guide
South Downs Way (British Walking Guide)
Thames Path (British Walking Guide)
Tour du Mont Blanc
Trans-Canada Rail Guide
Trans-Siberian Handbook
Trekking in the Everest Region
The Walker's Anthology
The Walker's Anthology – further tales
West Highland Way (British Walking Guide)

www.trailblazer-guides.com

TRAILBLAZER'S BRITISH WALKING GUIDES

We've applied to destinations which are closer to home Trailblazer's proven formula for publishing definitive practical route guides for adventurous travellers. Britain's network of long-distance trails enables the walker to explore some of the finest landscapes in the country's best walking areas. These are guides that are user-friendly, practical, informative and environmentally sensitive.

'The same attention to detail that distinguishes its other guides has been brought to bear here'.
THE SUNDAY TIMES

● **Unique mapping features** In many walking guidebooks the reader has to read a route description then try to relate it to the map. Our guides are much easier to use because walking directions, tricky junctions, places to stay and eat, points of interest and walking times are all written onto the maps themselves in the places to which they apply. With their uncluttered clarity, these are not general-purpose maps but fully edited maps drawn by walkers for walkers.

● **Largest-scale walking maps** At a scale of just under 1:20,000 (8cm or 3¹/₈ inches to one mile) the maps in these guides are bigger than even the most detailed British walking maps currently available in the shops.

● **Not just a trail guide – includes where to stay, where to eat and public transport** Our guidebooks cover the complete walking experience, not just the route. Accommodation options for all budgets are provided (pubs, hotels, B&Bs, campsites, bunkhouses, hostels) as well as places to eat. Detailed public transport information for all access points to each trail means that there are itineraries for all walkers, for hiking the entire route as well as for day or weekend walks.

Cleveland Way *Henry Stedman*, 1st edn, ISBN 978-1-905864-91-1, 240pp, 98 maps

Coast to Coast *Henry Stedman*, 9th edn, ISBN 978-1-912716-11-1, 268pp, 109 maps

Cornwall Coast Path (SW Coast Path Pt 2) *Stedman & Newton*, 6th edn, ISBN 978-1-912716-05-0, 352pp, 142 maps

Cotswold Way *Tricia & Bob Hayne*, 4th edn, ISBN 978-1-912716-04-3, 204pp, 53 maps

Dales Way *Henry Stedman,* 1st edn, ISBN 978-1-905864-78-2, 192pp, 50 maps

Dorset & South Devon (SW Coast Path Pt 3) *Stedman & Newton*, 2nd edn, ISBN 978-1-905864-94-2, 340pp, 97 maps

Exmoor & North Devon (SW Coast Path Pt I) *Stedman & Newton*, 2nd edn, ISBN 978-1-905864-86-7, 224pp, 68 maps

Great Glen Way *Jim Manthorpe,* 2nd edn, ISBN 978-1-912716-10-4, 184pp, 50 maps

Hadrian's Wall Path *Henry Stedman*, 6th edn, ISBN 978-1-912716-12-8, 250pp, 60 maps

London LOOP *Henry Stedman*, 1st edn, ISBN 978-1-912716-21-0, 236pp, 60 maps

Norfolk Coast Path & Peddars Way *Alexander Stewart*, 1st edn, ISBN 978-1-905864-98-0, 224pp, 75 maps

North Downs Way *Henry Stedman*, 2nd edn, ISBN 978-1-905864-90-4, 240pp, 98 maps

Offa's Dyke Path *Keith Carter*, 5th edn, ISBN 978-1-912716-03-6, 268pp, 98 maps

Pembrokeshire Coast Path *Jim Manthorpe*, 6th edn, 978-1-912716-13-5, 236pp, 96 maps

Pennine Way *Stuart Greig*, 5th edn, ISBN 978-1-912716-02-9, 272pp, 138 maps

The Ridgeway *Nick Hill*, 5th edn, ISBN 978-1-912716-20-3, 208pp, 53 maps

South Downs Way *Jim Manthorpe*, 6th edn, ISBN 978-1-905864-93-5, 204pp, 60 maps

Thames Path *Joel Newton*, 2nd edn, ISBN 978-1-905864-97-3, 256pp, 99 maps

West Highland Way *Charlie Loram*, 7th edn, ISBN 978-1-912716-01-2, 218pp, 60 maps

'The Trailblazer series stands head, shoulders, waist and ankles above the rest. They are particularly strong on mapping ...'
THE SUNDAY TIMES

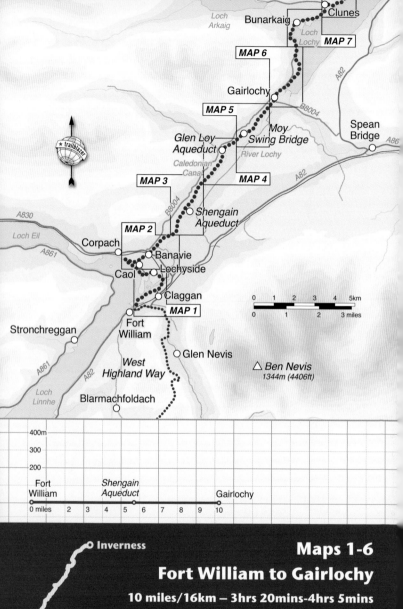

MAP 7

Loch
Arkaig

Bunarkaig

Clunes

Loch
Lochy

MAP 6

Loch
Lochy

A82

Gairlochy

MAP 5

B8004

Spean
Bridge

A86

Glen Loy
Aqueduct

Moy
Swing Bridge

River Lochy

MAP 4

Caledonian
Canal

A82

MAP 3

B8004

Shengain
Aqueduct

A830

Loch Eil

MAP 2

Corpach

A861

Banavie

Lochyside

Caol

Claggan

MAP 1

Fort
William

0 1 2 3 4 5km

0   1   2   3 miles

Stronchreggan

Glen Nevis

△ Ben Nevis
1344m (4406ft)

West
Highland Way

A82

Loch
Linnhe

Blarmachfoldach

- 400m
- 300
- 200

Fort
William

Shengain
Aqueduct

Gairlochy

0 miles   2   3   4   5   6   7   8   9   10

Inverness

Maps 1-6
Fort William to Gairlochy

10 miles/16km – 3hrs 20mins-4hrs 5mins

NOTE: Add 20-30% to these times to allow for stops

Gairlochy
Fort William

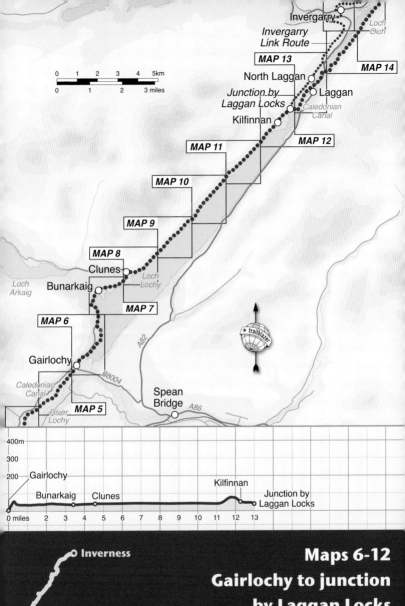

Invergarry

*Invergarry
Link Route*

Loch
Oich

MAP 13

MAP 14

North Laggan

Laggan

*Junction by
Laggan Locks*

Caledonian
Canal

Kilfinnan

MAP 12

MAP 11

MAP 10

MAP 9

MAP 8

Clunes

Loch
Lochy

Bunarkaig

Loch
Arkaig

MAP 7

MAP 6

A82

Gairlochy

Caledonian
Canal

B8004

Spean
Bridge

A86

MAP 5

River
Lochy

| 0 | 1 | 2 | 3 | 4 | 5km |

| 0 | 1 | 2 | 3 miles |

★ trailblazer

400m
300
200 — Gairlochy

Bunarkaig   Clunes

Kilfinnan

Junction by
Laggan Locks

0 miles   2   3   4   5   6   7   8   9   10   11   12   13

Inverness

Junction by
Laggan Locks

Gairlochy

Fort William

Maps 6-12
Gairlochy to junction
by Laggan Locks

13 miles/21km – 3hrs 50mins-4hrs 55mins

NOTE: Add 20-30% to these times to allow for stops

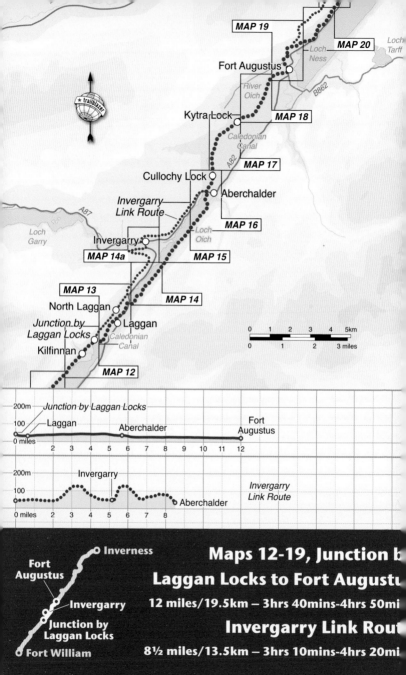

MAP 19

MAP 20

Loch
Tarff

Fort Augustus

Loch
Ness

River
Oich

B862

MAP 18

Kytra Lock

Caledonian
Canal

MAP 17

A82

Cullochy Lock

Aberchalder

*Invergarry
Link Route*

MAP 16

A87

Loch
Garry

Invergarry

Loch
Oich

MAP 14a

MAP 15

MAP 13

MAP 14

North Laggan

*Junction by
Laggan Locks*

Laggan

*Caledonian
Canal*

Kilfinnan

MAP 12

| 0 | 1 | 2 | 3 | 4 | 5km |

| 0 | 1 | 2 | 3 miles |

200m
100
0 miles
Junction by Laggan Locks
Laggan
Aberchalder
Fort
Augustus
2 3 4 5 6 7 8 9 10 11 12

200m
100
Invergarry
Aberchalder
*Invergarry
Link Route*
0 miles 2 3 4 5 6 7 8

Inverness

Fort
Augustus

Invergarry

Junction by
Laggan Locks

Fort William

Maps 12-19, Junction b

Laggan Locks to Fort Augustu

12 miles/19.5km – 3hrs 40mins-4hrs 50mi

Invergarry Link Rout

8½ miles/13.5km – 3hrs 10mins-4hrs 20mi

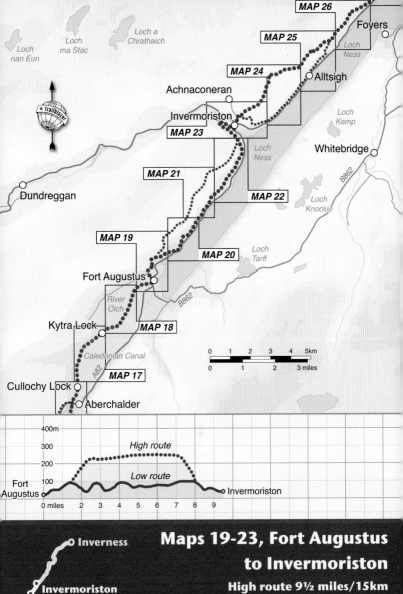

Loch nan Eun

Loch ma Stac

Loch a Chrathaich

MAP 26

Foyers

MAP 25

Loch Ness

MAP 24

Alltsigh

Achnaconeran

MAP 23

Invermoriston

Loch Kemp

Whitebridge

Loch Ness

MAP 21

MAP 22

Loch Knockie

Dundreggan

MAP 19

MAP 20

Loch Tarff

Fort Augustus

B862

River Oich

Kytra Lock

MAP 18

Caledonian Canal

A82

MAP 17

Cullochy Lock

Aberchalder

| 0 | 1 | 2 | 3 | 4 | 5km |
| 0 | | 1 | 2 | | 3 miles |

400m
300
200   *High route*
100   *Low route*

Fort
Augustus   Invermoriston

0 miles   2   3   4   5   6   7   8   9

Inverness

Invermoriston
Fort Augustus

Fort William

Maps 19-23, Fort Augustus to Invermoriston

High route 9½ miles/15km
2hrs 35mins-3hrs 45mins

Low route 9½ miles/15km – 2hrs 20mins-3hrs 20mins

NOTE: Add 20-30% to these times to allow for stops

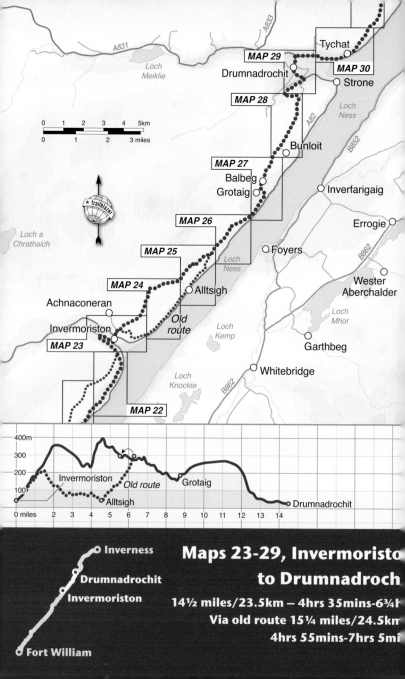

Loch Meiklie

A831

A833

Loch Ness

Tychat

MAP 29

Drumnadrochit

MAP 30

Strone

MAP 28

A82

Bunloit

B852

MAP 27

Balbeg

Grotaig

Inverfarigaig

MAP 26

Errogie

Loch a Chrathaich

MAP 25

Foyers

B862

MAP 24

Alltsaigh

Loch Ness

Wester Aberchalder

Achnaconeran

Old route

Loch Mhor

Invermoriston

Loch Kemp

MAP 23

Garthbeg

Whitebridge

Loch Knockie

B862

MAP 22

0 1 2 3 4 5km
0   1   2   3 miles

★ trailblazer

Elevation profile:

400m
300
200
100

Invermoriston

Old route

Grotaig

Drumnadrochit

Alltsigh

0 miles 2 3 4 5 6 7 8 9 10 11 12 13 14

Inverness

Drumnadrochit

Invermoriston

Fort William

Maps 23-29, Invermoristo to Drumnadroch

14½ miles/23.5km – 4hrs 35mins-6¾h
Via old route 15¼ miles/24.5km
4hrs 55mins-7hrs 5mi

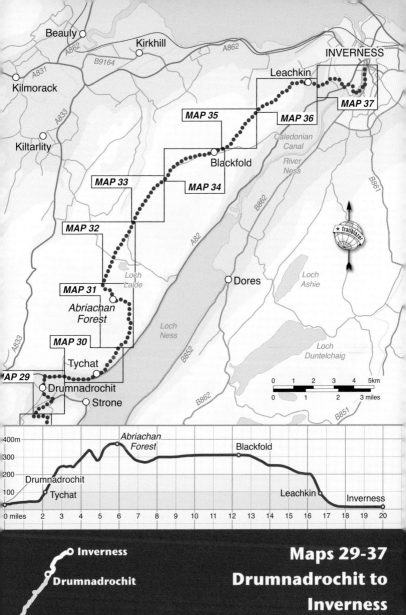

Maps 29-37

Drumnadrochit to
Inverness

20 miles/32.5km — 6¼hrs-8hrs 40mins

NOTE: Add 20-30% to these times to allow for stops

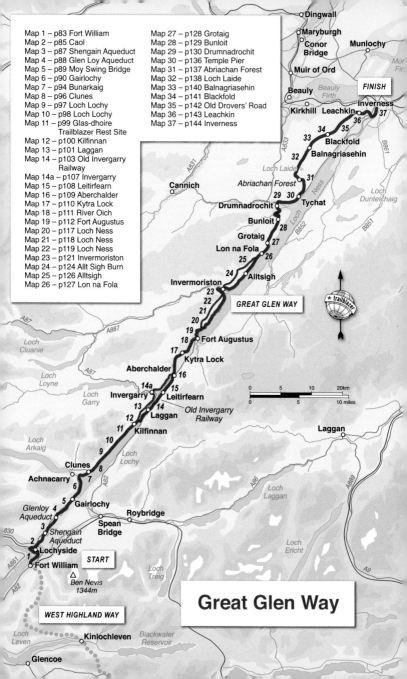

Great Glen Way